ALEXANDER THE GREAT

PAUL CARTLEDGE is Professor of Greek History in the Faculty of
Classics at the University of Cambridge, where he has taught since
1979; he is also a Fellow of Clare College. His undergraduate and
doctoral qualifications were obtained at Oxford, where he completed
a dissertation on the archaeology and history of early Sparta under
the supervision of Professor Sir John Boardman. He is the author,
co-author, editor or co-editor of a score of books, including most
recently *The Cambridge Illustrated History of Ancient Greece*; *The
Greeks: Crucible of Civilization*; *Sparta and Lakonia: A Regional
History c.1300–362 BC*; *The Greeks: A Portrait of Self and Others*
and *The Spartans: An Epic History*. He co edits two monograph series,
is on the editorial boards of three learned journals and serves as
consultant in ancient history to Duckworth publishers. He is a Fellow
of the Society of Antiquaries of London and holds the Gold Cross of the
Order of Honour awarded by the President of the Hellenic Republic.

Also by Paul Cartledge in Pan Books

THE SPARTANS: AN EPIC HISTORY

PAUL CARTLEDGE

ALEXANDER THE GREAT

THE HUNT FOR A NEW PAST

PAN BOOKS

First published 2004 by Macmillan

This edition published 2005 by Pan Books
an imprint of Pan Macmillan Ltd
Pan Macmillan, 20 New Wharf Road, London N1 9RR
Basingstoke and Oxford
Associated companies throughout the world
www.panmacmillan.com

ISBN 0 330 41925 0

9 8 7 6 5 4 3 2 1

A CIP catalogue record for this book is available from
the British Library.

Maps by ML Design
Battle plans by Map Studio

Typeset by SetSystems Ltd, Saffron Walden, Essex
Printed and bound in Great Britain by
Mackays of Chatham plc, Chatham, Kent

To Judith Portrait

(yet again)

Contents

Preface

There is really no need for any special justification, let alone apology, for a new history of Alexander. He is one of those very few genuinely iconic figures, who have both remade the world they knew and constantly inspire us to remake our own worlds, both personal and more global. What is needed, then, and I have aimed to provide, is a book that does full justice to Alexander's extraordinary achievement, while at the same time respecting the limits of the evidence and of the historian's craft. I have attempted to address that achievement both in its own terms (including some tentative probing into Alexander's deep psyche) and in terms of its subsequent impact – which continues to this day, when Alexander is still prayed in aid by fishermen in Greece, cursed as a 'thief' in Iran, and worshipped as a saint in the Coptic Church of Egypt.

It must also be a book with a distinctive interpretative approach, and mine is indicated in the book's subtitle: 'The Hunt for a New Past'. There are of course several possible keys to unlocking the enigma that was Alexander. Some modern historians, for example, have focused on the Greek word *pothos*, passionate yearning, which is associated in the sources with major projects of Alexander. Others have privileged Alexander's relationship with his father, Philip. One modern historian has tried to explain vital features of his career in terms of his alcohol dependency. My book will not minimize the influence of these factors on Alexander's outlook, personality and aims. But it will lay even more stress on his predilection, or rather grand passion, for hunting game: human as well as animal, and the bigger, more numerous and more dangerous the better. For that offered him a greater chance for enhancing his standing and his fame.

One of the very earliest probable images of Alexander (Figure 1) is painted in a fresco above the front entrance to what most of us refer to conventionally as 'the Tomb of Philip' (whether or not we actually believe it to be the tomb of Alexander's father, as I on the whole do). This monumental edifice was erected at the ancient Macedonian ceremonial capital of Aegae (modern Vergina) at some point in the last third or so of the fourth century BCE. The fresco depicts a series of hunting scenes, so that, if it does indeed feature Alexander centrally, it shows him engaged in what we know to have been one of his favourite pastimes. Except that 'pastime' may give a misleading impression, since hunting in Macedon – as in some other ancient societies, such as Sparta – was a culturally coded marker of social and political status and prestige. In Macedon, you did not become fully a man until you had passed the key manhood test of hunting and killing, without a net, one of the ferocious wild boar that roamed the heights of Upper (western) Macedonia. Only then could you recline – as opposed to sit – when participating in the daily ritual of the symposium: the evening drinking party, at which and through which the Macedonian elite celebrated together and mutually confirmed their elevated social and political status. Another kind of hunting – the killing of an enemy in battle – entitled a Macedonian to wear a special belt, as a visual signal and reminder of his attainment and prestige.

After the two introductory chapters I have aimed to combine sequential chronological narration with in-depth systematic surveys of a number of key themes of Alexander's career. A detailed Timeline right at the start of the book is intended to help convey the flow of events. All dates are BCE (Before the Common Era), unless otherwise specified. The concluding chapter explores Alexander's multiple legacies, from antiquity through the Middle Ages to the present day.

An Appendix explores the limits set by the available source materials to any attempted reconstruction of how it actually was in Alexander's day. The conclusions reached here condition and inform everything I write in the main body of the book, which ideally should be read in that light. The Appendix also explores in greater detail than usual two vital questions: first, how precisely did Callisthenes, Alexander's official historian, die in 327? and, second, what did really happen at the oracle at Siwah in 332/1? The contemporary narrative sources, as ever, do not survive as such, and the available reports of at least the main authors all tell different stories. This really does matter, because these were issues over which Alexander himself quite certainly took great care to control the flow of information, and one of the many paradoxes of his career is that, despite or because of that concern, the facts are so often murky and controversial. For reasons given here, too, various sorts of material objects lie at the very kernel of this historical enterprise. The illustrations of these objects are therefore not merely an optional extra but a key component of the history – any history – of Alexander. They have been selected with a view to combining the familiar with the unfamiliar, the spectacular with the ordinary, the decorative with the documentary.

The book concludes with a series of technical aids: a Table of Achaemenid Kings, a Dramatis Personae (register of prominent individuals), a Glossary (including place names) and a Bibliography. The authors and works referred to in the text can usually be found listed in the relevant chapter's suggestions for further reading in the Bibliography. Some of the suggestions are aimed more particularly at the scholar than at the general reader, but general readers too will assuredly find plenty here to interest and stimulate them further.

TERMINOLOGY – I use 'Macedon' as a political term to refer to the state or kingdom of Macedon that Alexander inherited and that was the ultimate basis of his position and power. 'Macedonia' is for me a geographical term, referring to the territory that formed the core of the state/kingdom of Macedon. Occasionally these two terms overlap. 'Greater Macedonia' refers to the enlarged territory conquered and consolidated as a state by Philip, the northern frontier of which Alexander sought to extend as far as the Danube. In much Western literature 'Persia' and 'Iran' have been used interchangeably, but strictly Persia (*Persis* in Greek) is the heartland of the Persian people, occupying a mountainous region northeast of the Persian Gulf; whereas Iran embraces also ancient Media to the north, and some more. In this book 'Iran' means the area of modern Iran, and 'Persia' the state or empire of the Achaemenid Persians.

MONETARY EQUIVALENTS – I have not tried to translate ancient monetary figures into modern equivalents. A silver Greek 'talent' (a word of Babylonian origin) contained 100 minas or 6,000 drachmas. Two to three drachmas a day was a skilled workman's wage in Alexander's time. To be seriously rich, the equivalent of a sterling or dollar millionaire, you had to be worth three or more talents, probably. So when Harpalus ran off with 5,000 talents in 324, or when Alexander gained access to Persian treasure worth perhaps 180,000 talents in 330, we are dealing with very big numbers indeed.

TRANSLATIONS – All translations from ancient Greek and Latin sources are my own. I have sometimes deviated slightly from a strictly literal rendering to ease the flow and cadence of the English.

Acknowledgements

The present book is distantly based on lecture courses I have given at Cambridge within the past twenty-five years, aimed chiefly at undergraduate students reading for either the Classical or the Historical Tripos. Audiences regularly included a sprinkling of graduate students and colleagues from both inside and outside the Classics Faculty, and sometimes more exotic visitors too: for example, Bob Strassler, editor of *The Landmark Thucydides* and benefactor of Classics extraordinary, and my Clare College colleague and Plumian Professor of Astronomy, Jerry Ostriker. To all of these I am grateful for the stimulus of having to convey succinctly, intelligibly and entertainingly something of the thrill of the chase involved in any hunt for a new Alexander.

In the course of researching and writing about Alexander and ancient Greek history and archaeology more generally I have incurred many other debts, especially to my many Greek friends. It is invidious to single out individuals but I must at least mention the following, in more or less alphabetic order: Nikos Birgalias and Nastassia Florou; Kostas Buraselis; Tassos Christidis (my guide to Alexander's Vergina and Pella); Soteroula Constantinidou and Costas Constantinides; Eleni Cubitt (*éminence* of the British Committee for the Reuniting of the Parthenon Marbles); Angelos Delivorrias; Katie Demakopoulou; Matti Egon and Nicholas Egon (an honorary Greek by association); Vincent Gabrielsen; Ariadni Gartziou-Tatti; Costas Grammenos; His Eminence Grigorios, Bishop of Thyateira and Great Britain; Vassilis Karasmanis; Paschalis Kitromilidis; Nota Kourou and Thanasis Kouros (my oldest Greek friends); Dimitris Kyrtatas; Vassilis Lambropoulos and Artemis Leontis; Edmee Leventis, Louisa Leventis and Tassos Leventis, and the late, much lamented Dino Leventis; Anna Missiou; Isidora Papadrakakis and Manolis Papadrakakis; Zenon

Papakonstantinou; Spyros Rangos; former Ambassador Alexandros Sandis (himself a native of Alexander's Egyptian Alexandria), Cultural Counsellor Victoria Solomonidis and Press Counsellor Nicos Papadakis, all of the Greek Embassy in London; Giorgos Steinhauer (but for whom I could not have got started on my archaeological research, as a graduate student of Professor Sir John Boardman); Antonis Tsakmakis; Evi Touloupa; Kostas Valakas; Kostas Vlassopoulos; Sofia Voutsaki; and, by no means least, Mary Yossi.

I am also more indebted than I can say to the following: Dr Jan Parker of the Open University (who read the whole book in pre-publication form, though she is not of course responsible for the published version's short-comings); Professor Graham Shipley, who generously and acutely read the proofs at the shortest of notice; my sympathetic and indefatigable agent, Julian Alexander; and my patient and practised editors at Macmillan, Georgina Morley, Natasha Martin and (picture-editor) Josine Meijer.

My daughter has been wonderfully supportive, if mainly from the other side of the globe – a side not even Alexander would have dreamed of. My greatest debt, however, as always, is to the book's dedicatee (though I do admit to being tempted to echo the words used by the great modern Alexander historian Ernst Badian when dedicating his *Studies in Greek and Roman History* to his wife).

PERMISSIONS

Extract from *After Nature* by W. G. Sebald reproduced by kind permission of Michael Hamburger, translator.

Extract from 'In the Year 200 BC' by C. P. Cavafy reproduced by kind permission of Evangelos Sachperoglou, translator.

Plan 3 based on 'Battle of Issus 333 BC' from J. B. Bury and Russell Meiggs, *A History of Greece* (1975), by permission of Palgrave Macmillan. All other plans based on plans from Campaign 7 – 'Alexander 334–323 BC', © Osprey Publishing.

Timeline

340/39		Alexander regent during Philip's absence at siege of Byzantium; founds Alexandroupolis in Thrace
338	autumn	Philip defeats Greek coalition led by Athens and Thebes at Chaeronea, founds League of Corinth, is chosen leader of Panhellenic expedition against Persian Empire
336		Accession of Darius III of Persia. Advance Graeco-Macedonian force under Parmenion establishes bridgehead in north-west Asia Minor
336		Philip assassinated at Aegae
336–323		Reign of Alexander III the Great
336	late summer	Alexander recognized as Philip's successor as head of League of Corinth and commander of Persian expedition
	c.2 Oct.	Alexander's first regnal year begins
335	spring to June	Alexander campaigns in Thrace against Triballi and in Danube region
	June to Aug.	Campaigns against Illyrians
	early Oct.	Destruction of Thebes
334	spring	Alexander assumes command of Persian expedition, crosses into Asia
	May	Battle of the River Granicus
	May to Aug.	Campaigns in western Asia Minor, disbands most of allied fleet

	Aug. to Sept.	Siege of Halicarnassus
	autumn/winter	Campaigns in Caria, Lycia, Pamphylia
333	spring	To Great Phrygia (Gordian knot incident).
	summer	To Ancyra, through Cilician Gates, to Tarsus and Soli
	Nov.	Battle of Issus in Cilicia
	Dec.	Parmenion captures Damascus
332	Jan. to July/Aug.	Siege of Phoenician Tyre
	Sept. to Nov.	Siege of Gaza
	Nov.	Alexander starts rule as Pharaoh of Egypt (?crowned at Memphis)
331	Jan. to Mar.	Foundation of (Egyptian) Alexandria (official 'birthday' 7 April). Consultation of oracle of Ammon at Siwah oasis
	spring	From Memphis to Tyre, reorganization of financial machinery
	July to Aug.	To Thapsacus
	autumn	'Battle of Mice' (Regent Antipater defeats Spartan revolt under Agis III at Megalopolis)
	20 Sept.	Evening eclipse of moon
	1 Oct.	Battle of Gaugamela

	Oct. to Dec.	Progress through Babylonia and Sittacene (army review and appointments) to Iran (Susa, then through land of Uxii and Persian Gates to Persepolis)
330	spring	Campaign in interior of Iran
	Apr./May	Return to Persepolis, burning of palace and departure for Media
	early June	Greek allied contingents dismissed at Ecbatana
	June	To Rhagae (ancient Teheran) and Caspian Gates
	July	Capture of Darius III's body, advance to border of Hyrcania, reception of Nabazarnes and Phrataphernes, dalliance with Amazon queen (alleged). Advance to Zadracarta, Alexander starts acting as Great King, adopts mixed oriental dress
	Aug.	Towards Bactria, then diversion to Artacoana (Herat); revolt of Satibarzanes
	Sept.	Trial and execution of Philotas followed by murder of Parmenion. Trial of Amyntas and his brothers
	winter	Through land of Drangaeans and Arimaspes, into Arachosia, through Paropamisadae to foot of Hindu Kush
330/329	winter	Foundation of Alexandria-by-the-Caucasus (near Begram and Charikar)

329	spring	Crossing of Hindu Kush, to Drapsaca (Kunduz) and Bactra; older men and Thessalian volunteers sent home. Crossing of Oxus river
	summer	Capture of Bessus (Persian pretender) by Ptolemy; murder of Bessus. Advance to Maracanda (Samarkand), summer capital of Sogdiana, to River Jaxartes. Foundation of Alexandria Eschate (Khodjend). Revolt of local Scythian tribesmen and of Sogdians, campaign against defected Spitamenes
329/8	winter	At Bactra Alexander receives embassies from Scythians and Chorasmians
328	spring	Systematic pacification of Sogdiana begins, guerrilla warfare against Massagetae of Turkestan steppes and against Spitamenes
	late summer	Return to Maracanda
	Nov.	Alexander murders Cleitus at Maracanda. Spitamenes killed by Massagetae
328/7	winter	Alexander quarters at Nautaca
327	spring	Capture of Sogdian Rock (?Baisun-Tau) and of Rock of Chorienes (Koh-i-Nor). Alexander marries Roxane, daughter of Oxyartes. To Bactria, defeat of last opposition. *Proskynesis* episode. Pages' Conspiracy. Arrest and execution of Callisthenes

late spring	Departure from Bactria, recrossing of Hindu Kush to Alexandria-by-the-Caucasus
late	Invasion of India begins
327/6 winter	Alexander quarters in Assacene (Swat and Buner). Capture of Massaga and Rock of Aornus (Bar-sar ib Pir-Sar); advance to Indus river
326	Progress to Taxila
May	Battle of the Hydaspes (Jhelum) against Porus (Rajah of the Pauravas)
May to June	Halt in Porus's kingdom
late June	Advance to Acesines river and Hyphasis (Beas) river; troops' mutiny followed by retreat from the Hyphasis and return to the Hydaspes. Death of Coenus. Fleets prepared
Nov.	Journey down the Hydaspes begins
325	Reduction of Malli tribe; Alexander near-fatally wounded. Down to the Indian Ocean
July	Pattala (Hyderabad?) reached
Aug.	Descent from Pattala begins
Aug. to Nov.	Approach to march through Gedrosian desert (Makran)
Sept.	Alexander reaches Oreitae

	Sept./Oct.	Nearchus leaves with fleet, Alexander marches through Gedrosia and reaches Pura
	mid-Dec.	Nearchus reaches Hormozeia (Hormuz)
	late Dec.	Alexander and Nearchus reunited in Carmania (? at Gulashird)
325/4	winter	Executions of satraps and generals; flight of Harpalus
324	Jan. to Mar.	Nearchus leaves Hormozeia, then round into Persian Gulf
	Jan.?	Alexander reaches Pasargadae
	Mar.	Alexander and Nearchus reunite at Susa
	Apr.	Susa weddings, paying off of soldiers' debts, voyage up Tigris
	June	Mutiny at Opis (Baghdad), banquet of reconciliation
	July	Harpalus arrives at Athens, hands over 700 talents
	Aug.	Promulgation by Nicanor of Alexander's Exiles' Decree at Olympic Games
	Oct.	Death of Hephaestion at Ecbatana
324/3	winter	Campaign against Cossaean nomads
323	early	Alexander in Babylon; preparations for Arabian expedition, visits of Greek envoys acknowledging Alexander's divinity

10 June	(evening of 28th Daisios by the Macedonian calendar): Alexander dies at Babylon (aged nearly 33, having reigned just over twelve and a half years)

Maps and Plans

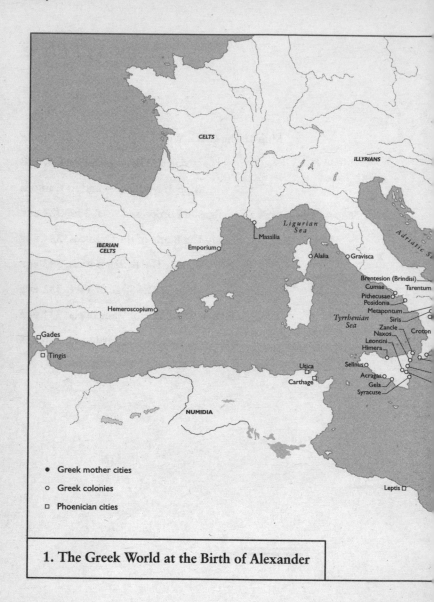

- ● Greek mother cities
- ○ Greek colonies
- □ Phoenician cities

1. The Greek World at the Birth of Alexander

SCYTHIANS

Tanais○

SARMATIANS

Olbia○

Tyras○ Panticapaeum○

Theodosia○

Istrus○

Black Sea

Phasis○

Callatis○

Odessus○ Sinope○ Trapezus○

Mesembria○ Amisus○

Apollonia○

THRACE Heraclea○

Byzantium○ ○Chalcedon

Abdera○

MACEDONIA Thasos○

CHALCIDICE Abydus○

Sigeum○

Aegean Sea

Sybaris ○Corcyra Phocaea●

Megara○ Chalcis●

Corinth▲ Eretria●

Achaea● Athens●

Sparta● Miletus● PERSIAN EMPIRE

Ionian Sea

Rhegium Paros○ Phaselis○

Catane Thera●

Megara Hyblaea CYPRUS ○Citum

Byblos□

Sidon□

Tyre□

M e d i t e r r a n e a n   S e a

○Cyrene

○Euesperides

200 miles

400 kilometres

Red Sea

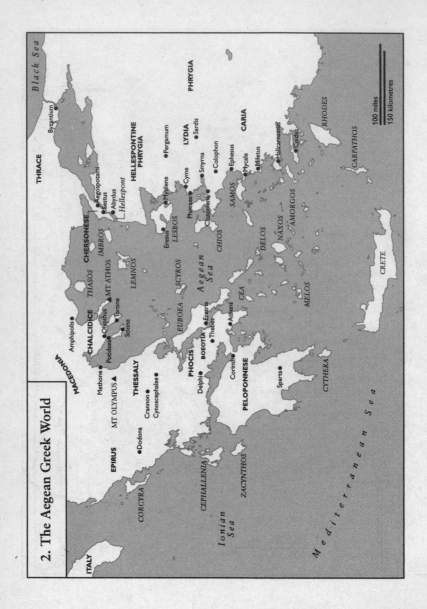

2. The Aegean Greek World

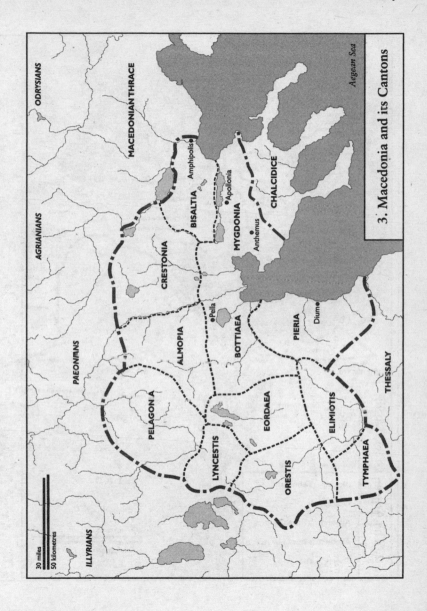

3. Macedonia and its Cantons

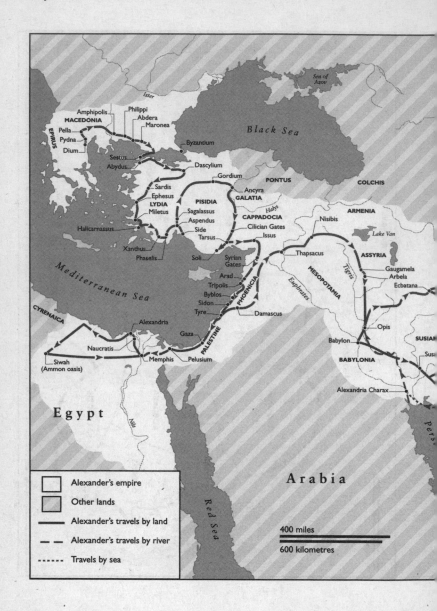

4. Alexander's Campaigns in Europe and Asia, 336–323 BCE

Lake Balkhash

Aral Sea

Issyk-Kul Lake

Caspian Sea

Oxus

Jaxartes

Bukhara
Maracanda
Alexandria Eschate
Cyropolis
SOGDIANA

Zadracarta

Alexandria Margiana
Nautaca
Alexandria of Oxiana

HYRCANIA
Susa
MARGIANA
Drapasca
PAROPAMISOS
Alexandria-by-the-Caucasus

Rhagae
Damghan
Hecatompylus
TAPORIA
PARTHIA
Bactra
BACTRIA

Caspian Gates
Artacoana

Nicaea
Alexandria Bucephala
Embolima
Alexandria Nicaea
Taxila

AREIA

Alexandria Arela

ARACHOSIA

Alexandria Arachosia
City of the Brahmans
Prophthasia
Sangala

Pasargadae
Persepolis

CARMANIA
DRANGIANA

Persian Gates

Hormozeia
Alexandria Carmania
Alexandria
Alexandria

PERSIA
Pura
GEDROSIA

Alexandria of the Oreitae

Cocala
Pattala

India

Gouadar
Alexandria Port

Arabian Sea

1a. The Battle of the Granicus: Phase 1

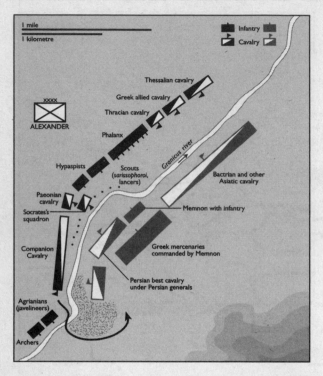

In the Granicus river battle, unlike in his other two set pieces on land, Alexander's forces actually outnumbered those of his opponents, led apparently by Arsites, satrap of Hellespontine Phrygia (see Dramatis Personae).

1b. The Battle of the Granicus: Phase 2

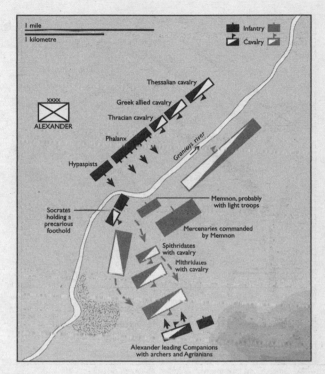

Having crossed the river unexpectedly far from the main concentration of Persian forces, Alexander compelled the Persians to transfer cavalry from the centre to defend their left wing. Dissipated and exposed, the Persian forces were overcome. (For further description see Chapter Seven.)

2. The Battle of Issus

Persian army	Macedonian army
A Greek Hoplites	1 Phalanx
B Cavalry	2 Hypaspists
C Kardakes (light Persian infantry)	3 Greek hoplites
D Other Asiatic light troops	4 Greek cavalry
	5 Macedonian cavalry
	6 Light troops

As at Granicus, the rival armies were divided by a river, but this time the Persians, led for the first time by Darius III, crossed before Alexander's army.

3. The Siege of Tyre

1 Cypriot ships   2 Other Phoenician and other ships   3 Tyrian ships

The walls of New Tyre were particularly thick on the landward side and thus difficult to penetrate. Lacking a fleet, Alexander built not one but two causeways (the first was destroyed by the Tyrian defenders) to attack the landward walls. Boosted eventually by a fleet of Phoenician turncoats, Alexander was at last able to attack the weaker seaward walls and finally completed the siege after seven long months.

4. The Battle of Gaugamela

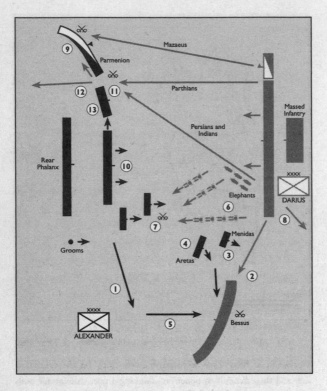

1. Alexander's initial oblique advance
2. Persian troops from Bactria and Scythia counter
3. Alexander orders mercenaries to break through Persian left
4. Attack on Bactrians and Scythians
5. Gap opens in Darius's line
6. Persian chariot attack
7. Resistance to chariot attack from archers and light troops
8. Darius flees
9. Parmenion defends against Mazaeus's cavalry
10. Alexander's infantry advance
11. Gap opens between infantry and Parmenion's cavalry
12. Breakthrough by Persian and Indian cavalry
13. Macedonian infantry resist Persian breakthrough

5. The Battle of the Hydaspes

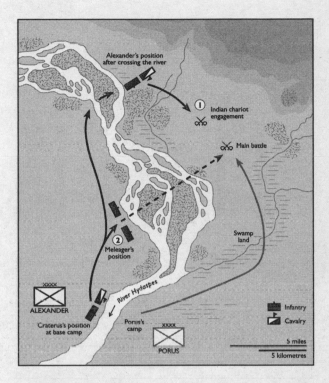

1 Alexander divided his forces into two, leading one himself and entrusting the other to Craterus. Alexander's 5,000 cavalry and 6,000 infantry crossed the river surreptitiously to attack Porus.

2 The main body under Craterus was left holding the right bank. Meleager was in command of the reserve battalions, which he led directly across the river after Alexander himself had crossed further upstream and moved to the attack.

ONE

THE FAME OF
ALEXANDER

The world remembers Iskander and his deeds.
Macedonia gave him its sceptre.
Iskander was the son of Philip.
His life was one long dream of glory.

– Abal, 'Iskander', trans. Richard McKane

INHERITING at the age of twenty his father Philip's position as
master of the Greek world east of the Adriatic, Alexander had also,
by the ripe old age of twenty-six, made himself master of the once
mighty Persian Empire. By the time he was thirty he had taken his
victorious arms to the limits of the known *oecumene* (inhabited world).
Yet, before his thirty-third birthday he was dead. Small surprise,
therefore, that he should have become a legend in his own lifetime.
That his legend has spread so far and so wide – from Iceland to China
– since his death in 323 BCE is due very largely to the so-called
Alexander Romance. This fabulous fiction took shape in Egypt, mostly
some five or more centuries after Alexander's death.

Thanks to this, and for other reasons too, of course, Alexander
became in various countries and at various times a hero, a quasi-holy
man, a Christian saint, a new Achilles, a philosopher, a scientist, a
prophet and a visionary. But in antiquity he was most famous of all as
a conqueror. Here is Arrian, writing in the early second century CE
under the influence of the Roman emperor Trajan's recent conquests
in Parthia (in modern Iran); his *Anabasis* ('March Up Country') is our
best ancient historical source on Alexander:

> *For my part I cannot determine with certainty what sort of plans*
> *Alexander had in mind, but none was small and petty, and he*
> *would not have stopped conquering even if he'd added Europe to*
> *Asia and the Britannic Islands to Europe . . .*

Arrian was quite properly alert to Alexander's fame. But that comment on his last plans (see Chapter Ten) is just the sort of measured and reflective remark that commends him to the modern critical historian and biographer of the world-conqueror. Apart, perhaps, from his casual remark about 'the Britannic Islands' – as if they were *not* part of 'Europe' . . .

A millennium and a half later, Shakespeare's Hamlet comments rather irreverently in the graveyard scene on the possible earthly fate of Alexander's corpse:

> *Alexander died, Alexander was buried,*
> *Alexander returneth into dust; the dust*
> *is earth; of earth we make loam; and why of*
> *that loam, whereto he was converted, might*
> *they not stop a beer-barrel?*

This is a chauvinistic English illustration of the fact that Alexander has featured in the national literatures of some eighty countries, stretching from our own Britannic islands to the Malay peninsula by way of Kazakhstan (home of Abai, its national poet). This, in its turn, is another way of saying that Alexander is probably the most famous of the few individuals in human history whose bright light has shot across the firmament to mark the end of one era and the beginning of another. As the novelist Mary Butts put it rather well (in a note to her 1931 fiction, *The Macedonian*): 'There are men who sum up an epoch, and men who begin another. Alexander did both.' She aptly cited, too, another passage of Arrian:

> *I am persuaded that there is no nation, city or people then in*
> *being where his name did not reach; for which reason, whatever*

origin he might boast of, or claim to himself, there seems to me to have been some divine hand presiding over both his birth and his actions, inasmuch as no mortal on earth either excelled or equalled him.

Another local testimony – and testament – to Alexander's fame is as British in its way as can be. To celebrate the 250th anniversary of the founding of the British Museum in 1753, the Royal Mail devised a set of special stamps illustrating just six objects out of the BM's collection of over seven million artefacts spanning some two million years of the human past. One of these six represents a stone bust of Alexander carved in the Hellenistic era (about 200 BCE)· Alexander, 'who', according to the promotional material, 'after his death, was worshipped as a god'.

That is not quite accurate; he was also, crucially, worshipped as a living god. But one ancient figure who certainly was worshipped as a god only after his death was the proto-Roman emperor Julius Caesar, in whose life Plutarch (as Shakespeare well knew) found a parallel to that of Alexander. Reasonably enough, since in some respects Caesar did come quite close to equalling Alexander – though only after many more years of trying – and he did give his name to a type of autocratic ruler (Kaiser, Czar). When Julius was on an early tour of imperial duty in Spain, Plutarch relates, he is said to have gazed at a statue of Alexander (perhaps like the one now in the Museum at Seville, which came from the Roman colony of Italica that produced two later Roman emperors). And he wept because, whereas Alexander had died at thirty-two, king of so many peoples, he himself at that same age had not yet achieved any brilliant success. I am no Julius Caesar. But I am fifty-six at the time of writing this – so you can, I hope, imagine how I feel.

Many many more illustrations of Alexander's fame could be given. St Augustine wasn't hugely impressed: he considered him (in Frank Holt's paraphrase of the *City of God* passage) 'a rogue with a global appetite for plunder' – a rather startlingly modern image. St John

Chrysostom, patriarch of Constantinople, objected to the way that coins bearing Alexander's image were often bound to people's heads and feet as apotropaic talismans. The modern equivalent of this is perhaps to be found on the tennis court: the Australian player Mark Philippoussis, whose father is Greek, carries an Alexander tattoo. Presumably Chrysostom would have been more in sympathy with Dante, who consigned Alexander to the seventh circle of his *Inferno*, along with (other?) thieves, murderers and tyrants. Even in Greece today sailors in distress are said to be confronted by a water-nymph who demands to know 'Where is the great Alexander?' To which the only satisfactory response is: 'Great Alexander lives and reigns.' Indeed.

Such in fact is his continuing fame even in today's very differently structured global world that business journalists write management books purporting to derive and to convey 'lessons from the great empire builder'. And American film-makers and their financial backers are prepared to commit millions of dollars to exploring, recreating and perhaps even, they hope, enhancing the fame of the original. But was fame or glory, as Abai would have it, the spur for Alexander – the holy grail that drove him to achieve what he did? And, though without question incomparably famous both now and in his lifetime, was he, is he, also 'great', let alone 'the Great'? These are just some of the major questions that we shall seek to answer in the course of our hunt for a new interpretation of Alexander's peculiar genius.

My answers, any answers, must necessarily be provisional, tentative and more or less speculative. For Alexander has been handed down to us ultimately as an enigma, thanks above all to the inadequate nature of our sources of evidence. Though the extant evidence is very far from slight in quantity, it is in several respects seriously deficient in quality. It is mainly non-contemporary, it is partisan (con as well as pro), and it tends to be sensationalist. Whichever of the major aspects of Alexander's career we study, therefore, we are usually unable to reach anything firmer than a high probability in explanation, and even that degree of probability is a rarity. The very facts themselves – what actually happened – are often unclear. Like that of the ancient Roman historian Tacitus, therefore, our prime watchword as historians of Alexander must be distrust of what we are told.

Some students of Alexander, indeed, believe that the best that can be done in the way of historical retrieval is to focus on the various images of the man that the different kinds and media of evidence provide, without hoping or expecting to be able to proceed further to uncover anything like the – or any sort of – truth about Alexander. The present book will indeed pay due attention to the image, or rather images, of Alexander, and to the abundant mythistorical tradition that sprang up around him in his own lifetime and has continued vigorously to our own day. But it will also argue that a careful reading of the most reliable ancient sources, both written texts and broadly archaeological data, can reveal something substantial about what made Alexander tick, and how and why he was able to achieve what he did.

I SHALL BEGIN by tracing in outline Alexander's career from his birth at Pella in Macedonia in summer 356 to the beginning of his campaign of conquest against the Persian Empire in 334. This will be only an outline account, but it will provide a geographical and chronological backdrop and framework for the subsequent thematic chapters; and, as I go through, I shall indicate those points at which the key themes singled out for detailed discussion are engaged. The purely geographical frame of Alexander's achievements will constantly be referred to. Polybius (a major Greek historian of the second century BCE) believed that a proper history couldn't be written except by someone who'd inspected all the scenes of historical action in person. Unfortunately, this has not been possible for me, not by a long chalk, but what I shall try to do is bring out the salient features of terrain and climate in every relevant case, beginning with Alexander's own home territory of Macedonia (Upper and Lower). I shall then dog

Alexander's footsteps for well over twenty thousand miles (thirty thousand kilometres) as he led victorious armies, first north towards the Danube then south into central Greece, before finally setting off for Asia, never to return to Europe, in 334.

Between 334 and 331 he defeated the Persian Great King's Mediterranean navy – paradoxically, unpredictably and perhaps undeservedly – by land. That is, he captured its bases one by one, especially in the Levant, where the siege of Tyre in 332 was crucial. This meant that, with mainland Greece under the firm control of Regent Antipater, Alexander could for the most part concentrate unswervingly on winning a series of major set-piece battles against Darius III. Of these there were three: the Granicus river in western Anatolia in 334, Issus in southern Anatolia in 333, and Gaugamela in Mesopotamia in 331. Much more, and very hazardous, fighting lay ahead. But to all intents and purposes from the middle of 329, when a kinsman and would-be successor of the dead Darius was executed, Alexander had no rival as ruler of a new, massively enlarged empire. Eventually, this would stretch from Greece to Pakistan, taking in on the way – among other countries or regions – Egypt, Syria and Babylonia, as well as, of course, the old Persian heartland of Iran.

The hardest fighting, and in its way the most admirable of Alexander's military successes, occurred in the uplands of central Asia between 329 and 327. This was episodic and irregular guerrilla fighting against tribal warrior bands, not a series of formal, traditional encounters with national or civic armies in open field of battle. Alexander's father Philip had, it was neatly said by a later biographer, 'fought his wars by marriages'. That is to say, he had combined straightforward fighting and conquest with marital diplomacy and bridge-building, either to lessen his enemies' resistance, or to ensure their quiescence after defeat; and he had done so no fewer than seven times. Alexander imitated his father only twice, in Sogdiana in 327 and in Iran in 324, and each was a sign not of power and success but rather of the difficulty with which the victory had been won, and the complexity of any subsequent maintenance of his authority. Later writers talked these marriages up in romantic terms, especially his first with Roxane, but the truth was surely more pragmatically prosaic.

Once he had Iran and its environs more or less securely under his control, by the summer of 327, it is arguable that Alexander did not need to embark on further conquest. He did not need, for example, to reconquer the land beyond the Hindu Kush mountains, in modern Pakistan, that had once belonged to the Persian Empire but long since been lost and abandoned. Yet not only did Alexander inspire, cajole or drive his men (and their sexual partners) across and into Pakistan and India, but he made as if to press on ever further eastwards, to the very edge of the world (as that was then generally conceived), to where the furthermost landmass was lapped by the engirdling Ocean. As the Roman author Quintus Curtius Rufus put it:

> *The fates waited for him to complete the subjugation of the Orient and reach Ocean, achieving all that a mortal man was capable of.*

A tremendous and astounding victory was gained in 326 over the Paurava Rajah (his name was Hellenized as 'Porus'), elephants and all, at the River Hydaspes (modern Jhelum; see further Chapter Seven). But when the men, the Macedonian core, reached the River Hyphasis (the modern Beas), their sufferings from long years of campaigning exacerbated by unheard-of natural torments like the monsoon, they delivered their – literal – ultimatum to Alexander, who was forced to concede his first defeat: at the hands of his own men. With ill grace and unappealing savagery Alexander cut a path to the mouth of the Indus, dispatching many Indians, on the one hand – and in another sense, on the other, a part of his troops back to Iran by sea. Perhaps recklessly he took the remainder in person through the gruelling Makran desert of Baluchistan.

This near-final – as it was to prove – military effort took some of the gloss off Alexander's previous astonishing military achievements.

His return to Iran, to the centre of his new empire, forced upon his immediate practical consciousness for the first time the nature and urgency of the problem of managing and administering this vast new entity. Not surprisingly, he did not always get it right. Not only did his Asiatic appointees as governors prove corrupt, inefficient or disloyal, or all three. Also, his childhood chum and now Imperial High Chancellor, Harpalus, decided in 324 to defect (for the second time) to mainland Greece, adding injury to insult by taking with him a vast sum of what should have been Alexander's treasure. Alexander's difficulties were compounded by the loss, this time merely to death from disease, of another intimate friend since childhood, his Grand Vizier Hephaestion. Rumour had it – and rumour was for once surely correct – that he and Alexander had once been more than just good friends. At any rate, Alexander's grief was truly Homeric, as if Achilles were grieving for Patroclus over again. And perhaps he never quite recovered the balance of his mind before he too died – of a fever, probably, though inevitably it was rumoured that he had been assassinated, like his father before him – at Babylon in June 323.

What exactly Alexander's plans for the future may have been, we shall never certainly know. Shortly after his death a set of alleged 'plans' was published. But they probably say more for the perceived state of his megalomania and the political ambitions of his rivalrous imitators than for any soberly conceived course of short-term and medium-term projects. At all events, the immediate outcome was a prolonged struggle between a handful of so-called Successors to carve up the corpse of the empire that had expired with its founder himself. By the early third century there were three major kingdoms in Greece and the Middle East: the Antigonid in Macedonia and old Greece (the heartland of the Aegean Greek World), the Ptolemaic in Egypt and the Seleucid in Asia, of which the latter two were the most powerful, and the Seleucid the nearest to retaining something like Alexander's Asiatic legacy intact. A fourth, the Attalid kingdom based on Pergamum, was added in the course of the third century. It was this 'Hellenistic' world that the Romans were to conquer between the late third and mid first century BCE, and it was within the Hellenized eastern Roman Empire that Christianity was first to emerge. St Paul, a Hellenized Jew possessing Roman citizenship, came from Tarsus in Cilicia, not all that far from the site of the second of Alexander's three major set-piece battles.

But were the Macedonians themselves Greek? This may seem an astonishing question, especially in light of the recent international brouhaha over the (Former Yugoslav) Republic of Macedonia. But actually many Greeks in Alexander's day were of the view that the Macedonians were either not very, or not entirely, or not at all Greek. In so far as there was any historical basis for that view, it rested on the perception of the Macedonians' language, often incomprehensible to standard Greek-speakers. Against it, however, was the symbolic language of shared and accepted myth, which spoke firmly for the inclusion of the Macedonians in the Hellenic family – both of all of them as descendants of the eponymous Macedon, and of the royal family, the Argeadae, in particular. The Argeads claimed direct lineal descent from one Temenus, who it was alleged had migrated from Argos in the Peloponnese to Macedonia in some dim and distant past. And so ultimately, since Temenus was a direct descendant of Heracles, they were descended from the hero–god Heracles himself. The location within Macedonian territory of Mount Olympus, home of the dozen major gods and goddesses, was a not inconsiderable reinforcement of such arguments. The Macedonians themselves, through the development of Dium on the mountain's north-east flank as a sacred city with its own truly Olympic Games, properly exploited this geographical contingency.

The territory of Macedonia falls roughly into two halves, an upland, western zone and a lowland, eastern zone, the latter distinguished by the fertile plain of Emathia. Some sort of monarchy was established in eastern Macedonia, with its capital at Aegae, by about 600 BCE, but the first Macedonian king to cut any kind of figure on a wider Greek stage was Alexander I, who reigned for most of the first half of the fifth century. Unfortunately, the figure he cut was more than a little ambiguous, as at the time of the Persian invasions of Greece in 490 and 480/79 he was merely a vassal and glorified messenger-boy of the Persian Great Kings Darius I and Xerxes. That he acquired the nickname 'the philhellene' was also ambiguous. On the one hand, it advertised his alleged loyalty to the Greeks as opposed to the Persians; on the other, it suggested that he was not himself a Hellene, or not Hellene enough.

Not until the very end of the fifth century did an Argead king achieve the political unification of Upper (western) and Lower (eastern) Macedonia, the indispensable condition for Macedon's becoming any sort of power. Archelaus (r. 414–399) simultaneously removed the capital further east from Aegae (which remained the ceremonial capital and royal burial ground) to Pella. Here he built a new palace (to which he welcomed, for example, Euripides), tamed the various local warlords of the Upper Macedonian cantons, established a network of fortifications to ensure their loyalty, and revamped the Macedonian army in partial imitation of the arms, armour and tactics that had been practised for over two centuries in Greece further to the south. Archelaus's unification and modernization were seriously jeopardized, however, as Macedon witnessed the coming and going of no fewer than four rulers within the decade following his death. But stability was reasserted by Amyntas III (r. 393–369), father of Philip II (r. 359–336) and grandfather of Alexander III (r. 336–323), our Alexander.

Of all his predecessors Alexander owed by far the most to his father, an unparalleled figure in European history, according to a not usually gullible Greek contemporary (Theopompus of Chios). Philip not merely established Macedon as the biggest thing in the north of the Greek peninsula and expanded its imperial control to both west and east, from the Adriatic to the Black Sea, and almost as far north as the Danube. He also extended his hegemony over the Greeks to his south, as far as the borders of Sparta's territory in the south-east Peloponnese. This hegemony he institutionalized within the framework of what moderns call the League of Corinth, actually more an instrument of empire than a league properly so called. And it was as appointed general of the League that Philip was on the point of commencing a Panhellenic crusade of revenge and reparation against the Persian Empire in 336.

But that summer Philip was assassinated in full public view by Pausanias, a disgruntled member of his own personal bodyguard, when taking part in the wedding procession of his daughter, Cleopatra, Alexander's full sister. The identity of the assassin was clear, but what never became clear was whether he had acted alone, or on behalf of a faction or cabal. Sexual shenanigans were alleged, but deeper political currents were swirling around the Pella court too. Fingers of suspicion were pointed at Philip's estranged wife Olympias, Alexander's mother, and indeed at Alexander himself, perhaps with some reason. It was Alexander at any rate who benefited most from the death of his father at that particularly pregnant moment in Macedon's, Greece's, the Middle East's and indeed the world's history.

Alexander seized the throne, had his authority as king recognized in the official way by the army, put to death a number of potential rivals and had himself elected in place of his father to the Panhellenic anti-Persian command. All that in the summer of 336. The following year he set about securing his rear on the European mainland in advance of crossing over to Asia. First, he quelled dissidence on his northern borders, particularly among the Thracians and Illyrians. Then he crushed Greek resistance led by Thebes – which suffered the same fate of physical annihilation as had Greek Olynthus under Philip in 348. Thus secure, and with the huge extra advantage – thanks to Philip's reforms – of commanding the one sort of army that could envisage seriously taking on and defeating the sort of armies that the Persian Great King would throw against him, Alexander set sail for Asia in spring 334. He was never to return to Macedon or indeed to leave Asia again.

Major controversy still surrounds the issues of when Philip of

Macedon first conceived the idea of an invasion of Persia, and just exactly what he aimed to achieve by his invasion. With Alexander, there is no doubt but that he intended from the first to conquer and rule all the existing Persian Empire – and then some. Not only areas such as Pakistan that the Persians had once ruled, but also new territories, indeed at the limit everything that lay between him and 'Ocean', the vast sea or river that was thought to encircle the earth's land masses. The question for us, rather, is what sort of a ruler he intended to be – always supposing that he ever intended merely to settle down and rule: in particular, how oriental – that is, in what way or ways, and to what extent oriental – a ruler?

Alexander died young and in mid-course, so we can't rule out that there might have been further, possibly significant evolution. But already there is, I believe, enough evidence to show that he aimed to establish himself as a new King of Asia by proving himself a legitimate successor to the Persian emperors. We can see him adopting versions of Persian regalia, using native Iranians in the highest of commands and administrative positions. We see him marrying two Persian and one Sogdian women, and encouraging his most intimate Companions to do likewise; incorporating Iranian troops in formerly exclusive Macedonian regiments, forming new elite units composed solely of oriental soldiers. And we see him bestowing honorific oriental titles such as 'Kinsmen' on orientals before doing the same to his Macedonians, and so forth. This, for example, is the – critical and not necessarily wholly accurate – account of the romanized Gaul Trogus (first century BCE) as preserved in Justin (third century CE):*

> *After this Alexander took on the dress of the Persian kings including a diadem, something previous Macedonian kings had never worn . . . He also told his friends to wear long, golden and purple robes. To imitate the Persians in their excessive customs as*

---

* See Appendix, pp. 255–6.

well as in their attire, he divided his nights among the horde of
royal concubines . . . To all this he added hugely sumptuous
banquets . . .

It was too soon to say how far he might also have altered the old
Persian methods of imperial administration. But the impression is that
he would have done so only for pragmatic reasons, not because he was
unhappy with the idea of maintaining inherited oriental practices and
institutions that had worked for many years.

We have seen already that it was a live issue whether Alexander
was truly 'Greek'. He himself, however, was in absolutely no doubt.
In culture above all, following the lead given by his father, he professed
himself a lover of Greek things and surrounded himself with Greek
courtiers – from his chamberlain Eumenes to his official historian
Callisthenes, his admiral Nearchus (a companion from boyhood) and
his official sculptor Lysippus. He proclaimed himself a new Achilles –
and his most intimate companion, Hephaestion, his Patroclus. He
advertised the Persian campaign as a (pan)Hellenic crusade, being
careful to return to Athens from the administrative capital Susa statues
stolen by the Persians in 480. He also sent there three hundred suits
of armour for dedication to Athena by 'Alexander son of Philip and
the [other] Greeks'. He celebrated Greek-style games and festivals
at regular intervals during the campaign, and he spread the worship
of the Greeks' gods, not least through the foundation of a number of
Greek cities at nodal points in the empire. There is even testimony, in
Plutarch's biography, to his Greek bookishness:*

> *When his campaigns had taken him deep into Asia, and he could*
> *lay his hands on no other books, he ordered Harpalus to have*
> *some sent to him. These comprised the [prose] histories of*
> *Philistus, many tragedies by Aeschylus, Sophocles and Euripides,*
> *and dithyrambic poems by Telestes and Philoxenus.*

---

* See Appendix, pp. 255–8.

There remain, however, major question marks over the nature of Alexander's Hellenism. How sincerely, for example, was he committed to the Greek freedom that he proclaimed after the Battle of the Granicus in 334? Why did he make no use of the Greek, that is mainly Athenian, navy, and relatively little of the forces provided by the League of Corinth, whom he cashiered immediately after the capture of the Persian heartland? Why did more Greeks fight against Alexander, as mercenaries, than for him, right down to and including the climactic Battle of Gaugamela? Why did so many Greeks join Athens in revolt against Macedon immediately after his death, in 323/2? And were the cities he founded really founded chiefly for cultural reasons, to spread Hellenism, or more narrowly for pragmatic political, military and economic reasons? Whatever the answer to that last question, however, the fact is unarguable that the Hellenistic world of the last three centuries BCE, with its major new centres in cities like Alexandria in Egypt and Antioch in Syria, was the direct outcome of Alexander's achievement of conquest and pacification.

There are those who believe Alexander to be the world's greatest military conqueror ever. Full stop. I, on the other hand, don't think it's realistic to try to make a global comparative judgement of that sort. Strictly non-comparable situations and contexts are involved. I am also one of those who believe that Alexander was – and had to be – very much more than just a conqueror. Arguably, though, it is above all, or perhaps solely, for his talents and achievements as a commander on the field of battle that he fully deserves the epithet 'the Great'. But those talents and achievements have to be contextualized in order to be properly appreciated, to be placed within the context of his diplomacy and other man-management skills off the field. They must also be situated, above all, in the framework of the almost miraculous military transformations wrought by his father Philip.

Five of Alexander's many and varied engagements will receive special attention in Chapter Seven, since they illustrate different facets of his military genius. These are his programmatic first season's campaigning as king, in 335, both in the far north, beyond the Danube, and in southern Greece; the arduous seven-month siege of Phoenician Tyre in 332; the decisive victory over Persian Great King Darius III in a titanic land battle at Gaugamela in 331; the guerrilla war in central Asia between 329 and 327; and, finally, the victory over Rajah Porus and his elephants at the River Hydaspes in 326. The other two major land battles, at the Granicus in 334 and Issus in 333, will also be given their due. Similarly, the often neglected campaign at sea in the Aegean and east Mediterranean between 334 and 332, in which Alexander deliberately but riskily chose to play no direct part.

Another of the major themes we shall be exploring with especial care is Alexander's perception of himself, and his desire for recognition by others, as more than merely mortal, as in some way superhuman or divine (see Chapter Eleven). He was not, quite, the first in the Greek world to become, literally, a cult figure. In 404 the oligarchs who had been restored to power on Samos renamed the city's principal festival, the Heraea (held in honour of the great goddess Hera, sister–wife of Father Zeus), as the Lysandreia in honour of their Spartan benefactor Lysander, who so far from being an immortal god was a very present and mortal human being. By thus bridging the gap between mortals and immortals they set a precedent not certainly imitated until the time of Alexander's father, Philip, some two to three generations later.

By the end of his reign, in 323, Alexander was quite certainly being worshipped by orientals as a god in Asia, both at Babylon where he died and further west, in Egypt, where religious worship of the ruling Pharaoh was traditional. But although there were these precedents, it must also be recalled that the Persian kings whom he had supplanted had not been regarded, or worshipped, as divine by their subjects. They were but the vicars on earth of the great Zoroastrian god of light, Ahura Mazda. Alexander would, then, have been taking a major step, if he wished to be or commanded that he be worshipped as divine by his non-Greek oriental subjects outside Babylonia and Egypt. He was also receiving lifetime divine worship from Greeks in the Greek cities of the Asiatic seaboard, filled as they were with gratitude for their liberation from Persian domination. Possibly too in mainland Greece – if, that is, we believe the very shaky evidence for a direct imperial order issued in 324 by Alexander himself that he should be so worshipped.

He might have been the more willing and eager to issue that order had he regarded himself as actually divine, that is, not merely to be treated as such. And there is a good deal of circumstantial evidence that such a self-belief did indeed grow exponentially in the course of his campaigning. A key moment seems to have been his consultation, at the Siwah oasis, with the Libyan–Egyptian god Ammon (Amun), after which he spoke of himself as being descended genetically from a god.* This gave rise to jokes about his 'so-called' father Philip. He tried to get his Greek and Macedonian courtiers to pay him the kind of obeisance which in Persia was a social, not a religious, custom, but which in Greek eyes was religious, not merely social, since it was due only to the gods. This may have been an indirect way of telling his Greek and Macedonian courtiers that he considered himself divine. But it may also be interpreted in a quite different way – as a method of amalgamating his Graeco-Macedonian and his Persian courts, by extending the Persian mode of ceremonial greeting to the Greeks and Macedonians.

In any case, whatever the motivation, it did not work diplomatically and was dropped. But this in no way diminished Alexander's own personal religiosity, which went beyond the merely superstitious and bordered even on the fanatical. The devotional element was a key ingredient of Alexander the man (see Chapter Ten). This raises in a sharp way the issue of Alexander's personality and character. We have no surviving direct testimony from any of his closest associates, and he kept no personal journal. So what made Alexander tick has to be inferred in the first instance from what he did, and did not do.

---

* See Appendix, pp. 263–5.

Beginning at the beginning, we may wish to speculate – there is no other way – about the characteristics, aptitudes and predilections Alexander inherited from his parents, Philip and Olympias (see Chapter Three). Here, for example, is Plutarch on the latter's alleged enthusiasm for ecstatic religious mysticism:

> Olympias was said to have outdone the other women in her desire to be possessed by the god [Dionysus]. She would introduce into the festal gatherings numbers of tame snakes, which struck fear into the male spectators as they entwined themselves around the wands and garlands of the women.

The information on Alexander's education is more solidly based, especially that presided over by Aristotle at Mieza from 343, though – notwithstanding the annotated copy of the *Iliad* that Aristotle gave his pupil – it remains doubtful that Alexander was persuaded the word was mightier than the sword. More influential were the lasting friendships that he struck up at Mieza that were to have important political consequences, especially with Hephaestion. Alexander seems actually to have referred to Hephaestion as his alter ego. Their relationship was almost certainly at one time sexual. Another key figure in his life from his boyhood or youth onwards was Bucephalas: possibly the only horse in history to have a city named after him (Bucephala in what is now Pakistan, though its remains have never been identified on the ground).

Men and horses at any rate seem to have taken precedence in his affections over women. A possible explanation might involve a Macedonian version of Freud's Little Hans case: as a very young boy Hans had seen a sexually aroused stallion, and the sight had put him off sex in adulthood. Or perhaps Alexander suffered from a repressed Oedipus complex (his relationship with his mother is one of the great unresolved puzzles of his life). This at any rate is more plausible than the suggestions that he was either impotent or/and a preferred homosexual. The alleged 365-concubine harem was doubtless more for ostentation than daily use, and, as already noted above, we surely shouldn't believe the love-match spin put on the marriage of convenience between Alexander and Roxane (daughter of a major Sogdian baron).

More important to him than women, or than sex with women anyway, was his religion. Alexander was the classic *deisidaimôn* (Superstitious Man). He relied above all others on his pet seer (*mantis*) Aristander; for conspicuous examples, see Halicarnassus in 334 and the Oxus River in 329. He was also something of a religious mystic, as was revealed above all by the Siwah episode. After this, he regarded himself as in some sense 'son of Zeus' and simultaneously contracted a special relationship of 'sonship' with Libyan Ammon (sometimes identified with Zeus by Greeks, though not by Alexander). It was to Ammon that he sent to enquire how Hephaestion should be honoured after his death in 324/3. The – acceptable – answer was, as a hero.

Another way of approaching the matter of Alexander's humanity and personality is through the word *pothos*, meaning 'passionate yearning' or 'irresistible desire', which crops up with noticeable regularity in Arrian's account and may go back ultimately to Callisthenes's heroic representation of his employer for the benefit initially of a sceptical Greek audience. The usage of the term by Arrian is at least consistent with the vision of Alexander as ever seeking after super-human achievement – maybe even to become superhuman. The authenticity of Alexander's so-called last plans, made public by Grand Vizier Perdiccas following his death at Babylon in June 323 and based allegedly on the official *Hypomnemata* or 'Expedition Note-books', is unfortunately suspect, even if they too are no less plausibly Alexandrine.

Both the neutral and the hostile sources paint a picture of Alexander as degenerating morally throughout his reign, until by its (premature) end he was showing distinct tinges of megalomania. The sobersided eighteenth-century Scottish historian William Robertson speaks of his 'wild sallies', while the disabused contemporary historian Ernst Badian prefers to see an ever-present ruthless streak coming out increasingly so as finally to predominate. Perhaps therefore it was a good thing for Alexander's reputation that he died when he did, so that rather than feeling massively let down (as some do, for example, by Napoleon) we are left only with the sense of what might have been (our own *pothos*?).

The politico-ethnic issue, as to whether or not he counted, wholly or in part, as 'Greek' under the act, is but one of Alexander's fiercely contested legacies, with an obvious contemporary resonance. Another, less immediately obvious perhaps, resides in the claim that modern business corporations can draw any number of useful 'life lessons' from a close study of Alexander's 'art of strategy'. More congenial, to me at any rate, is the study of his more direct legacy in antiquity to kings, would-be kings and imperial generals, who borrowed some or all of his powers and symbolic attributes to bolster their own claims to unswerving devotion and submission.

In another guise, Alexander himself became the one to cast spells, literally, as a practitioner of magic – just one of the many forms in which he was depicted in the so-called *Alexander Romance*. We have today versions of all the major ancient Romance traditions: Greek, Latin and Armenian. Parallel to this literary legacy, but with an even wider reception, was the dissemination of visual imagery of Alexander, and the proliferation of copies of some or all of it for the purpose of creating portraits of kings and generals who wished to bask by association in Alexander's aura. Finally, there are the modern equivalents of the ancient *Alexander Romance* and the ancient visual representations, respectively the historical novel and the movie. We for our part by dint of careful source criticism must scrupulously avoid succumbing to the temptation of becoming just latter-day purveyors or inventors of an *Alexander Romance* for the twenty-first century. That would be to reduce his genuine fame to mere celebrity.

To conclude: it has been well said that there are not one but many Alexanders, because every historian, or anyone seriously interested in him, creates an Alexander of her or his own. But that process of solipsistic Alexander-fashioning is by no means simple or straight-forward – as we are sharply reminded by one final illustration of Alexander's fame within the Western literary tradition. It comes from the American poet Robert Lowell's 'The Death of Alexander', published originally in a collection entitled simply *History*:

> *No one was like him. Terrible were his crimes –*
> *but if you wish to blackguard the Great King,*
> *think how mean, obscure and dull you are,*
> *your labors lowly and your merits less . . .*

TWO

ALEXANDER'S WORLD

ALEXANDER was born in 356 BCE. He was born into royalty. His mother Olympias was a princess from the Molossian kingdom of Epirus in north-west Greece. Just three years earlier his father Philip had arrogated to himself the throne of Macedon, although technically he was supposed to be acting merely as regent for an older brother's under-age son. The world Alexander was born into and grew up in had three main political and cultural dimensions. First, there was the kingdom of Macedon itself, consisting of the region of Macedonia alone until Philip vastly enlarged the kingdom's territory and sway during his meteoric twenty-three-year reign (359–336). Then there was the old Greek world to the south and east of Macedonia, embracing the Greek mainland, the Aegean islands and the east Mediterranean pale of Hellenic settlement. Finally, there was the Persian Empire, based in modern Iran, which stretched from the Hindu Kush in the east to the Aegean in the west, and periodically occupied or threatened to occupy the land of the Greeks who lived on the westernmost fringes of Asia.

Alexander's Macedonian inheritance from Philip is neatly summed up in the complex and subtle speech that Arrian puts into Alexander's mouth at Opis in 324 (where he was faced with a second mutiny by his Macedonian veterans). This is how it begins:

> Philip inherited you when you were resourceless vagabonds, the majority of you dressed in skins and pasturing a few sheep in the mountains and fighting on their behalf, feebly, against Illyrians, Triballians and the Thracians on your borders. Cloaks he gave you to wear instead of skins. He brought you down from the

mountains to the plains. He made you capable of fighting
worthily against the neighbouring barbarians, so that you no
longer put your trust in the natural strength of your mountain
strongholds to preserve you but rather in your own manly valour.
He made you city-dwellers. He civilized you through the
establishment of good laws and practices.

In its own idiosyncratic way this passage describes Philip's contribution to the economic, military, political and cultural development of Macedon and Macedonians. Alexander's picture of the Macedonian economy as totally pastoral at the time of Philip's accession to kingly power is overdrawn, though it does contain an important element of truth. The Macedonian economy was indeed still more heavily pastoral than the typical economies of the more developed, more urbanized Greek world to the south. This was due partly to Macedonia's geography, but also and no less – as Philip's reign was spectacularly to demonstrate in reverse – to its previous political disunity. For speaking simply of 'Macedonia' (the geographical area) or 'Macedon' (the political entity) is to disguise the fundamental duality of this large land mass, the duality of mountain and plain. Put differently, this is the distinction between Upper (western) and Lower (eastern) Macedonia.

It was Philip's major politico-military achievement to unify the two sectors politically and diplomatically, and thereby to gain unimpeded access to the whole range of Macedonia's generous native economic resources. These consisted of timber, pitch, and game from the uplands (one-fifth of this core Macedonia is still forest today), sheep and goats pastured on the foothills and mountain plateaux, and the grain grown in the fertile plains and valleys of the lowlands: especially that Emathian plain in which lay the city of Pella, the Macedonian capital since the end of the fifth century. Philip's extensive conquests along the northern Aegean seaboard, culminating in 348 in his destruction of Greek Olynthus, the capital of the Chalcidian federal state, had put at his disposal large tracts of spear-won land, his own personal property.

This he distributed mainly to leading Macedonians, and to some important Greeks too, on condition that in return he could demand and expect total loyalty – and in particular military service – from these bigshot beneficiaries. But some land was also distributed, in much smaller parcels, to humble Macedonian commoners, so as to produce a wider class of middling peasant farmers. These men were now, at least economically, not so very unlike the sort of citizens who composed the Greek heavy-armed militias further to the south. It is this process of 'gentrification' that Arrian's Alexander is referring to laconically when he says that Philip 'brought you down from the mountains to the plains'.

But what Alexander omits to say here is that Philip, in the process of expansion, also gained control of the vast mineral resources of the region, in particular the gold and silver mines of Mount Pangaeum in Chalcidian Thrace. These were said to yield him an annual revenue of 1,000 silver talents – which, if true, would have been the equivalent of the income of the fifth-century BCE Athenian Empire or of the Spartan Empire of the early fourth century at their respective heights. One of the major uses to which this mined wealth was put was to strike the ever more abundant coinage with which Philip both paid his large numbers of non-Macedonian mercenaries and advertised his power and piety.

To Philip's economic contribution Alexander rightly links his military contribution, even though he later falsely denies the success he himself owed, at least initially, to Philip's army. Theopompus of Chios, contemporary historian and the first to compose a history in Greek based on the exploits of one man (the *Philippica*), was nearer the mark when he claimed that Europe had not witnessed such a man as Philip before. This new army of Philip's naturally reflected the social structure of Macedon. In a society that is regularly labelled 'Homeric', the leading core of the Macedonian army was provided by the king and his noble advisers. The term for such royal advisers in Homer is *hetairoi*, 'companions' or 'comrades', and that term was applied as a technical usage in Macedon too. We know the names of some seventy-five Macedonians, fifteen Greeks and two orientals who at various points in Alexander's reign qualified for the honorific title Companion. And at Susa in 324 almost ninety of them were married to Iranian noblewomen in a famously controversial mass marriage ceremony.

It is not, though, the small size of this elite group that matters, so much as its composition. Before Philip, we must assume that the Companions would have been drawn almost exclusively from the leading families of Lower Macedonia. Philip, in order both to unify the territory politically and to weaken the old nobility, recruited in addition a significant number of Upper Macedonians. These included men like his premier general Parmenion, members of families which still thought of themselves as 'royal', despite the long establishment of the Argead dynasty at first Aegae and then Pella. Philip also established at Pella the body known as the Royal Pages. These were the late-teenage sons of Macedonian nobles, who officially performed the function of a ceremonial retinue and – less blatantly – royal bodyguard. But these select youths were also both being groomed for full adult Companion status and meanwhile serving as hostages for the good behaviour of their fathers.

If we want an illuminating analogy, the situation of the Argead dynasty was more akin to that of the English monarchy in the fifteenth century than to that of the Windsors in the twenty-first. Moreover, Philip's efforts at geopolitical unification are somewhat reminiscent of Louis XIV's struggle to tame his French barons in the seventeenth. Philip's cautious opening of the elite Companion group to some few Greeks as well as Macedonians ties in with his policy of Hellenization – that is, making Macedon culturally more Greek. Philip aimed to be a Hellenic, not just a Macedonian, ruler, and enthusiastically embraced the high culture that had been developed especially at Athens.

A little confusingly for modern observers, the term 'Companions' in the plural was not restricted to this close-knit circle of one hundred or so advisers of the king. It was used also to describe the Companion Cavalry, which was expanded by Philip on the same lines as the Companions in the narrow sense. We hear, for example, from Theopompus that Philip created eight hundred new Companion cavalrymen, both Macedonians and Greeks, by distributing among them an amount of land that in Greece would have had to support some ten thousand men. The economic standing of these eight hundred was founded on the more or less forced labour of a conquered and exploited peasantry, mainly Thracian by ethnic origin. Altogether, in 334 there were some 3,500 Companion cavalrymen, divided into eight squadrons. The premier squadron was known as the Royal Squadron and served as the king's bodyguard in battle.

The dilution – or dissemination – of the title 'Companion' did not end there. The backbone of Philip's Macedonian infantry phalanx was known as the Foot Companions (*Pezhetairoi*), an honorific title probably conferred on them first by one or other of Philip's two immediate predecessors as king. These were recruited on a territorial basis, in six battalions of roughly 1,500 men each. Thus we see how a title, *hetairoi*, applied originally in the fiction of Homer to a select band of high nobles advising the king, had become extended in the reality of Macedon to embrace the majority of the Macedonian army. There could be no more eloquent symbol of the personal importance of the army to the king, a theme on which Alexander was to play a significant oriental variation.

To complete the tally of properly Macedonian troops, it remains only to cite the *Hypaspistai* or Shield Bearers. These were another elite corps, of infantry – the Marines or Paras of the army. For the sake of mobility they were armed rather less heavily than the regular phalangites. They were divided into three battalions of about a thousand men each, one of the three being dubbed the 'Royal' battalion. This had the responsibility for the king's protection when he was using it for special exercises or operations. All these different sorts of troops were melded together by Philip, and combined in varying formations with non-Macedonians to create an ultimate fighting force. This would later hugely benefit Alexander the general.

It is not possible to calculate with precision the total number of Macedonians under arms at any one time in the reign of either Philip or Alexander. When Alexander took over command of the anti-Persian expeditionary force in 334, a figure in the range 35,000–50,000 seems quite plausible. This would indicate a fivefold increase since the start of Philip's reign twenty-five years earlier. The figures we have for the war of rebellion against Macedon that broke out in Greece in 323, immediately after Alexander's death, strongly suggest that his reign saw a population explosion in Macedonia. This was a predictable consequence of the political stability and economic prosperity engendered by his father. Under Philip, indeed, the total population of Macedonia, including a subject element of mainly Thracian origin, may have reached as high as half a million – perhaps twice that of Athens and its territory of Attica in the later fifth century. Under Alexander, we may safely infer, it grew considerably bigger even than that.

Besides its obvious military roles, the Macedonian army had functions that may broadly be called political. Philip clearly had seen the military as the key to the new national unity he was seeking to foster by breaking down or cutting across local and regional loyalties. We hear of no struggles or conflicts between lowland and upland Macedonians within the army, though the Foot Companions and Shield Bearers at least continued to be recruited territorially. It would be a gross misrepresentation, though, to say that under Philip the army became the state – except in the very broad and loose sense that the battlefield and the camp, rather than the council chamber or civilian assembly, were the theatres of the ordinary Macedonians' contribution to public life. It would be much truer to say that the king was the state (as in Louis XIV's 'L'état, c'est moi'). For the king united in his own person a near-monopoly of executive powers and privileges in the religious, judicial, diplomatic, political and military spheres.

The Macedonian monarchy was, to be blunt, an autocracy. In a polity without written laws such as Macedon, a king's power was what he could get done, or could get away with. Attempts to define or tie down his position in narrowly legalistic terms are inappropriate and seriously misleading. Like a Homeric king, he was what the Romans called a *primus inter pares*, a first among equals (equals, that is, in some respects only). So long as he could in the Homeric phrase 'rule by might', he became de facto an absolute ruler. There were, to be sure, some formal restraints on his exercise of that power. At a new king's accession the assembled army played an important role by officially ratifying by acclamation the selection of a successor to the deceased monarch. This prior selection, however, was not carried out by the army on its own initiative. It had been carried out already by the leading men within the inner Companionate. Only when the succession was disputed might the army play a genuinely, rather than formally, king-making role.

The army had a recognized role, too, in treason trials (by no means an unknown phenomenon), where the king himself was by definition an interested party and the prosecution was undertaken by another on his behalf. It was the army that reached the verdict, and decided and executed the sentence. Yet it would be wrong to exaggerate the degree of independence of the army's jurisdiction in such cases. Their decision could, of course, be swayed crucially by the known wishes of a powerful king such as Philip or Alexander. Finally, constraint was placed upon a king's freedom of action by factions within the Macedonian nobility that might seek to dictate policy to him or, failing that, to undermine his authority. To pre-empt this, a king might, like Alexander, seek to build up a faction unswervingly, even fanatically, loyal to himself and to use the rank and file of the army to crush or extirpate oppositionist factions. In short, when Arrian's Alexander says that Philip 'civilized you through the establishment of good laws and practices', we must understand that his strong, autocratic rule overrode internal struggles within the nobility and his dispensation of justice among the ordinary Macedonian people was generally respected.

It is important, too, not to misprize the statement that 'He made you city-dwellers.' To a Greek, a city or *polis* (whence our 'political', etc.) connoted full independence, and a man was a citizen of, say, Athens, an 'Athenian'. But in Macedon, cities were mere municipalities with, at most, some degree of local self-government, and a Macedonian was not a citizen of, say, Pella, a 'Pellaean', but a 'Macedonian from Pella'. Pella in such a formulation had a purely geographical connotation, and the ethnic designation 'Macedonian' was primary. There had been 'cities' in this Macedonian sense well before Philip, and it is not true to say that Philip had rendered Macedon a basically urban society.

On the other hand, so far as Macedon's civilization or culture is concerned, it is quite true that Philip had deliberately sought to Hellenize at least the nobility and had patronized Greek intellectuals and artists. This process had not trickled down to affect the populace as a whole, however, and the antics of the nobility, most conspicuously their crude drinking habits, suggest that even they had not thoroughly absorbed all aspects of Greek culture. The behaviour of Alexander himself is in this respect an entirely fair yardstick. Yet it would be out of place to depreciate Philip's own Hellenic culture in the way that Demosthenes of Athens, his diehard enemy, liked to do.

Demosthenes (384–322) called him a 'barbarian', or non-Greek-speaker, sneeringly adding that his country couldn't even provide decent slaves for true Greeks to employ. But even in the narrowest linguistic terms of Greek culture, this was strictly inaccurate. Philip was perfectly capable of conversing in standard Greek and reading Greek literature, even though the local Macedonian dialect was so interlarded with non-Greek (especially Illyrian) linguistic forms that it could be unintelligible to standard Greek-speakers. More importantly, the language of myth spoke for the Greekness of the Macedonian royal house. In 333, for example, Alexander absolved the Cilician Greek city of Mallus from paying to him the tribute that it had previously paid to Persia on the grounds that (as Arrian puts it) 'Mallus had been founded from Argos, and he himself claimed to be a descendant of the Argive Heraclids.' (The Heraclids were, according to a widely accepted myth, the descendants of Heracles who had settled at several places in the Peloponnese including Argos. The Argead royal house of Macedon, as mentioned earlier, claimed descent from the Heraclid Temenus, who had allegedly migrated from Argos to Macedonia.)

This claim to Greekness was one that the state of Elis, which organized the Panhellenic (all- and only-Greek) Olympic Games, was prepared to accept. For religion too was an intimate bearer of identity in ancient Greece, and the Macedonians' religion paid divine worship to the usual Hellenic pantheon. For example, at Alexander's new foundation of Calindoea we find an inscribed list of priests serving the cults of Asclepius and Apollo (Figure 10). On the other hand, it is noteworthy that only the reigning king of Macedon, and no other Macedonians, was considered sufficiently Greek to be permitted to enter the sacred Olympic Games as a competitor.

In the first half of the fourth century, during the early years of both Aristotle's and Philip's lives, there had been three major Greek powers: Sparta, Athens and Thebes. This fateful triangle's constant wrangling eventually played into Philip's hands as he sought to extend the power of Macedon over the whole Greek mainland. Sparta had been the first of the three to achieve a sway far outside its already large home territory in the southern Peloponnese (some five thousand square miles, or eight thousand square kilometres). This was done through its Peloponnesian League alliances that embraced most of the cities of the Peloponnese (except, notoriously, Argos) and several outside it, such as Megara and Thebes. Athens was a relative latecomer as a big power. It exploited its key role in repulsing the Persian invasion of 480/79 in order to build up a naval empire that would dominate the Aegean and indeed much of the eastern Mediterranean over the next half-century. In 431 the two power blocs dominated respectively by Sparta and

Athens came to blows in what we know as the Peloponnesian War. This mutually disastrous conflict lasted on and off for a generation (431 to 404) and had major consequences, not least militarily.

The eventual victor, but only with the aid of vast amounts of Persian cash, was Sparta. But Sparta then sought, inappropriately, to add much of what had been Athens's sea-based empire on to its existing land-based Peloponnesian League. The result was serious imperial overstretch and the alienation of such an important ally as Thebes, which joined forces with Athens to resist Spartan encroachment north of the Peloponnese. Sparta thereupon coolly renewed its rapprochement with Persia. Sparta's hard-line King Agesilaus II joined the Persian Great King (Artaxerxes II) in co-sponsoring in 386 the first of a series of Common Peaces (see Chapter Five) that notionally guaranteed autonomy to all Greek cities great and small. As interpreted by Agesilaus, however, with Persian connivance, the Peace entailed the abandonment of the Greeks of Asia Minor to Persian imperial sway once more. This was combined with a particularly aggressive settling of scores in mainland Greece – not just in the Peloponnese but as far north as Olynthus, in Macedon's backyard as it were.

Fatally, as it turned out, Sparta made the mistake of occupying Thebes in 382 and placing a garrison on its acropolis. This encouraged Athens to join forces with Theban exiles in order to expel the Spartans in 379. The following year, 378, Thebes re-established the Boeotian federal state that the Spartans had disbanded in 386, but on new and democratic lines, and put in hand a major army reform that included the creation of the Sacred Band, consisting of 150 pairs of homosexual lovers. This elite strike force was commanded by Pelopidas, one of the liberator-exiles who had spent part of his exile at Athens and no doubt had been influenced there to some degree by democratic ideas and ideology. But the overall organizing political and military brain was that of Epaminondas, who was something of a philosopher as well as a statesman, diplomat and general. He was shortly to prove a liberator of other Greeks (the Messenian Helots) on the grandest scale.

Eventually, the Thebans built up a sufficiently powerful military at home and a sufficiently large alliance abroad, including Athens, to take on the once invincible Spartans in pitched battle on land. In 371, at Leuctra in Boeotia, the Spartans were at last decisively defeated, a 'single blow', as Aristotle put it, from which they could not recover. The following year, the Spartans' home territory was invaded for the first time in centuries, by a massive Theban-led force under Epaminondas. Within a decade they had lost both their principal economic basis of the Helots (state serfs) at home in Messenia and their Peloponnesian League alliance abroad. The new federal capital city of Megalopolis in Arcadia, founded under Epaminondas's aegis, was a permanent bone lodged in Sparta's throat and a manifest symbol of Sparta's fall from great-power grace.

Thebes, briefly, was in the ascendancy, and one nicely relevant illustration of its temporary sway was that between 368 and 365 the young Philip was forced to kick his heels under confinement in Thebes itself, as a hostage for a weak Macedon's good behaviour. In 362, however, the Thebans' ascendancy melted away after the indecisive Battle of Mantinea in Arcadia – the result of which, according to the contemporary Athenian historian Xenophon, left Greece 'in an even greater state of confusion and upheaval than before'. Naturally, Philip had absorbed all the lessons he could, negative as well as positive, from his enforced stay in Thebes, the city of the great Epaminondas (who died at Mantinea in 362) and Pelopidas (who had died in 364 in Thessaly). He would put them to excellent effect in the coming decades as king of Macedon – and then of Greece.

In 378 the Athenians had at last established a successor to the naval alliance that had been the foundation of their empire in the fifth century, before defeat in the Peloponnesian War. This was an explicitly anti-Spartan organization, though it claimed to be legal within the terms of the Common Peace, and as such it included among its six founder-members Thebes, which could hardly boast anything of a naval tradition. At first the new alliance prospered greatly. Within a few years it had grown to a membership of some seventy-five states. But as with the Spartans in the aftermath of the Peloponnesian War success went to the Athenians' heads, and they started to use the Second Naval League for purposes that were more narrowly Athenian than communal. In particular, they tried again and again to recover the city of Amphipolis in the Thracian Chalcidice, which they themselves had founded in 437 but which had defected to the Spartans in 424 and remained independent ever since. Injury was added to insult in 357, when Amphipolis was besieged and captured by Philip, taking advantage of the widespread disaffection that put paid to the Athenian alliance as an effective military unit after the mid 350s. It was the loss of Amphipolis as much as any other single factor that accounted for the Athenians' deep distrust of Philip – a distrust exploited to the hilt by Demosthenes, democratic Athens's most famously effective politician after the great Pericles.

Athens was a Greek *polis*, culturally speaking the most famous of all, as it was the home of – to name but two contemporaries of Alexander – Plato and Demosthenes. But it was only one among the fifteen hundred or so Greek cities that stretched from Spain in the west to what is now Georgia at the eastern end of the Black Sea. Plato in his *Phaedo* conjured up a nice image of Greeks living 'like frogs or ants around a pond', since most Greek cities were coastal or in regular and close touch with the shores of the Mediterranean and Black Seas. This huge diaspora was the result of a movement of 'colonization' whereby many thousands of Greeks from about 750 BCE left their original homes in the Aegean and east Mediterranean basins and fanned out, first west, then north-east, then south, in an attempt to find more congenial or more profitable surroundings. A combination of economics and politics was the main driving force behind this massive population movement. A few of the Greek cities founded in this way were on the coast of Macedonia – cities like Pydna and

Methone, which Philip took over in the 350s. This merely emphasized the difference in conception between an independent and separatist Greek *polis* and the towns and villages in which the Macedonians lived as members of a tribal or ethnic group under either a local, cantonal 'baron' or a king who sought – usually unsuccessfully before Philip II – to impose his will over all.

For a few heady years in the late 340s Philip's son and heir Alexander was tutored at Mieza to the west of Pella by the greatest Greek intellectual of his day, Plato's pupil Aristotle. We don't know how far advanced Aristotle's thinking on politics was by then, but within a decade he had produced the first version of his treatise entitled *Politics*, or 'Matters to Do with the *Polis*'. In this he stated as an axiom that man (humankind generally) was a 'political animal', that is, a living creature designed to achieve the complete fulfilment of his or her nature within – and only within – the framework of a *polis* type of political entity. The Macedonians therefore were in his opinion some way off this state of perfection. On the other hand, in Aristotle's surely correct view, the Greek *polis* in the fourth century BCE was seriously defective in two main respects. First, it was all too liable to be racked by internal dissension, even civil war – what the Greeks called *stasis*. Aristotle spent one whole book out of the eight of the *Politics* in analysing the causes of *stasis* and prescribing preventive and curative remedies. One of the most horrific examples occurred at Argos in the Peloponnese in 370, when Aristotle was in his early teens. Over a thousand of the wealthiest Argive citizens were simply clubbed to death by a mob of impoverished and enraged ordinary people.

The second major defect of the exclusivist and separatist Greek *polis* was a chronic inability to form stable political alliances at any level above the ethnic/tribal. Herodotus at the end of his *Histories* had given a famous definition of 'Greekness': a compound of common blood, language, religion, customs and mores. Spot the deliberate omission – a common political organization. Here, in a way, the Macedonians scored relatively more highly than the other Greeks, apart from federal states like that dominated by Thebes in Boeotia. Kings might be assassinated in Pella, but the cantons and towns of Macedonia pulled together for the most part. In his exasperation Aristotle was moved to expostulate in the *Politics* that 'if only the Greeks could achieve a single *politeia* [political organization or constitution], they would rule the world'. Perhaps when he wrote that he had one eye on what his former pupil, Alexander, was doing in Asia at the time. Perhaps he even hoped Alexander would bring about some sort of global Hellenic unification at the expense of the non-Greek 'barbarians', whom Aristotle considered to be naturally and unalterably inferior to Greeks. But, interestingly, Alexander did not share his master's view of barbarians. Far from it: his empire was to be one in which 'barbarians', including – or especially – former enemies, could play a major, even a dominant role.

For most Greeks the barbarians *par excellence*, the quintessential 'Other', were the Persians. On more than one occasion before Alexander's day Persia featured crucially in the story of Greek affairs. The evidence for the first Persian Empire, that of the Achaemenids, is, alas, scrappy. No royal chronicles have been discovered, if indeed they ever existed, at any of the three royal capitals – Pasargadae (built by the Empire's founder Cyrus II the Great), Susa or Persepolis (the two latter built by Darius I, the Empire's re-founder) – or at the summer palace of Ecbatana in Media (the modern Hamadan). We do have isolated official texts, such as this inscription of Cyrus on a brick from Ur in Babylonia (now in the British Museum):

> *Cyrus, king of the world, king of Anshan, son of Cambyses, king of Anshan. The great gods delivered all the lands into my hand, and I made this land to dwell in peace.*

Most notably of all, we have the famous Bisitun (or Behistun) inscription carved in the living rock near Ecbatana. Here Darius I recorded in three languages (Old Persian, Elamite and Babylonian) his official version of how he came to the throne in 522 BCE and re-established order in the Empire (Figure 12). It was on the basis of this text that the Englishman Henry Rawlinson was able to decipher the Old Persian language in the nineteenth century. But such texts do not provide the materials for a history properly so called, unless it is a history precisely of Persian official imperial ideology and propaganda.

Quite recently, though, a huge advance in our knowledge and understanding has been made possible by the publication of official texts from Persepolis, in the local Elamite language. These show that the Achaemenid Empire was indeed a bureaucratic monarchy in the age-old Middle Eastern tradition. But as yet these documents are rather isolated and restricted chronologically to roughly the half-century between 525 and 475. Archaeological and art-historical evidence, especially from the various capitals, reveals a hybrid Achaemenid palace style of architecture. Formal and informal inscriptions demonstrate how multinational were the materials and craftsmen employed in its creation, including Greeks (whom the Persians, like the Hebrews, called 'Ionians'). Here is a telling sample, from Darius's Foundation Charter, or official account of the construction of the great complex at Susa:

> I am Darius, the Great King, the king of kings, king of the lands, king of this earth, son of Hystaspes, an Achaemenid . . .
>
> This palace which I built at Susa: its materials were brought from afar . . .
>
> The cedar timber was brought from a mountain called Lebanon. The Assyrian people brought it to Babylon. From Babylon the Carians and Ionians brought it to Susa. The sissoo-timber was brought from Gandara and from Carmania. The gold which was worked here was brought from Sardis and from Bactria. The precious stone lapis lazuli and carnelian which was worked here was brought from Sogdiana. The precious stone turquoise, which was worked here, this was brought from Chorasmia. The silver and the ebony were brought from Egypt. The ornamentation with which the wall was adorned was brought from Ionia. The ivory which was worked here was

brought from Ethiopia, and from India and from Arachosia.
The stone columns which were worked here were brought from a
village called Abiradu, in Elam. The stone-cutters who worked
the stone were Ionians and Sardians. The goldsmiths who worked
the gold were Medes and Egyptians. The men who worked the
wood were Sardians and Egyptians. The men who worked the
baked brick were Babylonians. The men who adorned the walls
were Medes and Egyptians . . .

Again, this evidence by itself does not explain how the system came into being or how it operated in detail. But a flood of light on economic and military organization is shed by the records of two banking houses in Babylonia and by official correspondence written in Aramaic, the Empire's lingua franca, unearthed on papyrus in Egypt. These, however, were just two of the more than twenty provinces of the Empire, and, though they were both vitally important, they differed greatly from each other and cannot be used to make generalizations about the Empire as a whole. Above all, it has to be remembered that virtually all this documentary evidence is relevant only to the late sixth and early fifth centuries, arguably the heyday of the Empire, and not to the period of its relative decline in the fourth century BCE, the time of Philip and Alexander.

We are forced, therefore, to place more reliance than we should ideally have liked on Greek evidence. In other words, by and large on the evidence of the victors in a two-centuries-long struggle, to whom the Persians were 'barbarians' and – with the sole exception of the Great King – 'slaves'. This hellenocentric vision is perfectly illustrated by a quotation from Strabo, a Greek geographer from Asia Minor writing some three centuries after Alexander: 'The Persians of all the barbarians became the most famous among the Greeks, because none of the other barbarians who ruled Asia ruled Greeks'!

The Persian Empire was founded in the mid sixth century by Cyrus the Great, son of a Persian father and a Median mother, who traced his ancestry to one Achaemenes (as the Greeks pronounced that

Persian name). What Cyrus did, in effect, was to reverse the political relationship between the Persians of southern Iran and their kinfolk, the Medes of northern Iran. In the late seventh century the Medes had succeeded the Assyrians as the 'great power' of the Iran–Iraq region, and among their vassals were the Persians (*Parsa*, in their own language). Cyrus turned the tables on the Medes, though without by any means totally altering the institutions through which they had ruled. He was also responsible for ending the Babylonian captivity of the Jews, but his successors preferred to retain population transfer as a means of imperial control. Darius I, for example, compulsorily transferred Greeks from Miletus and Eretria to inland Iran and the shores of the Persian Gulf.

The Persian Empire under the Achaemenid dynasty founded by Cyrus (see the Table of Achaemenid Kings, p. 271) was heir to the long tradition of Middle Eastern bureaucratic and monarchical empire. Cyrus, however, and his immediate successors went further and faster than either the Assyrians or the Medes along the path of empire. By the time Darius I's son Xerxes sought to annex old Greece in 480, the Achaemenid Empire stretched from the River Indus in the east to the Aegean in the west, from the River Jaxartes (Syr-Darya) in the northeast (which flows through modern-day Uzbekistan and Kazakhstan) to the first cataract of the Nile in the south. The figure most responsible for setting the Empire on a durably workable administrative footing was Darius I, author of the Bisitun and Susa inscriptions cited above. Yet it is characteristic of the nature of our evidence that the only surviving connected account of his administrative reorganization is in the history of the Greek Herodotus. He was himself born within the Persian Empire at Halicarnassus (modern Bodrum on the Aegean shore of Turkey) shortly before the invasion of Greece that he set himself to explain, while simultaneously celebrating 'the great and wondrous deeds of both Greeks and non-Greeks'.

The post-Darius Empire, according to Herodotus, was divided into twenty satrapies, or provinces, and each of them was required to pay an annual tribute in either cash or kind, valued in terms of its silver equivalent. But his account leaves out those satrapies that paid their tribute in kind rather than cash – there were perhaps some twenty-six satrapies in all. Each was ruled by a satrap – the Greek word *satrapês* is the Hellenized form of an originally Median word, indicating that the system was first developed under the Medes. Satraps were royal appointees, often indeed members of the royal dynasty by birth or marriage, and anyway until the fourth century always Iranians. There was a tendency for satrapies to become virtually hereditary domains. Moreover, the Great King – who in theory (like the Crown of England) owned all the land in the Empire – made land grants to other Persian grandees and to non-Persian notables, including Greeks. We have evidence for this practice from Asia Minor, Egypt and Babylonia.

The prime responsibility of the satrap was to ensure that the relevant tribute was collected and delivered to one of the central treasuries in Iran. In the time of Alexander's opponent, Darius III, the largest treasury was at Persepolis in modern Fars (which preserves the ancient name Parsua), the most remote and therefore most defensible part of Iran. To facilitate the smooth collection of tribute, the satrap was entrusted with military powers; and to speed its delivery to Iran the Empire was provided, in anticipation of the Roman Empire, with a network of roads suitable for horses. The most famous of them was the Royal Road from the main administrative capital, Susa, to Ephesus in Ionia, a distance of some two thousand miles (three thousand kilometres). It is estimated that by using the system of horse relays positioned at its 111 staging-posts a courier might traverse the length of the Road in ten days, whereas an army on foot and burdened with animals and other impedimenta would require three months to go the same distance. Some Persepolis tablets reveal the intricately bureaucratic system of rations allocations for couriers who travelled these roads.

There is some evidence that the early Achaemenids had attempted to limit the power of satraps by appointing separate garrison commanders and financial officials directly responsible to the Crown and by employing officials known as the King's Ears. But in the fourth century the tendency was for the satrap to arrogate to himself all civil, military and financial functions. That, coupled with the tendency for satrapies to become virtually hereditary domains, was an index of the weakening of the power of the centre over the periphery. Of course, it is important not to follow the pro-Alexander sources too closely in magnifying the degree of central weakness by the time of Darius III. This was a device for encouraging Greeks to line up behind Alexander and for persuading them to desist from serving as mercenaries for the Persian Great King or his satraps. But there does seem to be enough objective evidence to confirm that the Empire ruled by Darius III was probably weaker than that of Darius II (r. 424–404) and certainly than that of Darius I. This weakening was very much a personal matter, since the power of a Great King to a crucial extent depended directly on the authority exercised by his own personality.

In official Persian parlance, which Greeks seized on with glee, even satraps were technically 'slaves' of the Great King. But that was too easily misinterpreted, since the Achaemenid Empire had never been just the slavish kingdom of an all-powerful master, the classic oriental despotism. The Great King was chosen by the warriors from the Achaemenid royal house, and in theory the succession passed from father to son. But as early as the third (legitimate) king, Darius I, father–son succession broke down; Darius was at best a distant relative of his official predecessor Cambyses. A further complicating factor was the multiplicity of sons always potentially available thanks to the harem system developed by Xerxes. Intrigue followed by assassination became endemic – not altogether unlike the situation within the Macedonian monarchy. And this was not the only point of similarity between those two dynasties and kingdoms. Thus Darius III was a very distant relation of the previous kings and had secured his elevation thanks to the murderous machinations of the eunuch Bagoas, who had removed Artaxerxes IV (in 336) and many others of the ruling house.

Even a weak king, however, such as Darius III looks to have been, was provided with enormous institutional and symbolic buttressing. He was, to quote the formula from an inscription of Darius II, 'the Great King, King of Kings [*Shahanshah*], King of peoples with many kinds of men, King on this great earth far and wide'. His person was sacred, and though not himself a god, he ruled by the grace of the great Zoroastrian god of light Ahura Mazda, whose symbolic presence dominates, for example, Darius I's depiction in the rock at Bisitun. Darius I's Foundation Charter opens with this invocation to him:

> *Ahura Mazda is a great god, who created this earth, who created the sky, who created man, who created happiness for man, who made Darius king, one king among many, one lord among many.*

The Great King presided over an elaborate court whose officials included staff-bearers, a spear-bearer, a bow-bearer, a cup-bearer (the biblical author Nehemiah was cup-bearer to Artaxerxes I), a captain of the King's bodyguard, a grand vizier (in Greek the Chiliarch, or ruler of a thousand) and, not least, assorted eunuchs. These court eunuchs included the Bagoas with whom Alexander was to consort, the 'Persian boy' of Mary Renault's excellent novel (see p. 312) – not to be confused with his murderous homonym who brought Darius III to the throne. Among their other functions, the court eunuchs supervised a vast harem of both Persian and non-Persian wives. The Bible's Esther was one of these, and the Book of Esther contains a Jewish-oriented description of the search for a replacement senior wife at the time of King 'Ahasuerus' (that is, Xerxes I, r. 486–465):

> *The young women were given beauty treatments for one whole year. The first six months their skin was rubbed with olive oil and myrrh, and the last six months it was treated with perfumes and cosmetics. Then each of them spent the night alone with King Xerxes. When a young woman went to the king, she could wear whatever jewellery or clothes she chose from the women's living quarters. In the evening she would go to the king, and the*

following morning she would go to the place where his wives
stayed after being with him . . . Only the ones the king wanted
and asked for by name could go back to the king.

– Esther 2:12–14, Contemporary English Version

The King's decision in matters of policy was final, but he was advised by seven special counsellors, by royal judges, and by an indefinite advisory group drawn from the so-called Honoured Equals, King's Friends and Royal Relations. Some of these titles were to be bestowed by Alexander, too, as part of his policy of orientalization. These advisers would all be Persians, or more broadly Iranians, by whom and in whose interests the Empire was ultimately run. The King was also commander-in-chief of any imperial army and, symbolically, took up his position in the dead centre of the Persian host. There he would be protected by a special guard of one thousand. This elite royal bodyguard was drawn from the crack infantry force known to the Greeks as the Ten Thousand Immortals (so called, they wrongly thought, because losses were instantly made good by fresh recruits held in reserve for the purpose). These Immortals had been instrumental in bringing their former commander, Darius I, to power. He returned the compliment by having them depicted as bowmen in immediate attendance on him in coloured brick reliefs decorating his palace at Susa. It was also as an archer that Darius had himself depicted on the coin of the realm, the silver and gold daric that took its name from him (see Figure 14). The premier strike force of the Persian army, however, was the west Iranian cavalry. For infantry in the fourth century, the Great King preferred to liquidate his vast reserves of silver and gold bullion in order to hire Greek mercenaries. Some 235,000 silver talents' worth was in store in 331, and up to fifty thousand such mercenaries fought against Alexander between 334 and 331.

A number of internationally minded Greeks first suspected that the Great King was not the power he made himself out to be after the internal dynastic struggle for the Persian throne in 401/400. Cyrus, the younger full brother of the reigning King Artaxerxes II, had allegedly been encouraged by their mother Parysatis to usurp the throne. To help him, he had recruited more than ten thousand Greek mercenaries. The decisive battle had been fought at Cunaxa in Mesopotamia, but, though the Greek mercenaries had defeated their opponents, Cyrus himself had been killed. The survivors managed to extricate themselves from the very heart of the Persian Empire and return to Greek civilization at the southern shore of the Black Sea without undue military difficulties – though they suffered miserably from the rigours of the terrain and weather.

The story was immortalized by the man who led them at the end, Xenophon of Athens. But already before his account appeared, the tireless Athenian pamphleteer Isocrates had made propaganda at the time of the Olympic Games of 380, advocating a Panhellenic crusade against the Persian Empire partly on grounds of its perceived weakness. He subsequently redirected this plea opportunistically at Alexander's father, Philip, who for his own reasons initiated just such a campaign but was forced to leave the completion of it to Alexander.

The *peripeteia*, or reversal of fortune, that Alexander's victory over the Persians represented was neatly commented on at Athens in 330, by the Athenian orator Aeschines:

> *Was it not the Persian King who demanded earth and water from the peoples of Greece on the ground of his mastery of all mankind from the rising to the setting of the sun? And is not that monarch now fighting, not for the supremacy of the world, but to preserve his life?*

As it turned out, Darius lost both his life and his kingdom. The world – now Alexander's world – would never be the same again.

THREE

YOUNG ALEXANDER
(356–334 BCE)

ALEXANDER was born on or about 20 July 356 BCE. The Greek biographer Plutarch, who is our best and often indeed our only source for the first twenty years of Alexander's life, reports a famous story. Philip, he says,

> had just taken Potidaean in Chalcidice, when three messages reached him pretty much simultaneously. The first informed him that Parmenion had won a great victory over the Illyrians, the second message told him that a race-horse he owned had won at the Olympic Games, and the third told him of Alexander's birth.

Philip and Parmenion we have already met. The Illyrians were Macedon's traditional enemies on their western border. The Olympics were the most prestigious of the Panhellenic festivals. Alexander's mother was Philip's fourth wife, Olympias, a Greek princess from Molossia in Epirus (to the south of Illyria), who had given birth at the Macedonian administrative capital of Pella. Alexander's name was already a royal one within the Macedonian kingly house. But the fact that it was also the alternative name of Homer's Paris may not be irrelevant either, given our Alexander's passion for all things Homeric.

We are not, of course, bound to accept the strictly literal historicity of the remarkable chronological coincidence that Plutarch reports. But this one passage does nevertheless neatly introduce all the major facets of Alexander's complex and sometimes troubled inheritance. The Illyrians, together with the Paeonians to the north and the Thracian tribespeople to the north-east and east, had been a major cause of the weakness of the Macedonian kingdom. Their crushing by Philip was a prerequisite for the wider international role he envisaged for Macedon;

and that they were crushed was due to his creation of the finest land army in the Balkan peninsula under the outstanding leadership of either himself or the powerful Parmenion. Philip's victory at the Olympic Games symbolizes both the process of cultural Hellenization that he promoted in his kingdom and the more extensive and ultimately dominant role he sought and managed to play in the Greek world to the south of the vale of Tempe (the southern border of Macedonia with Thessaly). And Philip's union of body with Olympias is thought, plausibly, to have had something to do with Alexander's own peculiarly potent combination of leadership qualities and passionate mysticism. On the other hand, the disunion of hearts between his parents was to lead to his estrangement from his father – a threat, as he apprehended it, to his succession to the Macedonian throne. And it probably also helped to foster a permanent deep-seated sense of insecurity for which he compensated in a variety of ways, not all of them pleasant or positive.

It is important, though, to avoid getting too Freudian. We can judge Alexander's career only from the outside, in other words. The two tutors of his earliest youth were both Greeks, a kinsman of Olympias from Epirus and another Greek from rugged Acarnania. They were responsible for seeing that he received not only the basic education in literacy, numeracy and physical exercise that any Greek or Macedonian boy might get but also some inkling of what lay ahead of him as a royal prince destined sooner or later for the Macedonian throne. Until Alexander reached his late teens he had no obvious rival to succeed his father, and his mother Olympias would have done nothing to discourage the idea that he was destined by heaven as well as by nature to succeed Philip – not least because this put her in the position of senior among Philip's several (eventually seven in all) wives and queens.

We may be sure, too, that Alexander's Greek tutors did nothing to inhibit his early passion for the hunting of wild game, since this was both a suitably royal pursuit – with oriental associations that Philip may have been not at all unhappy with – and played a key role in the development of youths into manhood among the Macedonians generally. Yet even they, presumably, were as astonished as we are told their employer Philip was at one particular precocious demonstration of Alexander's cool self-possession. In about 344, when he was aged only twelve or so, he succeeded where many before him had failed in taming a magnificent, and quite extravagantly expensive, horse: the Thessalian stallion Bucephalas ('Ox-Head') – so called either from a natural marking on his muzzle, or from a generic stamp branded on horses of his specially elite breed (see Figure 6). No one, however, could have then foretold that one day he would set a precedent by naming a city after this favourite hunter and warhorse.

Presumably Alexander spent most of his early life in or in the vicinity of the palace at Pella, in close and regular contact both with his mother and with his full sister Cleopatra, of whom he was said to be exceptionally fond. Philip, by contrast, was an ever more distant figure, almost always on campaign somewhere, in winter and summer alike, and often very far away. Partly to compensate for this lack of paternal guidance, and partly to stimulate what was clearly an exceptional intelligence in his son, Philip in about 343 made an even more remarkable educational appointment. He chose as Alexander's tutor the most distinguished pupil of Plato's Academy in Athens. There were perhaps also personal reasons for the choice: Aristotle's father, Nicomachus, had been personal physician to Philip's father, Amyntas III. And maybe political ones too, since in 348 Philip had ordered the total destruction of Aristotle's home city, Stageira, and possibly wanted to make some gesture of reconciliation towards the scattered survivors.

Above all, probably, Philip had intellectual ends in view, though the precise extent of Aristotle's lasting influence over Alexander remains controversial. Certainly, he would have helped to stimulate his pupil's lifelong interest in and love for Greek literature, especially Homer, and no doubt he also had something to do with Alexander's penchant for biology, botany and zoology. (He was careful to send unusual and exotic specimens back from Asia to his old master in Greece.) But it would probably be wrong to regard Alexander as ever anything remotely like an intellectual of Aristotle's own stripe. He certainly had ideas, including some big ones, but essentially Alexander was a doer rather than a thinker, Action Man incarnate and not a philosopher in arms.

Apart from his relationship with Aristotle, Alexander struck up also a number of friendships among the pupil group at Mieza (near modern Lefkadia) that were to prove both long-lasting and historically of the highest importance. Easily the closest and most significant of these was with Hephaestion, already mentioned, who became Alexander's principal confidant and aide-de-camp and eventually the Grand Vizier of his new orient-based empire. Another Upper Macedonian in this intimate royal circle was Harpalus, whom Alexander was to appoint Treasurer of his empire. No less interesting in its way was the inclusion in the circle of at least three Greeks. One, the Cretan Nearchus, not only rose to be Admiral of the Fleet in India but also wrote a book about it, a book that our major source Arrian knew and used.*

It is an accurate measure of Alexander's precocious development as a leader of men, and as a man who would be king, that in 340/39 Philip appointed him regent of Macedon during one of his many absences, this time at the sieges of Byzantium and Perinthus. Alexander was still only sixteen, but he made the very most of his opportunity. For he found himself obliged – or so he contrived to make it appear – to campaign against the Thracian people called Maedi on his eastern border. And not only did he defeat them, but he also dropped a loud hint of things to come by founding a new Greek-style city on the site of their capital and giving it his own name: Alexandroupolis. One wonders what his father, founder already of a Philippi (modern

* See Appendix, pp. 251–2.

Philippi) and a Philippopolis (modern Plovdiv in Bulgaria), thought about that.

By 340, then, Philip's expansion to the north of mainland Greece had taken him as far east as the approaches to the Black Sea, to the Propontis (Sea of Marmara). This was a bold campaign that excited the interest, and perhaps apprehension, of two very disparate powers above all: the Achaemenid Persian Empire, ruled by the Great King, and the democratic Greek city-republic of Athens. By 340 the Persian Empire was something of a ramshackle edifice, as suggested in Chapter Two. Always rather loosely knit together, the weave had threatened to burst asunder during a major revolt of several of the satraps of the western provinces during the 370s and 360s. This revolt coincided unhappily with a prolonged revolt since 405 by Egypt, a province of strategic and economic importance. In fact, it was only three years or so before 340 that the Persian Great King Artaxerxes III had managed at last to reimpose a semblance of unity. He sent help to Philip's beleaguered Greek enemies at Perinthus, perhaps because he feared that Philip had designs on his own sphere of Asia – as may well already have been the case.

As for Athens, although by then a shadow of its great fifth-century BCE self, it did still control the largest navy in the Aegean. This was used among other things to convoy the grain ships bringing to Athens's port of Peiraeus the literally vital annual supply of wheat from the black-earth lands of the Ukraine and Crimea. Philip's attack on Perinthus and Byzantium threatened the passage of these ships through the Bosporus and the Hellespont (Dardanelles). It also apparently confirmed what the patriotic Athenian politician Demosthenes had been preaching to his fellow-countrymen for the past dozen years: namely, that it was Philip and not any other Greek state, nor even Persia, who was Athens's public enemy number one.

Anomalously, Philip's sieges of Perinthus and Byzantium both failed; these were practically his only failures in a military career of over twenty years. But later in that same year of 340 he did manage to capture an entire grain fleet en route to Peiraeus. Then, in 339, he proved Demosthenes spectacularly right about the danger he posed to Athens by conducting a lightning march across Thessaly and, possibly avoiding the famous 'Hot Gates' of Thermopylae, into Phocis, where he seized the town of Elatea. Demosthenes was obliged to employ all his powers of persuasive oratory and considerable diplomatic skills to cobble together some sort of Greek alliance to resist Philip. This was based primarily on Thebes, once the major land power of Greece and still the strongest Greek land power after Philip. But in autumn 338 Philip's troops cut the Greek allies to pieces at Chaeronea in Boeotia.

Alexander, as we have seen, had been regent of Macedon at sixteen. At eighteen, at Chaeronea, he was appointed by Philip to the overall command of the crack Macedonian Companion Cavalry. This in itself speaks worlds both for Alexander's prowess and for Philip's faith in his command abilities. He is said to have distinguished himself by leading the Companions' decisive cavalry charge. The freedom of the Greek cities, it has been claimed or lamented, died on the field of Chaeronea. Thereafter, politically speaking, much of the Greek world was one of territorial absolutist monarchies rather than sovereign republics – though we must be careful not to exaggerate the freedom of independent action that most of those cities had really had before 338. After the battle Philip entrusted to Alexander a task of enormous symbolic significance. The corpses of the Athenian dead were cremated in accordance with their traditional practice, and the ashes ceremonially poured into wooden urns which were returned to their relatives for proper burial. Philip chose Alexander to lead an honour guard to accompany those urns back to Athens. It was the one and only time in his life that Alexander set foot in what Aristotle's teacher Plato had called the 'city hall of Wisdom'.

Thereafter, Philip was the undisputed – or at least incontestable – political and military master of Greece. He guaranteed his mastery by garrisoning Thebes and some other cities of central Greece, and by establishing in 338/7, as noted earlier, the League of Corinth. Philip, as *hêgemôn* or leader of the League, concluded a series of bilateral treaties with his individual subordinate Greek allies, almost all of which were governed by oligarchies (small or very small groups of seriously wealthy citizens). Following the precedent set by the Second Athenian Naval League (378–338), Philip's subordinate Greek allies were to send delegates to a permanent *synedrion* or ruling Council, the function of which was to decide, or rather to rubber-stamp, League policy. Corinth was chosen as the Council's seat partly for its strategically central location in the Greek peninsula. But Corinth was also the host of one of the major Panhellenic religious festivals, the biennial Isthmian Games, and it was here that in 481 the handful of Greek states had taken a joint oath to resist the invasion threatened by Great King Xerxes of Persia. The very first decision taken by Philip's allied Council on behalf of the League was to undertake a Panhellenic crusade against the Persian Empire, ostensibly in revenge for Xerxes's sacrilegious invasion and destruction of Greece in 480/79.

Naturally enough, Philip was appointed commander-in-chief of the prospective League expedition, with full powers. But there was to be no role, apparently, for Alexander on the campaign. Now rising twenty, he was to be left behind, as in 340, to act as regent of Macedon, while the labour – and the glory – of the Persian conquest were to go to his father alone. However, before Philip himself could join the advance force that he had sent across to Asia Minor under Parmenion, he was assassinated, at the youngish age of forty-six. Whatever its motivation, the assassination was carried out in the most public and symbolically impressive manner imaginable, while Philip was in the midst of celebrating the marriage of his daughter Cleopatra at the old Macedonian ceremonial capital of Aegae (where Macedonian kings were still buried).

Many Greeks, especially those from cities which, like Thebes, had had a Macedonian garrison imposed upon them to guarantee their 'liberty and autonomy', were thrilled. It must have seemed to them that Macedon was running true to its old form: the barbarians (as they saw them) would now be embroiled in yet another primitive dynastic struggle, and the centrifugal forces temporarily tamed by Philip would again tear the kingdom apart. They had reckoned, of course, without Alexander. Whatever his role (if any) in Philip's assassination may have been (see the beginning of the next chapter), it was he who most of all benefited from it – from its happening at all and from its happening in that way and at that particular moment.

Winning the crucial allegiance of the noble Antipater (Antipatros in Greek), he exploited his father's murder as a pretext and excuse to rid himself both of potential rivals to the throne and of actual political opponents. In such matters Alexander would always show himself prudently ruthless. The Macedonian army, prompted by Antipater, then exercised its legal power – or customary prerogative – of electing Alexander king. Whereupon he at once marched south to Corinth and terrorized the Greek representatives of the League of Corinth into confirming his position as hereditary *hêgemôn* in succession to his father. This had the not unwelcome consequence of handing over to him the responsibility for Philip's already started invasion of the Persian Empire.

First, though, before going out to Asia in person, he was obliged to deal with urgent business nearer to hand. Like some Greeks to the south, some of Macedon's barbarian neighbours in the north had interpreted Philip's murder as a welcome signal that the happier days of internecine Macedonian strife before Philip's reign were about to return. They were to be no less seriously disappointed. In a brilliantly conceived, coordinated and executed campaign in 335, Alexander struck east against the Thracian Triballi through the high Shipka Pass (8,500 feet; 2,600 metres). He then moved north before actually crossing the Danube, which he apparently intended to make the northern frontier of Greater Macedon. This campaign was a classic demonstration of Alexander's constant attention to the strategic necessity of safeguarding his rear, and it showed too that as a strategist he was much older and wiser than his mere twenty years had led contemptuous critics like Demosthenes wishfully to suppose. He then struck west against the Illyrians (Philip's enemies of the early 350s), on this occasion giving a smart demonstration of the overriding importance that he (like Napoleon) always attributed to the factor of morale in warfare.

Alexander's good fortune became a proverbial topic – the young Plutarch, for instance, wrote essays about it. But it should not be blown out of proportion, since a great general to some extent creates his own good luck. Nevertheless, it was certainly fortunate for Alexander in autumn 335 that he had just subdued the Illyrians before he received the news of another major revolt against Macedonian power in Greece, led again by Thebes. The revolt had in fact been sparked off by a rumour that Alexander had been killed in combat in the far north. Within a fortnight, the revolted Greeks received a rude double shock. A Macedonian force was besieging Thebes, and at its head was a very much alive Alexander whom the disaffected Greeks were beginning to have to take rather more seriously. Again characteristically, Alexander had deployed extraordinary speed (covering some three hundred miles (five hundred kilometres) in just twelve days) to effect surprise – two factors that before Philip had played a relatively restricted role in conventional Greek warfare.

Early in October 335 Thebes was duly captured. But only those already conversant with Alexander's consistent conception of realpolitik could have anticipated the sequel. The order was given, formally on the decision of the Council of the League of Corinth but really at Alexander's behest (we may safely infer), to destroy Thebes utterly. The city was therefore torched and laid waste, barring some few but highly important symbolic exceptions – sacred buildings (it would not do for Alexander to sink to the level of the barbarian Xerxes) and the house where the lyric poet Pindar, composer of odes celebrating victors in all the Panhellenic games, had lived at the time of Xerxes's invasion. Alexander was ever the master of the grand propaganda gesture. But this was not so much a gesture as a calculated decision to terrorize any potential Greek opposition into either supporting or at least not actively opposing and jeopardizing the Persian campaign. For it did not do much genuinely to foster the Panhellenic spirit in which the decision to attack Persia had supposedly been taken. In this respect, as in many others, Alexander showed himself to be an apt pupil of his father Philip, rather than of Aristotle.

FOUR

ALEXANDER AND
THE MACEDONIANS

When he [Alexis Zorba] speaks, the whole of Macedonia is
immediately spread before my gaze, . . . with its mountains,
its forests, its torrents, its hard-working women and great,
heavily built men.

– Nikos Kazantzakis, *Zorba the Greek*

In the summer of 324, at Opis on the River Tigris north of Babylon (near where modern Baghdad stands), Alexander found himself with a mutiny on his hands. This was not the first time his Macedonian soldiers had been sufficiently provoked, and sufficiently brave, to oppose their king's will. It was, though, the first genuine mutiny of the extraordinary, unprecedented ten-year campaign of conquest. Alexander, however, was entirely ready for it. Indeed, there is some reason to suspect that he may actually have provoked the showdown as a test of strength. In either case, the way in which he was able to ride roughshod over the mutiny is highly revealing. It is an accurate index of the change that had come about during the twelve short years of his reign in the relations between Alexander and the Macedonians, including the governing elite of courtiers, officers and administrators as well as the ordinary soldiers.

To mark the gravity and significance of the Opis mutiny, our best historian Arrian composed for Alexander a long set-piece harangue, in the rhetorical tradition of historiography set by Thucydides and Polybius. It amounts to a justification and glorification of his entire career as conqueror of the Persian Empire. No doubt, Arrian did somehow base the speech on his two main contemporary sources, Ptolemy and Aristoboulus.* But the result is his own composition, and it is a mishmash of exaggerations, half-truths, plain untruths – and some facts. One basic detail, at least, rings true. Alexander begins by rehearsing the achievements of his father Philip. However, he does so only in order to emphasize the more sharply how much greater have been his own services to the Macedonians. And this raises a question mark that hangs over, and indeed shadows, Alexander's entire career, both before and after he became king. All comparison is said to be odious, but undoubtedly Alexander found especially odious any comparison that ranked the achievements of his father higher than his or suggested that his own were in some way crucially indebted to Philip's. How far this attitude was due to his own innate ambition or to a culturally conditioned reflex of competitiveness, how far to the goading of his mother or the slights he received from Philip, must remain conjectural.

In the late 1970s CE three extraordinary tombs were unearthed under a huge tumulus at Vergina, the ancient Aegae. Almost inevitably the most important of the three, Tomb II, was dubbed by its excavator Manolis Andronikos 'the Tomb of Philip'. In the absence of foolproof corroboration of the occupants' identities, the dating of the tomb must rest on subjective aesthetic judgements. At any rate, the style of the associated artefacts is consistent with a dating in the third quarter of the fourth century. Their high quality and sheer quantity, too, not to mention the location and lavish construction of the tomb itself, leave little room to doubt that we are dealing with a royal Macedonian burial. Moreover, the find of a number of small ivory heads including apparent representations of Philip and Alexander (see Figure 9) lends the identification much colour. And the evidence of the bones and teeth of the male skeleton suggests that death occurred when he was

---

* See Appendix, p. 250.

between forty and fifty years of age. Philip died in July 336 BCE aged forty-six.

Philip, however, did not just die. He was assassinated, as we have seen, during celebrations of his daughter Cleopatra's marriage, and shortly before he was due to take over command of the expedition that he had already dispatched against the Persian Empire. Why was he murdered? The official story went like this. The assassin, Pausanias, who was not merely a Companion but one of Philip's seven most intimate bodyguards, had allegedly been motivated by a personal grudge against the king arising out of a gross homosexual violation and humiliation that Philip had not redressed. Moreover, Pausanias had been aided and abetted by others, in particular two brothers from the 'royal' house of Lyncestis (one of the Upper Macedonian cantons). There are several good reasons for doubting this official story – at least as it has been transmitted by our surviving sources. Indeed, there are even reasons for suspecting Alexander himself of complicity in the deed. The charge of patricide against him can never be proved, but that it can be contemplated at all conveys a good notion of the edgy quality of life at the top of Macedonian society.

Alexander, for a start, deeply resented the influence over Philip of the noble Attalus. The previous year Attalus had married his niece and ward Cleopatra to Philip (she became his seventh wife, or consort), while he had himself married a daughter of Philip's senior general and chief of staff, Parmenion. At the wedding of Cleopatra and Philip Attalus had very pointedly and publicly prayed that the union might produce a son and legitimate heir to the Macedonian throne. The clear implication was that Alexander, whose mother Olympias was an Epirote Greek and not a pure-bred noble Macedonian like Cleopatra, was illegitimate, or not fully legitimate. Alexander had reportedly reacted with such fury that his father felt obliged to send both him and Olympias away from the court into a sort of internal exile. Olympias had retired to the court of her brother Alexander, king of the Molossi. Perhaps to effect a reconciliation, or at least to prevent the Molossians from turning against him, Philip married his daughter by Olympias, another Cleopatra (Alexander's full sister), to her maternal uncle, Alexander. It was at their marriage celebrations that Philip was assassinated: two weddings and a funeral.

Furthermore, some ancient sources alleged that Alexander and Olympias jointly conspired to bring about Philip's death, fearing that Alexander would indeed be pushed aside from the succession. One episode is particularly noteworthy in this connection. After Alexander's banishment order had been revoked and he had been recalled to Pella by Philip, he allegedly entered into secret negotiations to marry the daughter of a minor Persian satrap or sub-satrap, Pixodarus of Caria. This was apparently because he feared the dynastic implications of a marriage bond favoured, for diplomatic reasons, by Philip between the girl and Alexander's only half-brother, Arrhidaeus. When Philip found out about these clandestine negotiations, he banished five of the prince's closest friends, who had been conducting them on his behalf. They were Ptolemy and Harpalus, from Upper Macedonia, and three Greeks – the Cretan Nearchus who settled at Amphipolis, and the brothers Erigyius and Laomedon from Mytilene on the island of Lesbos.

The 'Pella Five' constitute an interesting cross-section of the internationalized Macedonian elite that Philip had done so much to encourage and foster. But they also illustrate sharply how Alexander found his most intimate friends from outside the circles of his father's closest adherents. All five became Companions of Alexander and most were elevated to the highest positions during the Asiatic campaign. Whether Alexander was right in thinking or suspecting that Philip intended to oust him from the succession is not the point. The point is that Alexander very probably did suspect and fear this.

A third reason for entertaining the idea of his complicity in his father's murder is his treatment of the assassin. Instead of having Pausanias arrested and put on trial, Alexander ensured that he was killed more or less at the scene of the crime by three more of his closest friends, two of whom were destined to rise high in his service. The fourth and final reason for pointing the finger at Alexander is that the role attributed to the other alleged conspirators in the official version is curiously shadowy. In none of our extant sources do we find concrete and plausible allegations being made against the two Lyncestian brothers. It seems far more likely that Alexander simply seized on the murder of his father as an opportune moment to do away with actual or potential sources of disloyalty and resistance to his own rule, if not rivalry for the throne itself. This at any rate is the obvious explanation of the murder of his cousin Amyntas, whose claim to the throne in 360/359 Philip had successfully overridden. And it was for similar dynastic reasons of state that Alexander had Attalus and his niece and her child (or children) by Philip killed as soon after his father's death as could expeditiously be arranged.

This, then, is a possible case for Alexander's guilt, at least by association – cumulatively impressive, but not proven beyond a shadow of reasonable doubt. It is also illegitimate to infer his guilt just from the fact that it was he who undoubtedly benefited most from Philip's dying when he did. It could as easily be argued that the assassination occurred coincidentally at an opportune moment for Alexander. He was feeling isolated at court and rattled about the succession, and by taking immediate advantage of what he saw as the enemy's temporary weakness he displayed the same sort of cool opportunism that would characterize his brilliant generalship. Especially noteworthy, and a recurrent feature of his career, is the way that Alexander rewarded friends who showed themselves conspicuously loyal to him personally. We have also to remember that, in the context of late summer and early autumn 336, he was not yet remotely qualified even to be considered for the title 'the Great'. He had no string of military successes under his belt as yet. Instead, he was a twenty-year-old – admittedly precocious – with one foot only insecurely placed on the first greasy rung of the ladder of supreme power.

That his foot was there at all was due very largely to the support of the old noble Antipater. His reward was to be made regent (*epitropos* – the word also means 'guardian' in a familial sense) of Macedon and to be given control of Greece as deputy leader of the League of Corinth when Alexander departed for Asia in 334. It is highly significant that, when Antipater presented Alexander to the army for formal acclamation as king in 336, both Parmenion and his new son-in-law Attalus were in Asia spearheading Philip's advance force. Had they been still at Aegae, Philip might not even have been assassinated. History, though, deals in facts, not might-have-beens.

Alexander, as noted, had Attalus murdered soon after becoming king. Indeed, if we are to believe the historian Curtius,* the murder was carried out with the connivance of Parmenion himself. We can only conjecture Parmenion's motives, if so. Loyalty to Alexander's father, perhaps – or pragmatic calculation that his own personal advantage, and that of his immediate family members, would be better served by sticking with Alexander, at least for the time being? At any rate, Alexander's reasons for treating Parmenion with deference and retaining him in his post as senior general, besides himself, are rather more obvious. Militarily, Alexander needed Parmenion's proven expertise as battlefield commander going back over a quarter of a century, at least until such time as he should himself assume the supreme command in person. There were pressing concerns, too, on both the northern and the southern borders of Macedonia, preventing his immediate departure for Asia. Politically speaking, moreover, Parmenion carried enormous political clout. He himself was Alexander's chief of staff. One of his sons was commander-in-chief of the Companion Cavalry, another of the Hypaspist Shield Bearers. A brother probably held the same position over the light cavalry, and there were clients of his, some related by marriage, among the subordinate officers. Besides, Parmenion was an Upper Macedonian, his loyal adherence vital for maintaining the political integrity of Macedon as a whole.

---

* See Appendix, p. 256.

But if these were reasons why Alexander could not take hostile action against Parmenion at the beginning of his reign, even supposing he had wanted to, they were also reasons why he should very much wish to take such action against him in the longer run. For if anything is clear about Alexander's personality and character – at least, it is clear to me – it is that he was not the sort of man to be willing to bask in the reflected glory of an old soldier more than three times his age (in 336 Parmenion was about sixty-four). Especially not when that old soldier had won his rank and position from Philip, not from himself, and was an individual whose cautious temperament and narrowly Macedonian outlook would soon clash with the mercurial temper and broad outlook of the young king. This is the case regardless of what Parmenion may have thought or felt about the fact, and especially the manner, of Alexander's accession.

One of the dangers of writing history is to abuse the gift of hindsight and pass anachronistic judgements. But if this picture of Alexander's behaviour and attitudes in 337/6 is substantially correct, his relationships with high-ranking Macedonians were fraught with tension from the outset; and the downfall, perhaps even violent death, of Parmenion at Alexander's behest would seem to have been only a matter of time. In what I shall call for short 'the Philotas syndrome', Alexander revealed just how ruthless he was prepared to be in his struggle to achieve an incontrovertibly autocratic position of command and rule.

Philotas was Parmenion's eldest son and commander-in-chief of the crack Macedonian strike force, the Companion Cavalry. In autumn 330 came the denouement of what is presented in the official account, as retailed by Arrian, as the conspiracy by Philotas against Alexander. In actuality, it was a conspiracy *against* Philotas actively endorsed if not initiated by Alexander. (We might compare the alleged plotting of Sejanus against the Roman emperor Tiberius, when really it was Sejanus who was the victim of Tiberius's plot against his former favourite.) This conspiracy had been hatched some time before, possibly in Egypt, but the circumstances and timing of the denouement are revealing of Alexander's methods. Craterus, an Upper Macedonian noble who commanded one of the six battalions of Foot Companions and was also a Companion of Alexander in the intimate sense, began to lay information against Philotas in the winter of 333/2. His source of evidence for Philotas's alleged anti-Alexander treachery was his Greek mistress, but the most damning evidence he could obtain, apparently, was Philotas's boasting that Alexander's victories were really owed to himself and his father Parmenion.

Philotas may also have been known to disapprove of Alexander's claim – as articulated and broadcast after his visit to Ammon's oracle in the Siwah oasis – to be the son of Zeus (or/and Ammon). He could therefore have appeared to be an obstacle to the implementation of Alexander's policy of orientalization. At any rate, his demise came a few months after Alexander, as self-proclaimed successor to the Great King of Persia, had begun to wear a modified version of Persian regal attire (see Chapter Eight). Severe as it was, Philotas's extreme treatment does fit in with Alexander's general tendency to seek to rid himself of all encumbrances to the free exercise of his untrammelled will and to develop intimate attachments outside the circle of his father's appointees.

The problem for Craterus and Alexander was how to get rid of a man so powerfully and deeply entrenched in the army and court. Late in 330 they were blessed with a stroke of good fortune. A conspiracy against Alexander's life led by a Macedonian called Dimnus was alleged, and it was further alleged that Philotas, although he had known about it, had failed to report it. The timing of this 'revelation' is unlikely to be accidental. Philotas had been attending to the obsequies of his brother Nicanor in Areia and had not yet rejoined the army, which had reached Phrada in Drangiana in eastern Iran. His father Parmenion was over eight hundred miles (nearly thirteen hundred kilometres) away at Ecbatana in Media, where Alexander had left him in June the same year. When Philotas did return to the camp, the air was thick with rumours surrounding the alleged conspiracy of

Dimnus. For his complicity, or neglect, Philotas was arrested on a charge of treason, tortured and put on trial before the army.

According to Ptolemy, as reported in Arrian, the persons who had revealed Dimnus's plot brought forward 'irrefutable proofs' of Philotas's guilt. But, since Ptolemy considered failure to report the alleged conspiracy to be the most damning, there probably was no good evidence to convict Philotas as charged. This puts the conspiracy against Philotas in its true light. His trial before the army in the presence of Alexander (the unspoken principal accuser) was actually a vote on a motion of confidence in Alexander's leadership. Hardly surprisingly, the army decided in favour of the man who had proved himself eminently capable of 'ruling by might', and who alone was likely to be able to lead them to final victory over the Persians. Dimnus and six associates, all Macedonians of standing, shared Philotas's fate, but Alexander had an even fatter fish to fry – or rather to catch.

Philotas's end may be described as judicial murder. That of his father Parmenion was undisguised assassination. Even Arrian, usually an apologist for Alexander, was unable to give it a moralizing or legalistic gloss. Parmenion was murdered for reasons of realpolitik, out of a calculation of political expediency pure and simple, since – despite being left behind at Ecbatana, in command only of non-Macedonian troops – he still had great influence with the army. It is noteworthy too that Parmenion's second in command Cleandrus, brother of his son-in-law Coenus, helped in the assassination of his chief. This opportune and perhaps opportunistic change of allegiance probably helped the army to change theirs. Nor was that the end of the round of accusations and executions. The four sons of one Andromenes, probable adherents of Parmenion, were fortunate to escape with their lives. But Alexander of Lyncestis, who had been lucky not to be killed along with his two brothers in 336, was now quietly put out of the way.

In the case of the assassination of Philip, the evidence was too murky to allow a simple inference of Alexander's guilt on the grounds that he was its chief beneficiary. But we need not be so cautious in interpreting the 'Philotas syndrome'. Alexander now split Philotas's sole command of the Companion Cavalry into two. His new appointees were Cleitus nicknamed 'the Black' (there was also a Cleitus 'the White'), who was brother of his wet nurse and had saved Alexander's life at the Granicus river battle, and Hephaestion, Alexander's boyhood friend and also probably boyfriend, who thus obtained his first major command. These appointments were a brilliant compromise. Cleitus, like Philotas, opposed Alexander's monarchical aspirations. His elevation to a key command would have been welcomed by the old guard as an assurance that the purge was over. Hephaestion, Alexander's alter ego, owed his position directly to the king. His loyalty had recently been reaffirmed by his role in the arrest and torture of Philotas. He would serve, besides, as a counterbalance to, and check on, Cleitus.

It was, however, Alexander himself who had profited the most. The army had been used successfully against those commanders who had up until then enjoyed its full confidence and respect, and Alexander had, at last, gained his full kingly independence. How was he going to use it? Our best historical source, Arrian, provides a persuasive answer in a uniquely instructive passage of seven chapters in the fourth book of his *Anabasis*. In addition to his two preferred, official sources, Ptolemy and Aristoboulus, he was drawing on the Vulgate tradition* and, above all, on his own judgement. This extract, with its repeated use of the invidious pronoun, indicates how personally Arrian took the whole thing:

> And I do not only disapprove of this excessive punishment of
> Bessus, but consider the cutting-off of the extremities to be
> barbaric. I agree too that Alexander was motivated by rivalrous
> envy of the Median and Persian wealth and adopted an

---

* For an account of the Vulgate tradition, see Appendix, pp. 254–6.

inegalitarian style of life towards his subjects in the manner of non-Greek kings. In no way do I approve either of the Median dress that he exchanged for traditional Macedonian apparel, even though he was a descendant of Heracles, or of the tiara proper to the Persians whom he had defeated that he took to wearing instead of his customary headgear.

What makes this passage so revelatory is the sequence of Arrian's thought and exposition. He starts with the mutilation of the Persian pretender Bessus according to oriental norms (his nose and ears were sliced off) as a preliminary to his execution in summer 329. He then breaks his usual chronological sequence and proceeds via Alexander's manslaughter of Black Cleitus in summer 328 to the Pages' Conspiracy and the arrest of the Greek official historian Callisthenes in spring 327. Arrian gives no other than artistic reasons for this decision to abandon his standard narrative mode. But Plutarch, writing his biography of Alexander several decades earlier and, like Arrian, using the Vulgate as well as the Official source traditions (see the Appendix), had spelled out the connecting link between these episodes – Alexander's increasingly despotic behaviour. Indeed, Plutarch had begun the sequence of damaging episodes earlier, precisely with the judicial murder of Philotas. But from a historical rather than a moralizing standpoint, was Alexander really acting increasingly despotically between 330 and 327? And, if so, why?

The key is his policy of conciliating the traditional ruling elite of the old Persian Empire to their new Macedonian overlord, so that he could tap their inherited expertise and prestige within a new administrative structure and framework. This was Alexander's orientalization policy. After the victory at Gaugamela in late 331, he had begun to act as if he – and not any Achaemenid Persian – was the rightful occupant of the Achaemenid throne. It was unfortunate that he had failed to capture Darius III alive after the battle, since this had allowed Darius to be deposed and murdered by Bessus, a distant relative who made bold to assume the Achaemenid tiara (symbol of monarchical authority). It was not until the summer of 329 after fierce guerrilla-style campaigning that Bessus was at last captured in central Asia by Ptolemy and put to death Persian-style by Alexander. The point of the prior mutilation of Bessus, missed by Arrian, was to demonstrate especially to his Iranian subjects that Alexander was now in effect Great King and that any oriental rebels would be put down in the symbolically appropriate oriental fashion.

The same point was being made by Alexander in his adoption of a modified oriental style of dress, a mixture of Persian and Macedonian features, and of the trappings of an oriental court (harem included). However, he was mindful of the sensibilities and sensitivities of his Macedonian officers and troops. Hence, precisely, his mixed Macedonian–oriental form of royal garb. Hence, too, his decision at first to maintain two distinct courts, a Persian and a Macedonian–Greek, and two distinct chancelleries. Yet even this relatively restrained orientalism apparently proved too much for Black Cleitus, who for some time had made it plain that he was 'aggrieved both by Alexander's move to a more eastern style [Arrian literally says 'a more barbaric'] and by the sycophantic expressions of his courtiers'. But he would have had personal reasons for feeling aggrieved too, so we should probably not place too much weight on Cleitus's principled opposition to Alexander. At any rate there was a massive flare-up between them at Maracanda (Samarkand, in Uzbekistan) in autumn 328 during a wild drinking binge. Cleitus made the mistake of accusing Alexander of minimizing his father Philip's achievements in order to magnify his own, and Alexander, blind drunk and out of control, ran Cleitus through with a pike.

The army, by now eating out of Alexander's hand, retrospectively adjudged Cleitus guilty of treason. Alexander was stricken with no doubt genuine remorse at his unthinking action. Yet no personal feelings were to be allowed to get in the way of the orientalizing programme. In 327 he attempted the momentous step of amalgamating his Persian and Macedonian–Greek courts, placing the onus on the Macedonians and Greeks to behave like the Persians rather than vice versa. It was at this point that he obliged them to perform before him the ritual gesture of *proskynesis*, or obeisance, which in Persian court circles was a matter of social etiquette. All ranks performed it before the Great King, as their social superior, regardless of how exalted their own rank might be. Perhaps commoners alone were obliged to grovel on hands and knees, whereas the elite honorary Royal Kinsmen needed only to bow stiffly from a standing position. For a Greek – and, we must assume in this context, for a Macedonian too – *proskynesis* implied divine worship. Although Callisthenes was perfectly willing to describe Alexander in writing as 'son of Zeus', he was not prepared to treat him as a genuine divinity face to face. His resistance would have been stiffened by the general Greek perception of Persians as naturally inferior oriental barbarians, who were, besides, a recently defeated enemy.

The experiment in amalgamation was concerted in advance by the good and faithful Hephaestion, but it all went horribly wrong, thanks above all to the opposition of Callisthenes. For the time being, Callisthenes was spared. But his recalcitrance had been noted, and it seems that Alexander was just waiting for a suitable opportunity to do away with him. This arose soon enough in the spring of 327. A plot – apparently genuine – was hatched among the Royal Pages, led by Hermolaus. Like Philip's assassin Pausanias, Hermolaus is said to have plotted because he had been humiliated by his king and immediate employer. The cause of his humiliation was said to be punishment for a grave breach of protocol during a wild boar hunt, when he had stepped up and killed the main prey rather than leaving it for Alexander. Hermolaus and at least six other Pages, all by definition the sons of high-ranking Macedonians, were convicted and executed by the army. Conveniently, much too conveniently, Callisthenes's name was linked with theirs, and, as Ptolemy reported, he was at once tortured and hanged.

Alexander, in other words, was prepared to stake all on his policy of orientalization. Clearly, in the process he decided that the only way to silence any serious opposition was to kill it off and to promote to the highest positions men who were prepared to give him personally their unconditional loyalty.

Against this tense background Alexander began in 327/6 the greatest adventure of his campaign, the expedition into 'India' (modern Pakistan and Kashmir). There he won what is in some ways his most impressive set-piece victory of all, over Porus (the Rajah of the Pauravas) at the Hydaspes (Jhelum) river. After that, it is easy to imagine the bitterness he felt at his first real 'defeat': the refusal of his Macedonian veterans to proceed yet further east beyond the River Hyphasis. There is nothing very remarkable about their refusal, in the trying circumstances. What is remarkable is Alexander's uncharacteristically irrational reaction to it. He appears to have wanted to make the soldiers pay heavily for their disloyalty (as it seemed to him) by imposing on them an unnecessarily wearing and bloody progress to the mouth of the Indus, followed by a march back to Iran through the baking desert of Gedrosia (the modern Makran, in Baluchistan). This proved a serious error of judgement. To cap it all, when he finally emerged from the desert in winter 325/4 he learned that more than half of the provinces of the Empire were showing signs of either disturbance or outright revolt.

Alexander's reaction to this situation has been called, probably correctly, a reign of terror. At least eight satraps were deposed, and three (or four) of the men involved in the murder of Parmenion almost six years earlier were now removed, including Cleandrus, brother of Coenus. Coenus himself had made the mistake of speaking up for the men at the Hyphasis and died soon afterwards. What seems to have motivated Alexander was a fear that the army, since 330 a pliant tool in his hands, might now be turned against him by some leading Macedonian nobles. One of these, the Grand Imperial Treasurer Harpalus, his friend from boyhood, so feared Alexander's wrath that he chose this moment to flee from Asia to Greece. Not for the first time: he had done likewise just before the Battle of Issus, but had been pardoned and reinstated. Harpalus took with him a vast sum of money by Greek standards, part of which became available for public purposes at Athens. This indirectly contributed to the rising of Greeks against Macedon in the immediate wake of Alexander's death in the summer of 323. Indeed, by the time of his death he had still not repaired the administrative and political damage done in the winter of 325/4. The struggle that broke out after his death among his closest Companions and senior commanders was very much a harvest of the suspicion and fear that he had consciously sown.

Two further major episodes illustrate the changing relations between Alexander and the Macedonians. At Susa in Elam (in southern Iran), in perhaps April 324, no fewer than eighty-seven of Alexander's Companions together with Alexander himself were married formally, according to the oriental rites, to Iranian noblewomen. Alexander at the same time officially recognized the informal liaisons between some ten thousand ordinary Macedonian soldiers and oriental women as legitimate marriages, and provided each couple with a wedding gift. What the noble Macedonian grooms really thought of their marriages is probably demonstrated by the fact that all but one (Seleucus, the future King Seleucus I) repudiated their oriental wives after Alexander's death. Even clearer, though, is what Alexander had in mind by accomplishing this grand act of union. The new ruling class of his empire was to be mixed-race Irano-Macedonian.

This message he complemented and reinforced by his approach to the recruitment of the military infrastructure of his new imperial army. In early summer 324 some thirty thousand Iranian infantrymen arrived at Susa. They had been recruited in 327 and deliberately trained to fight in the Macedonian manner as what Alexander accurately if tactlessly called his 'successors'. Their job was to succeed and replace, for good, his time-expired Macedonian veterans. Even massive monetary handouts merely postponed the inevitable Macedonian explosion, which occurred at Opis. Alexander, however, was ready and prepared for it. His quite brutal actions spoke louder than any words he may have uttered. Ten thousand veterans, including men who had just been 'married' to their oriental partners with Alexander's blessing, were discharged forthwith and ordered back to retirement in Macedonia. Their offspring by oriental women were required to be left behind as children of the camp. In the case of the male children, these were seen as further potential recruits to his new model imperial army.

By 324, then, Alexander's determined policy of orientalization had succeeded in alienating not only many of the Macedonian nobility but also many ordinary Macedonian soldiers. It is a measure of the (metaphorical) distance he had travelled during the past twelve years that he was in a position to ignore both groups. Having first abandoned the Panhellenic crusade in 330, he was now abandoning a narrowly Macedonian imperialism. True, his senior officers – such as the four marshals of the empire, Hephaestion, Perdiccas, Craterus and Ptolemy – were all still Macedonians. And it was from their ranks that would come the rulers of his fragmented empire after his death. But these were men who had climbed to their stations of high favour over the bodies of fellow-Macedonians who for one reason or another had been considered insufficiently loyal to Alexander. These *arrivistes* were, above all else, Alexander's men.

FIVE

ALEXANDER AND
THE GREEKS

D ONNING his father's mantle at the tender age of twenty, Alexander assumed the roles of king of Macedon and leader of the Greek League of Corinth. Boldly, he identified himself with the Homeric hero Achilles, and committed himself formally to the liberation of the Greeks of Asia (Minor), who had been subjects of the Persian Empire – once again – for the past half-century. In his treatise entitled *Politics* Alexander's former tutor Aristotle wished for the establishment of a single *politeia*, or common political organization, for all Greeks, remarking casually that if they could achieve this aim they could rule the world. At the time Aristotle was composing the *Politics* at Athens in the 330s and 320s, his former pupil was engaged across the sea in Asia on a mission that might conceivably have been construed as the creation of a single *politeia* for all Greeks – under one man.

Aristotle was a Greek with close familial Macedonian connections and intimate personal knowledge of the king of Macedon, so he might not have found that prospect entirely daunting. Yet the vast majority of Greeks (as distinct from Macedonians) saw things very differently indeed. Right down to the final decisive battle against the Persian Great King, Alexander had more Greeks fighting against him than for him. Between 336 and 322 a significant number of Greek cities and federations of the mainland were at one time or another up in arms against him (or his deputy, Antipater, who served as regent in old Greece). Between them Alexander and Antipater were responsible, as these Greeks saw it, for the final annihilation of Greek political liberty both in old Greece and in Asia.

How is this seeming paradox to be explained? I shall argue that there is, in fact, no paradox at all, and that Alexander's treatment of the Greeks – all Greeks, both collectively and individually – was entirely consistent. Consistent, that is, with the fulfilment of his one demonstrably overriding and abiding ideal, the power and the glory of Alexander. This is not to say that he did not also hold high ideals of Hellenism and seek to promote them widely; only that he would not allow the promotion of that or any other altruistic ideal to come in the way of his self-promotion as – ultimately – the son of a non-Greek god and as a new god in his own right.

The second year of Alexander's reign, before he left Europe for good, as it turned out, provides us with a perfect litmus test of his attitude to Greeks and Greekness – the destruction of Thebes in 335. Thebes in the 360s, following its defeat of Sparta, had been briefly the greatest power in mainland Greece. Philip, not irrelevantly, had spent there the years from 368 to 365, his mid to late teens, as a royal hostage. During the Third Sacred War (356–346) over control of the shrine of Delphi, when Thebes was no longer such a great power, it had been an ally of Philip to the north and an implacable foe of its neighbours to south and west, Athens and Phocis. But in 339 the Athenian politician Demosthenes pulled off perhaps his greatest diplomatic coup by persuading the Thebans to join a Greek anti-Philip coalition.

In the following year, a decisive battle was fought at Chaeronea in Boeotia north-west of Thebes, the result being a total victory for Philip. A magnificent stone lion memorial marks the battlefield to this day (Figure 17). The Boeotian federal state that Thebes had dominated since 378 was perhaps now dissolved, but certainly the anti-Macedonian leaders were killed or banished. A Macedonian garrison was placed on the Theban acropolis (the Cadmeia), and a supposedly tamed and quiescent Thebes was enrolled along with most other cities of mainland Greece south of Macedonia in Philip's new League of Corinth.

Freedom is often said to be indivisible. Whether or not that is true as a general rule, a significant number of influential Thebans chafed at the division of theirs. In 336, as soon as news of Philip's assassination at Aegae was known, Thebes was among those Greek states that sought to recover their independence from Macedon but were forestalled by Alexander. Again, in 335, following the rumour that Alexander had been killed (like his uncle Perdiccas in 359) fighting against the Illyrians on his north-west frontier, the Thebans openly raised the standard of rebellion. This time they were aided and abetted by Demosthenes's Athens and some other Greek states. The luck of Alexander understandably became proverbial, though to an important extent he made his own. Anyhow, by a great stroke of good fortune he had just finished off his Illyrian business when news reached him of the Thebes-led Greek revolt. Within two weeks, like a lightning flash, he was before the walls of Thebes with an army. The Thebans were rudely surprised. But if Alexander had hoped that they would be terrorized into submission and take advantage of his advertised clemency, he too was in for something of a rude shock.

The Thebans' democratic Assembly not only voted to continue the struggle for autonomy, as they understood it, but also (in the words of Diodorus*) 'proclaimed from a high tower that anyone who wished to join the Great King and Thebes in freeing the Greeks and destroying the tyrant of Greece should come over to them'. This proclamation was addressed to the members of the League of Corinth, including other Boeotian cities, who were obediently serving in Alexander's army. Mention of it does not, however, appear in what is on the whole our best surviving narrative source on Alexander, Arrian's *Anabasis*, since his picture of the Theban episode is seriously biased. We would not have expected to find in Arrian, who chose to rely mainly on the court historians Ptolemy and Aristoboulus, a proclamation such as this.[†] It blew the lid off the whole Panhellenic project – or fraud – that

---

* See Appendix, pp. 255–6.
† For a more detailed discussion of the vexed question of Arrian's sources, see the Appendix, pp. 249–51.

Alexander, following Philip, was seeking to perpetrate. Not only did the Thebans call Alexander a tyrant, a despot rather than a legitimate or constitutional monarch, just as Demosthenes had labelled – and libelled – his father Philip. But they were actually appealing for aid in liberating Greece from Alexander's tyranny to the Great King of Persia – that is, to the very figure who was supposed to be the bogeyman of the united freedom-loving Greeks.

Again, it is Diodorus not Arrian who bluntly states and explains Alexander's reaction to the Theban proclamation: 'he realized that he was held in contempt by the Thebans and so decided to destroy the city utterly and by this act of terror take the heart out of anyone else who might venture to rise against him'. Put differently, Alexander decided to cow into submission by an act of extreme political violence the allies whose anti-Persian crusade he was supposed to be leading. This is, I believe, an accurate indication of Alexander's mature character and methods, fully formed already at the age of twenty-one. It is likewise an accurate sample of our sources' strengths and weaknesses.*

Against Diodorus's blunt, realistic and plausible statement quoted above, we find only the Official version – or spin – in Arrian. According to this, the decision to destroy Thebes was taken not by Alexander on his own initiative, but rather by the members of the Council of the League of Corinth, whose judgement Alexander merely respected and implemented. What they allegedly intended by it was to punish Thebes most severely for its past record of 'Medism': that is, either its outright collaboration with Persia against Greeks, or at any rate its insufficiently vigorous resistance or opposition to the Persian invasion in 480/79. It was Alexander, according to Plutarch, who then deliberately softened the blow somewhat by insisting on sparing from the general destruction the sacred precincts of the gods of Thebes, together with one secular structure – as we saw earlier, the house in

---

* These are fully discussed in the Appendix, pp. 243–70.

which the famous lyric poet Pindar had lived at the time of that Persian incursion of the early fifth century.

In order to assess the bias of the Official version, we must revisit first Alexander's own much-paraded Hellenism. One of the most sober and respected historians of Alexander of the last century was the German scholar and papyrologist Ulrich Wilcken. It was his considered but controversial opinion that Alexander 'remained to the last a thorough admirer of Greek culture'. In favour of that view is the fact that Greek philosophers (such as Anaxarchus of Abdera) and littérateurs (most conspicuously Callisthenes) frequented his court. All across Asia and as far as India (the Punjab and Kashmir) Alexander staged athletic, literary and musical contests for his troops on the Greek model (borrowed already by Philip for the local Macedonian version of the Olympic Games held at Dium). He himself is said to have kept constantly at his bedside a special copy of the *Iliad*, annotated for him by Aristotle; after the Battle of Issus in 333 he stored it in a golden chest captured from Darius III.

Finally, and probably most importantly, the cities that Alexander founded in Egypt and Asia were Greek in culture, and through them and by other means Greek culture was spread all over the Middle East. After Alexander, as Robin Lane Fox has neatly pointed out in his biography, Sophocles was read in Susa, Euripides inspired artists in Bactria, comic mimes were performed at Alexandria-by-the-Caucasus, a Greek treatise was written in Babylon, the Trojan Horse story became a favourite tale in Ai Khanum on the banks of the Oxus in central Asia, and Alexander's adored Homer found his way even to India.

Not everyone, however, as suggested earlier, is equally convinced of either the depth or the sincerity of Alexander's Hellenism. The critics of Wilcken's view point out that Asiatic tyrants who ruled in the Persian interest, and even Persian satraps or sub-satraps like Mausolus of Caria (Chapter Two), might be as Hellenic in culture as Alexander. The array of goods stowed in the tomb at Aegae that may or not be Philip's (Figures 18, 19) displays, they feel, a regrettable lack of tasteful restraint. The Macedonian court and Alexander's general headquarters give them the impression less of a polished Hellenic court than of a rough officers' mess. They believe that Alexander's cities were founded and sited for strategic, economic and political purposes, not cultural ones. They also believe that – as a general rule, to be applied across the board – Alexander never sacrificed policy to sentiment or passion. In other words, so the critics would hold, if Alexander did indeed speak up for sparing Pindar's house (and the lives of his descendants), he did so because this was a cheap way of sugaring the pill of the total destruction of a hostile state with the best land army in Greece, not out of a patriotic love of Greek lyric poetry.

Both sides probably overstate their case, but on the whole I side with Wilcken's critics on this one. I am prepared to allow Alexander a more sincere and deep attachment to Hellenic culture than they would: Yet I believe that he advertised and disseminated his attachment only so long as it furthered, or at least did not obviously hinder, his other, more basic aims – above all else, conquest and glory-bringing empire.

Similarly, as with Alexander's Hellenism, there are broadly two lights in which to view Philip's formation in 338/7 of the League of Corinth, depending on whether we see it as fostering the Greek states' self-governance or as promoting Macedon's self-interested realpolitik. The apologetic view is beautifully summed up in the final section of the general history of Greece written by the late Nicholas Hammond, himself a war hero with the most profound knowledge of Macedonian topography and history. The relevant section of his *History of Greece* (first published in 1959) is entitled 'Different Ideas of Freedom'. Philip, according to Hammond:

> *gave to the Greek states a charter of freedom and self-government, conditioned by co-operation and respect for others, and Alexander followed his example in 336. Garrisons were indeed placed in some citadels; but this measure was approved by the Council of the Greek League as the self-governing organ of the whole.*

Hence, Hammond argued, the Council of the League was availing itself of the freedom of cooperation granted it by Philip and Alexander in order to curb the freedom of oppression in Boeotia claimed by the Thebans. This it did first by voting for the imposition of a Macedonian garrison on Thebes and then, after the city's revolt of 335, voting for its near-total destruction.

The alternative, diametrically opposed view sees the issue in terms not of legality and morality, but of power. In other words, so far from granting to the Greeks a new and improved cooperative freedom, it can be argued with equal or greater plausibility that Philip and Alexander were exercising the all too familiar, time-hallowed freedom to oppress politically in virtue of superior military might. Certainly, the League Council did vote to destroy Thebes in 335. But the ultimate source of that decision was Alexander (as Diodorus makes plain). This is the proper light in which the Theban episode should be viewed: might neither makes right, nor equates to legality. Hammond himself was aware of this dimension of the issue, too. For after seemingly arguing in terms of morality, he then writes a few sentences later that the Theban rebel leaders of 335 had 'failed to understand the power of Alexander'. Likewise, when he comes to discuss the so-called Lamian War (see pp. 100–3), the much more widespread and effective Greek anti-Macedonian revolt that broke out after Alexander's death in 323, Hammond writes that the Greek rebels were 'much inferior to the power of Macedon'.

Let us therefore linger a little longer over this supposed 'charter of freedom and self-government, conditioned by co-operation and respect for others'. It is an absolutely fascinating instrument of, and experiment in, Greek interstate relations – generally fraught at the best of times (see Chapter Two), and these were not by any means the best of times. As one would expect of a military and diplomatic genius like Philip, the League of Corinth embraced the main features of the two types of association most likely to conduce to a managed and controllable Greek unity under unchallengeable Macedonian domination:

Common Peace, and military alliance under a *hêgemôn*, or supreme leader.

The essential ideas of a Common Peace were as follows. It embraced all Greek states, whether or not they were actually party to the swearing of the religious oaths that brought it into being and were meant to guarantee its observance; and it provided for the 'autonomy' of all states great or small – that is, their freedom from all external control or interference. The first such Peace had been sworn among Greeks in 386, under the joint presidency of Sparta and – another irony – the Great King of Persia. Yet the conclusion of this Peace and its subsequent renewals had not prevented outright war or even infringements of autonomy, but only minimized or mitigated them, to some extent. In 338/7 the sole president and guarantor of the new Common Peace was the Macedonian Philip. He had the power to see that the terms were not infringed – or infringed only in ways that were congenial to him. Thus before outlawing domestic political revolution and the freeing of slaves for the purpose of making such a revolution, Philip had taken care to ensure that 'his' men – oligarchs or even tyrants – were in nominal power in important cities.

The most immediately relevant model for a hegemonic military alliance was Athens's Second Naval League, formed in 378 and dissolved by Philip's new League. The Athenian Assembly had had sole authority to initiate Naval League policy, but for the Athenians' wishes to be put into effect they had had to be confirmed by a permanent Council (*synedrion*) of allied delegates or representatives sitting in Athens. The permanent Council of Philip's new League was sited in Corinth rather than Athens for a number of reasons – geopolitical, religious (Corinth hosted the biennial Panhellenic Isthmian Games), and symbolic (it was at Corinth in 481 that the handful of Greek resisters had met to swear resistance to Xerxes's impending Persian invasion).

In theory, then, from 338 or 337 all Greek cities and states were to be free and autonomous. Yet Thebes revolted in 335 precisely to regain the autonomy of which it had in its view been deprived. There were two main reasons for this judgement. First, the terms of the League's charter were so drawn up that there was plenty of scope for ostensibly legal intervention by the *hêgemôn* in allied states' internal affairs. And in order to enable him to intervene effectively, he could call on a mysterious body known as those 'in charge of the common defence' – presumably, a special task force for ensuring that his wishes were swiftly executed. Second, there was no effective check on the *hêgemôn*'s free initiative. There was no court that could rule that Alexander was acting beyond his legal powers or sentence him for illegality. And in any case what League law there was would be laid down, applied and interpreted by the king himself – as we shall indeed see him doing in some of the few surviving contemporary documents. So, in case one is tempted to place a great deal of faith in the supposed freedom and independence of decision accorded to the League's Council, one should recall that relations between Alexander and the Greeks, like all interstate relations everywhere at all periods (as Thucydides's history of the Peloponnesian War had taught), were based ultimately on power and force. This is the true spirit in which the League Council voted in 335 for the destruction of Thebes, having already acquiesced in 338/7 to the imposition of Macedonian garrisons on Thebes, Corinth, Ambracia and perhaps Chalcis.

Philip had decided upon his Persian expedition, then, both to exact revenge for the Persian invasions of European Greece in 490 and 480/ 79 and to liberate the Greeks of Asia from Persia. They had been Persian subjects since 386 under the terms of the first Common Peace, alternatively known as the (Persian) King's Peace or (after the Spartan chief negotiator) as the Peace of Antalcidas. Alexander was initially happy enough, at least outwardly, to embrace such liberation propaganda too. It could be used tactically against Thebes (a notorious 'Medizer' in 480/79) and might be expected to encourage the Asiatic Greeks to defect openly from Persia and contribute men, money, equipment and supplies to the Panhellenic crusade. And yet he was also rather revealingly slow to make use of it once he had actually reached Asia in spring 334. Likewise Parmenion, in command of the advance bridgehead force, had shown no qualms in 335 about storming Greek Gryneum and selling its citizens into slavery. In other words, the Macedonian high command's message to Greeks as the campaign got under way was: cooperate – or else. It was not until the summer of 334 that Alexander decisively broke with this unsentimentally aggressive conception.

The turning point came at Ephesus, always most vulnerable to Persian influence as it lay close to the western end of the Royal Road that ran west for some two thousand miles (three thousand kilometres) from Susa, and was within easy striking distance of the Lydian satrapal capital, Sardis. Envoys from Greek cities further inland came to Alexander at Ephesus and invited him to their own cities, which presumably implies that they had already freed themselves from Persian control. But what might such 'freedom' mean in this context?

Ever since our Greek evidence begins, with Herodotus in the third quarter of the fifth century, the Great King of Persia had laid claim as of right to all of 'Asia' – that is, the entire land mass up to the Aegean coastline of Anatolia in the west. The physical tokens of earth and water that conventionally expressed submission to the Great King symbolized his physical ownership of this space. And in practical terms the irreducible minimum of submissive obedience required was the payment of tribute in cash or kind. As far as the political, religious, social and economic institutions of the individual Greek states went, the King preferred not to have to intervene directly, whether in person or via his satraps. Instead, he ruled indirectly through what we might want to call quisling governments and regimes, consisting either of one man (a 'tyrant' in Greek parlance) or of a few men ('oligarchies'). This was the political situation when in midsummer 334 Alexander dispatched Alcimachus and a force of about five thousand men to, in Arrian's words:

proceed to the Aeolian towns and all the Ionian ones still subject to Persia. Throughout the country [the coastal strip of western Anatolia] he dispossessed the oligarchies and established democracies in their place, allowing every community to enjoy its own laws and customs and to discontinue payment of the tribute it had previously paid to the Persians.

Does this mean that Alexander was, for preference, an ideological democrat? Far from it. As we have noted, under the terms of the League of Corinth established by Philip which Alexander had seen no reason to alter, domestic revolution was outlawed as well as external interference in the internal affairs of another Greek state. So far, so, apparently, respectful of the Greek allies' autonomy and of their freedom to choose, including the freedom to choose democracy. But Philip in hard actuality had been very careful to ensure that, before the oaths were sworn, his partisans were in control of their cities. In this, as in other ways, the Macedonian Empire was little distinguishable from the Persian. Where the security of complaisant pro-Macedonian oligarchic rule was jeopardized, there Philip had garrisons installed: at Thebes, Corinth, Ambracia and perhaps Chalcis, as we have seen. These later came to be known, understandably, as the Fetters of Greece. Athens, as so often, was an exception, and treated exceptionally by Philip. But if he allowed it to retain its democracy and to be free from a garrison, this was not wholly or even mainly out of sentiment. It was because this was the price he calculated he had to pay in order to have at his disposal for the upcoming Persian campaign by far the largest and most efficient Greek navy – a necessity, surely, for a campaign that would be amphibious, and a *hêgemôn* which in Macedon's case lacked a navy altogether.

In all these respects Alexander followed his father's example. It is particularly noteworthy that he seems to have countenanced the rule of tyrants at Pellene, Messene and Sicyon, all in the Peloponnese, and at Elatea in Phocis in central Greece. So, the support that Alexander gave explicitly to democracy in Greek Asia in the summer of 334 has to be interpreted as a purely pragmatic and opportunistic move – as a somewhat tardy and perhaps reluctant agreement to swim with the dominant democratic current of Greek anti-Persian sentiment in a milieu where the Persians had systematically backed and operated through non- or anti-democratic forces, movements and individuals. What, then, are we to make of Alexander's further decisions to allow every Greek community to enjoy its own laws and customs, and to remit their tribute?

It does not take much insight, I think, to perceive that the very act of establishing and supporting democracies at the expense of oligarchies was itself formally a breach of the cities' autonomy. But, given that Greek *dêmokratia* was the sovereign authority of the *dêmos* – in the sense of either the people as a whole or of the majority of the citizens – such a breach of autonomy would not generally have been considered oppressive or tyrannical, since it accorded with the wishes of the majority. On the other hand, Alexander's further interventions at Ephesus were not necessarily quite so welcome. For he did not stop at straightforwardly remitting the old Persian tribute. Instead, he ordered that it be redirected to the city's patron goddess Artemis. A pious objective, true, recalling his sparing of the shrines of Thebes the previous year. But ought piety to be compulsory? And who would get the major credit for it – the Ephesians or Alexander?

At Priene, also in Ionia, Alexander seems to have been even more strongly interventionist, to judge from a contemporary official document that (in the apt words of Michele Faraguna) 'introduces us to the basic principles of Alexander's administration'. It was significant enough in its way that there is mention of the payment of a *syntaxis*, or 'contribution'. This is precisely the word that the Athenians had used for their Second Naval League allies' sake in order to avoid the stigma of imposing on them again (as they had in the fifth century) the hated *phoros*, or 'tribute'. In other words, Alexander's proclaimed remission of tribute did not exactly mean remission of tribute. But more significant still was that, instead of entering into treaty relations with Priene and binding himself by oaths, even to the – relatively small – extent of those that constrained his relations with the Greek allies of the League of Corinth, Alexander simply issued an edict to Priene, unilaterally. In tone the Priene document strongly recalls a recently discovered contemporary official document from Philippi, in Chalcidian Thrace. (Philippi had originally been founded by Greeks under the name of Crenides, in order to exploit the local mineral wealth. Philip II, once he'd taken it over as part of his eastward march, refounded it and gave it his own name, signifying that it was part of the new order of Greater Macedonia.) Whatever the precise legal status of these newly liberated Asiatic Greek cities may have been, Alexander's intervention created its own legal forms.

The case of a third Greek city of Asia, Aspendus in Pamphylia to the south-west, raises yet further issues, again with regard to Alexander's handling of the tribute question. The old Persian tribute of Aspendus had been paid in kind – in the form of horses – rather than in cash. In this case, perhaps because he was feeling strapped for this particular sort of resource, or perhaps because there was a large and wealthy non-Greek element in the population whom he felt he could usefully penalize for their loyalty to the Great King, Alexander did not remit it. Rather, on top of that tribute in horses, he slapped on a huge demand for a monetary 'contribution' of fifty talents, something like ten to fifteen individual 'millionaire' fortunes. Not surprisingly, Aspendus demurred. Perhaps this was the reaction Alexander had intended to provoke. At all events, his response was swift and ferocious. Of course, he could not enslave Aspendus as Parmenion had enslaved Gryneum, since that would have made a total mockery of his Panhellenic 'liberation' propaganda. So Aspendus 'escaped' with having to hand over a doubled monetary contribution plus hostages, together with the original equine tribute, and to suffer the imposition of a garrison, with possibly some loss of territory and full satrapal control. Alexander (as we shall see in more detail in Chapter Eight) fundamentally maintained the old Persian satrapal system, though at this early stage of the campaign he was altering the personnel across the board.

By no stretch of the imagination – or stroke of terminological spin – could the autonomy of Aspendus be said to have been preserved, let alone honoured. It was, in fact, a kind of Asiatic Thebes, a terrible warning example of the likely consequences of less than total and immediate compliance with Alexander's orders and demands. Normally, as the exceptional case of Aspendus reveals, an Asiatic Greek city at this time might have expected only to have to pay a 'contribution' and perhaps receive a garrison for as long as it took to ensure a smooth transition from the old Persian order to a new, tame democratic regime. 'For the rest,' as Ernst Badian put it in a phrase of which Tacitus would not have been ashamed, 'they [the Greek cities of Asia] were free, provided they obeyed.'

It would be quite wrong to imagine that the narrowly legal–political aspect of the cities' relationship to Alexander was always uppermost in their minds. Centuries after Alexander's death, Asiatic Greeks were still celebrating or at least commemorating their gratitude to him by paying him religious homage. As I shall argue in Chapter Eleven, Alexander was being spontaneously worshipped as a living god by the Asiatic Greeks before he was deified – perhaps at his demand – by the Greeks of old Greece. On the other hand, the question of their legal status vis-à-vis Alexander was not merely a formality. For if the Asiatic Greeks were indeed enrolled in the League of Corinth, then Alexander would at the very least have had to swear certain oaths towards them and, to that extent, restrict his own freedom of action by going through the procedures (or motions) of consultation.

There is no positive evidence that the Asiatic Greek cities were so enrolled. Yet there is such evidence for the enrolment by Alexander of Greek cities on the offshore Aegean islands of Chios (a contemporary document), and Tenedos and (Mytilene on) Lesbos (literary references). So the question is really whether there would have been a pragmatically awkward inconsistency in Alexander's treating the Greeks of the European mainland and the Aegean islands on a different legal basis from the way he treated those of the Asiatic mainland. I have an open mind. But perhaps Alexander's use of the term *syntaxis* in regard to the latter is a bit of a clue. Since this was the term employed to mean tribute in the Second Athenian Naval League, the coincidence of terminology is at least suggestive, especially as the League of Corinth was obviously modelled in its military alliance aspect on this now superseded organization. It suggests that on liberation the Asiatic Greeks were indeed incorporated in the League of Corinth.

The issue of the numbers of Greek troops that Alexander did – or did not – recruit and use for the Asiatic campaign of conquest sheds further light on his relations with Greeks. A reasonable estimate of the situation in spring 334, after the link-up with Parmenion at Abydus in the Hellespont, might go something like this. Out of the perhaps 43,000 foot and something over 6,000 horse only 7,000 foot and 2,400 horse were contributed by member states of the League of Corinth. This was in the context of a potential of perhaps 200,000 infantry and 15,000 cavalry. Moreover, such League troops as were used were, apart from the valued Thessalian cavalry, before long taken out of the front line and left on communications and garrison duty. Alexander's inadequate fleet was wholly Greek, and mainly Athenian, but numbered only 160 ships, although Athens alone could have manned more than that. On top of the Greek troops contributed by the member states of the League, Alexander had 5,000-plus Greek mercenaries in his employ in 334, and by 331 he had hired another 7,000-plus – at least so far as our unsatisfactory sources reveal. To put this in perspective, Darius III was able to employ some 50,000 Greeks as mercenaries in pitched battles down to and including the decisive Battle of Gaugamela in 331, and many others on fleet and garrison duty.

How, then, are we to explain the following: that Alexander

enlisted so few Greek League troops – relatively to both their potential and to the actual numbers of Macedonians used; that, despite the crucial strategic importance of sea power, he took along an inadequate fleet; and, not least, that more Greeks fought against him than fought for him in all engagements before Gaugamela? The obvious answers, it might seem, are that Alexander did not consider he needed more Greek troops or a larger fleet, and that Darius offered higher pay and a better chance of survival to Greek would-be mercenaries. But obvious answers are not necessarily the right ones.

By the time of Gaugamela in late 331, Alexander had sent for and received fourteen thousand or more men as reinforcements, half of them mercenaries, the other half Macedonians; once again, this is a striking underuse (or rather non-use) of League troops. Then, too, Alexander's naval policy nearly was, as it really ought to have been, a disaster. His decision to disband most of his fleet in 334 and his paradoxical determination to defeat the Persian navy by land both slowed down his eventual victory over Darius and laid him open to a stab in the back from the Aegean. As for the mercenaries, we have to remember that men did not usually become such from an act of pure, free choice, but sold their services from a mixture of economic and political motives. Politically, revolution had been outlawed by the terms of the League of Corinth, so anti-Macedonian exiles naturally gravitated to the service of Alexander's enemy Darius III. Economically, there was no good objective reason why poor Greeks should have preferred to fight for Darius rather than Alexander, since the Great King was notoriously a bad payer and in any case mercenary wages were not high. Therefore they either calculated that Darius was the more likely to win (a reasonable enough supposition, at least until the Battle of Issus). Or, more interestingly, they wanted to fight against Alexander on principle, perhaps the same principle that had motivated the revolt of Thebes.

To sum up: the most plausible explanation of the composition of Alexander's forces, as it seems to me, is that he mistrusted the Greeks' loyalty, with good reason after all, and that an awful lot more Greeks disliked or feared Alexander's Macedonian rule than positively favoured or embraced it. This impression seems confirmed by none other than Arrian, retailer of the pro-Alexander Official version of events for the most part. At the Battle of Issus, he reports, there was among Alexander's troops 'even a degree of emulous antagonism between members of the Greek and Macedonian peoples' – that is, between troops who were supposed to be fighting on the same side in a common cause. This was because for many Greeks, the Macedonians too – not just the Persians – were 'barbarians'. Furthermore, it was Macedon, not the Great King, which they thought was the real, or at any rate the more immediately present, danger and enemy. For many Macedonians, conversely, Greeks were members of a recently defeated and so despised people who did not know how to conduct their political and military life sensibly. This, I think, is the true light in which we must view Alexander's inherited Panhellenic propaganda. If he kept it up until 330, despite its increasing awkwardness, this was because it was his only means of attempting to conciliate the considerable amount of hostile Greek opinion and so of helping to keep the Greek mainland quiet.

THERE is one Greek state that has not been mentioned so far in this chapter which, after Thebes and before Athens, posed the most serious threat to Macedonian rule in mainland Greece: Sparta. Philip had been careful both to weaken Sparta humiliatingly in 338/7 (by mulcting it of territory in favour of its hostile neighbours in Arcadia, Messenia and the Argolid, whose support Philip cultivated) and to leave it firmly outside the framework of the League of Corinth. His impeccable reasoning followed the 'my enemy's enemy is my friend' principle – if he treated Sparta in this contemptuous way, Sparta's hostile neighbours would remain fervently loyal to him. This he thought would be especially true of the men of Messene, whose fathers and grandfathers had been Helot serfs but achieved their personal and political emancipation and enfranchisement, thanks to the great Epaminondas's Thebes, in 369 (see Chapter Two). And so indeed it proved. What Philip considered policy, Alexander in this instance considered duty. Under his regime, Sparta remained firmly out in the diplomatic cold; and in 334, after the Battle of the Granicus, he took pains to remind the Greeks, including the Spartans, of this fact, in the most blatant possible way.

As part of that battle's victory celebrations, Alexander had sent back to Athens three hundred captured suits of armour and ordered that they be dedicated to Athena on the Athenian acropolis, with this accompanying message (recorded for us by Arrian):

> *Alexander son of Philip and the Greeks except the Spartans*
> *dedicate these spoils taken from the Persians who dwell in Asia.*

Note first the absence of the royal title; then the phrase 'who dwell in' – not 'who control' – Asia. Of course. But the real sting lay in the two suitably laconic Greek words translated in English as 'except the Spartans'. In actual fact, the victory at the River Granicus had been won essentially by the Macedonian contingents, not by the Greeks. Alexander's propaganda, in its specific Athenian religious context, was designed to hark straight back to 480/79, when Sparta and Athens had jointly led the Greeks' successful resistance to Persia. Why precisely three hundred suits of armour? Because that was the number of the immortally famed band of selected Spartans who were sent to defend the pass of Thermopylae under their king Leonidas. The defence was, inevitably, a failure, and Xerxes's troops forced the pass. But in terms of morale-boosting Thermopylae was a mighty victory for the Greek resisters, and especially for the Spartans, since it showed that the Persian horde could be effectively confronted. From Thermopylae the way was opened to the Greeks' eventual decisive victory in 479 at Plataea, where again it was the Spartans who played the leading role.

How different was the Spartans' situation in the late 330s. Smarting from their all too public humiliation by first Philip and then

Alexander, and reduced to the status of a second-rate Peloponnesian wrangler, the Spartans under Agis III spent the next few years preparing to lead a Theban-style rising in Greece behind Alexander's back. They even entered into negotiations with his enemy Darius through his agents and commanders in the Aegean and eastern Mediterranean. They were particularly active in recruiting mercenaries on Crete. In 331 they felt they were as ready as they would ever be. With the outcome of Alexander's expedition against Persia not yet finally decided (this was before the Battle of Gaugamela), they went into open revolt in the Peloponnese.

In one sense, this was yet another demonstration of Greek hostility to Macedonian rule. But its real significance lies elsewhere. For Agis's revolt demonstrated finally and beyond doubt that for the majority of Greeks Sparta was an even more unpopular proposition as *hêgemôn* than Macedon. Perhaps twice as many Greek citizen soldiers fought for Macedon, under Regent Antipater, as fought under Agis at Megalopolis in Arcadia. States like Argos and Messene in the Peloponnese did not support Agis in his anti-Macedonian revolt but did revolt later, under the leadership of Athens, in 323. As for the Athenians, they had powerful reasons of their own for not following Agis's lead, above all because they thought the revolt was ill-timed and unlikely to succeed for lack of general support. Alexander, from his Middle Eastern vantage point and perspective, is said to have referred to the Megalopolis battle sneeringly as a mere 'battle of mice'. This was hardly just, at any rate as regards the scale of the battle: perhaps as many as forty thousand troops under Antipater confronted Agis's maybe thirty thousand or so. But the Spartan mice made no impression on the Macedonian cat. Agis lost his life. Sparta lost a role of any significance in Greek affairs for almost a century thereafter.

FOLLOWING the victory at the Granicus river in 334, Alexander had not only sent back to Greece three hundred inanimate and barbarian suits of armour for dedication to Athena in Athens. He had also dispatched some two thousand very much alive Greeks, prisoners of war who had served under Darius as paid mercenaries, to work for no pay as chain gangs in the gold and silver mines of Greater Macedonia. He no doubt calculated that in propaganda terms this tune too would play well, back in the homeland. But actually, so far from encouraging Greeks to enlist as mercenaries under his banner, it persuaded those already in Persian service that it would be preferable to fight to the death than to be captured by Alexander and die a prolonged and ignominious death in the Macedonian equivalent of the salt mines of Siberia.

More successful was an act of restitution of cultural property that Alexander carried out in December 331, when the war against Darius was essentially won and Alexander had started to rule as King of Asia. He then sent back to Athens from Susa the statues of the liberator-heroes Harmodius and Aristogiton that the wicked Xerxes had plundered from there in 480. Not only was this entirely in line with the expedition's legitimating propaganda of Panhellenic revenge. It also had the not inconsiderable benefit of reinforcing Alexander's anti-tyrannical credentials. For Harmodius and his older lover Aristogiton had been executed for conspiring to overthrow a tyrant of Athens, Hippias, and the Athenian democracy that was instituted not long afterwards (in 508/7), following the overthrow of Hippias by the Spartans in 510, treated them as founder-heroes. Moreover, the exiled tyrant Hippias conveniently went over to the Persian side, thereby firmly establishing in ordinary Athenians' minds an association between opposition to tyranny and opposition to Persia. Hippias hoped to secure both the overthrow of the democracy and his own restoration by the Persians, but his journey to Marathon with the invading Persian forces in 490 was in vain. John Stuart Mill was of the thought-provoking view that the Athenians' victory at Marathon was a more important event in *English* history even than the Battle of Hastings.

So far as Alexander's formal military cooperation with the League of Corinth is concerned, it ended in June 330 when he dismissed the League's contingents at Ecbatana in Media (near the site of Darius I's Bisitun inscription). He thereby abandoned the Panhellenic pretence, which had never brought him any solid gain in old Greece, though it had helped to promote the defection from Persia of Asiatic Greeks and cement their loyalty to him. This leaves us with a final major puzzle: the flames over Persepolis – that is, the burning to the ground at the Achaemenid Empire's ceremonial capital in late April or May 330, of the huge and immensely rich palace built by Darius I and subsequently augmented or adorned by several of his Achaemenid successors. Why did Alexander order this, if he did order it? Or countenance it, if he did not?

So scandalous and exciting was this act of major arson that all sorts of stories got out. One – much favoured in the taverns of Greece – told how drunken revelry had led to a wild suggestion by the famous Athenian prostitute Thaïs (Ptolemy's sexual partner at the time), to which Alexander in his cups agreed. In this version, the burning of the Persepolis palace was almost an afterthought, and at any rate not the final implementation of a carefully considered and rational plan. There is an alternative, and very different, modern view. This holds that the burning of the Persepolis palace should be seen, like the total destruction of Thebes, as an act of coldly calculated policy, if on a global or Empire-wide rather than a locally Hellenic scale. According to this less romantic but probably more accurate view, the bonfire was both an integral part of the Panhellenic campaign of revenge and the signal that it was now ended. It was (to quote Ernst Badian) 'the brilliant funeral pyre of the Hellenic crusade against the Barbarian'. The dismissal of the League of Corinth troops the following month would at any rate seem to corroborate that.

However, there is a difficulty with this view too. By May 330 Alexander had long since ceased to present himself as a peculiarly Greek sort of ruler. Rather, he was putting himself across as the successor to the Achaemenid Kings in the sense that he was intending to rule and wanting to be viewed as king of a new oriental empire of Asia. For this reason he was hoping above all to harmonize his leading Macedonians and those members of the old Persian ruling elite who were prepared to endorse his aims and ideals, or at least to work with rather than against him. Within this new Macedonian–Persian governmental and ideological framework the Hellenic crusade had no further meaning or purchase.

So why carry out a Panhellenic bonfire that would please only or mainly Greeks? Moreover, burning the major ceremonial palace of the Achaemenids was hardly the most suitable way to conciliate leading Persian nobles to the new regime. There are indeed still Zoroastrians in Iran and neighbouring lands to this day who condemn Alexander as a devil for this act of wanton vandalism against not only their people but also their religion. Reaction among observant Zoroastrians in May 330 is unlikely to have been less uncomprehending and ferocious. So, the burning of the palace at Persepolis remains a bit of a conundrum, by no means the only one we have encountered – and regrettably have to leave as such – in our search for Alexander.

TO ROUND off our account of Alexander and the Greeks, we must consider finally a major Greek enterprise of summer 323. The Athenians, we saw, had refused to join Agis's revolt in 331. In summer 323 they began their own. It is generally known as the Lamian War, after the town in Thessaly, Lamia, where Regent Antipater was for a time blockaded. The very fact that Thessaly had mostly come out for Athens and against Macedon was itself highly revealing of the changed state of Greek–Macedonian relations. But the revolt was referred to at the time, very significantly and oddly, as the 'Hellenic War'. Normally – as in 'Persian War' or 'Peloponnesian War' – we would expect this to have meant a war *against* Greeks. But here it was being used to designate a war *by* Greeks, against in this case Macedon. Perhaps the point was that this war, like the Peloponnesian War a century earlier, was an internecine inter- and intra-Greek conflict. Another possible explanation of this singular usage is the extent of Greek cooperation that the Athenians were able to muster. For once, 'Hellas' was not merely an ideal to which conventional lip service was being paid, but a lived actuality.

The origins of the revolt of 323 may be traced to Alexander's execution of Callisthenes in 327,* which may have marked the extinction of Alexander's Panhellenic consciousness or conscience, and more immediately to his Exiles' Decree of 324. The latter required, or rather ordered, the Greek cities of old Greece to receive back both their political and their economic exiles. Possibly he did go through the motions, as in the case of the destruction of Thebes, of having the Decree passed by the Council of the League of Corinth – if this was still a going concern. Certainly, he had the Decree announced by a Greek adjutant (Nicanor, a future son-in-law of Aristotle) at the Panhellenic Olympic Games of late summer/early autumn 324. But such formalities hardly altered the fact that the Decree was a flagrant breach of the cities' autonomy, under any ordinary construction of that weasel word. Nor did Alexander take any steps to forestall or ease the appalling practical difficulties that its implementation necessarily entailed. A contemporary public document from Arcadian Tegea graphically illustrates the terrible problems caused, especially over the settlement of contested claims to agricultural land and other property. Humane concern for the exiles, such as Alexander's modern supporters have alleged, doesn't enter into it.

Nor, perhaps, was the Exiles' Decree the only assault on Greek political sensitivities and sensibilities that Alexander chose to launch. For at about this time he also either explicitly demanded, or – in the softer version – let it be known that he would welcome, his own deification by the Greeks. The official divinization of a living human

---

* See Appendix, pp. 263–5.

being was not actually unprecedented (and will be discussed in more detail in Chapter Eleven). But a formal request for it – if indeed Alexander made one – certainly would have been. Such a request following hot on the heels of the Exiles' Decree would have served to convince many Greeks, at any rate in old Greece, that Alexander no longer had their best interests at heart. It is very striking that even cities whose governing regimes were on balance well disposed to Alexander were unable to view the Exiles' Decree as a beneficent, let alone benevolent, act.

Diodorus was therefore partly right to trace the origins of the Lamian War to the Exiles' Decree, though that extreme measure had up to a point been forced on Alexander by the problem of hordes of wandering, cashiered mercenaries in Asia. Greek anti-Macedonian opinion was led by Athens, which opportunely received a windfall of seven hundred talents from Alexander's errant ex-Treasurer Harpalus. The catalyst of open revolt was the news of Alexander's death at Babylon in June 323. One Athenian politician famously affected to disbelieve the report, because, if it were true, he said, the stench of his corpse would already have spread over the whole world. But true it was, and the Athenians' revolt quickly proved enormously more attractive to the Greeks generally than had that of Agis. At least twenty Greek states and peoples joined forces against Regent Antipater, and for a brief moment *to Hellênikon*, Greekness, acquired a political identity. It took on something like the quality of ethnic or national solidarity that Aristotle had ardently desired – though ironically he himself was to be a victim of the revolt, as an alleged Macedonian sympathizer. Forced into voluntary exile, he became ill and died at Chalcis in Euboea in 322.

Herodotus a hundred years earlier had given a famous, if hugely optimistic, definition of *to Hellênikon* (literally, 'the Greek thing'): common language, common blood and common customs, especially religious, were what set the Greeks as a group apart from the 'barbarians'. What that definition signally lacked, however, was any political component, since – as Herodotus's own *Histories* laid painfully bare – the Greeks were unable to establish for themselves a single *politeia*, or overarching political framework. But although they could not agree on that, they did all share a fierce customary attachment to the free and autonomous political unit, whether individual city or federal state or people, to which they defined themselves as belonging. Despite his education by Aristotle, Alexander came from, and declared his allegiance to, an alien tradition of charismatic monarchy. To him, freedom and autonomy were gifts that he bestowed, or withheld, at his pleasure, whereas to the Greeks they were fundamental, irrefragable political rights.

Thus, it was the Lamian War, won eventually by the Macedonians in 322, rather than the Battle of Chaeronea in 338, that hammered the last nail into the coffin of Greek political freedom and independence – a coffin that Philip had commissioned and Alexander all but finally closed.

SIX

ALEXANDER: CONQUEROR OF PERSIA (334–327 BCE)

As is tolerably well known by now, Alexander had no sex-life whatsoever and my theory is that he got his fun doing to countries what normal people do to women, cities being the tangible outcome.

– 'Euxenus' in Tom Holt's *Alexander at the World's End*

Dᴜʀɪɴɢ the central years of Alexander's kingship and campaign, he defeated the Persian Great King and began replacing the old Persian Empire with an empire of his own. He also began re-placing himself as a new style of emperor or Great King. But why did Alexander assume, and with such eagerness, his late father's role as hammer of the Persians? At one level, it probably never occurred to him not to do so. He had been bred for the tasks of royal leadership, not least in war, and his deeply competitive and ambitious nature and love of glory could hardly fail to rise to the challenge. Perhaps he was also goaded subliminally by a sense that, but for Philip's assassination, the opportunity would not have been his in the first place. Indeed, he had not been part of his father's plans for the conquest at all, apparently. But there were also positive reasons, both public and private, that might have impelled him irresistibly in that same direction.

Above all there was the fact that, ostensibly, this was to be a Panhellenic expedition. It was explicitly designed first to exact revenge for the great Persian invasion of Greece in 480/79, and then to liberate those Greek cities of Asia that had been delivered over to Persian control in 386 under an agreement sanctioned by the then leading

Greek power, Sparta. Alexander, as a man imbued with Greek culture, would not have been insensible to the Panhellenic appeal. Yet his thoroughly pragmatic approach to his existing and future Greek allies and subjects was most notoriously displayed in his harsh, destructive treatment of Thebes in 335 (see Chapter Five). This suggests that his Panhellenism was romantic, at most, and always dispensable in favour of more deeply felt aims, pre-eminently his yearning to conquer at least the existing Persian Empire and add it to his own inherited imperium.

Whatever sort of a conqueror Alexander was, there is no question but that he was superbly equipped for the role. Even before 335 his strategic and tactical flair, his personal leadership, his speed and use of surprise, and his good fortune were on conspicuous show. But potentially his greatest asset of all was the basically Macedonian army he inherited from Philip. This is not said to take away from Alexander his due glory, but rather to emphasize how slight was the military role played in this ostensibly Panhellenic enterprise by the allied Greek troops. From the start of the expedition proper in 334, Alexander treated them not as front-line troops but rather as very unreliable allies indeed.

This attitude of mistrust was far from irrational. Right down to the decisive battle at Gaugamela in 331 the Greeks fighting as mercenaries for Persia, as noted in the last chapter, outnumbered those fighting for Alexander and the 'Panhellenic' cause. It is this same mistrust that explains Alexander's otherwise puzzling behaviour towards Athens. Although he remained outwardly scrupulous in his consideration for the city that had been Persia's chief target in 480/79, he refrained none the less from making any active use of Athens's fleet – even though this was the largest in the Aegean, and his only hope of challenging Persia's Phoenician and Cypriot fleet in the eastern Mediterranean. This mistrust, too, was to lead Alexander to adopt a highly risky and nearly disastrous strategy in southern Asia Minor and the Levant. Yet, whatever errors of judgement he may have made, they pale somewhat beside those committed by his opponents.

Darius III and the Persians' first big mistake was to allow Alex-

1. 'Tomb of Philip', Vergina (Archaeological Museum)

Tomb II, the second of three major royal tombs enclosed within the Great Tumulus at Vergina (ancient Aegae), has a good chance of being the Tomb of Philip (as it is conventionally labelled). See also Figs 9, 18, 19. The fresco adorning its front-elevation architrave depicts hunting on horseback in wooded terrain for mountain lion, wild boar and deer. The central figure, depicted boldly in rear-profile view, is thought to represent Alexander alongside his father Philip.

2. 'Alexander Sarcophagus', from Sidon, Lebanon (Archaeological Museum, Istanbul)

The 'Alexander Sarcophagus' is so named because on one long side Alexander is depicted on horseback in combat against a Persian (Fig. 8). Traditionally, the coffin has been attributed to Abdalonymus, king of Sidon, since that is its findspot; but an alternative view attributes it to the much more important Mazaeus, a noble Persian whom Alexander appointed to govern Babylon. The scenes on the short sides show scenes of the hunting of lion and (as here) panther.

3. Lion Hunt mosaic, House of Dionysus, Pella (Archaeological Museum)

This pebble mosaic originally adorned a floor in a luxurious Hellenistic-period house in Pella. It may show Craterus (R) famously supporting Alexander (L) in a hunting park in Syria, imitating bronze statue-groups in the round by Lysippus and Leochares. A mummified lion of the Ptolemaic (Hellenistic) period has recently been found in an ancient Pharaonic tomb at Memphis, indicating the continued Macedonian interest in the king of the beasts.

4. Stone relief from Messene (Inv. no. 858, Musée du Louvre, Paris)

This carved relief served as the facing of a large base or altar, set up in Messene in the south-west Peloponnese in the early Hellenistic period. From L., a horseman in Macedonian dress (tunic, cloak and broad-brimmed hat) attacks a lion being harried by specially bred smooth-coated hunting hounds. The hunter on foot is clad in a lionskin, which is reminiscent of Heracles and so may be meant to allude to Alexander.

5. Coin-shaped gold medallion of Olympias, found at Aboukir, Egypt (Archaeological Museum, Thessaloniki)

Struck to celebrate the 'Alexander Olympic Games' held at Beroea *c.* 250 CE, this fine medallion depicts Olympias demurely veiled as a proper Greek matron – not quite the picture that emerges consistently from the largely hostile literary sources presenting her as a bit of a wild woman.

6. Bronze figurine (Archaeological Museum, Florence)

Alexander alone was able to tame the Thessalian stallion Bucephalas ('Ox-Head') who served him faithfully for some twenty years until his death in 326 and posthumous immortalization in the town of Bucephala in the Punjab. This non-contemporary figurine was made in the Hellenistic period.

7. Bust of Aristotle (Musée du Louvre, Paris)

This Hellenistic-period bust of Aristotle is said to be derived from an original by Alexander's Sicyonian Greek court sculptor Lysippus.

8. (ABOVE) 'Alexander Sarcophagus', from Sidon, Lebanon (Archaeological Museum, Istanbul)

Alexander fighting a Persian. See Fig. 2.

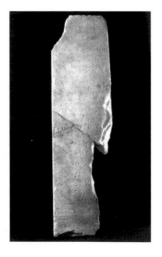

9. (ABOVE) Fragmentary ivory heads, 'Tomb of Philip', Vergina (Archaeological Museum)

Of the fourteen miniature ivories recovered from Tomb II and originally adorning a chest, these two are thought to depict Philip (bearded) and Alexander.

10. (LEFT) Inscription from Kalindoia (Archaeological Museum, Thessaloniki)

Kalindoia was a new foundation of Alexander in eastern Macedonia. This official inscription lists priests of Asclepius (hero-god of healing) and Apollo.

11. Funerary stele from Aiane (Musée du Louvre, Paris)

The deceased male is shown seated and surrounded by his mourning family on this funerary stele of the fourth century BCE from Aiane in south-west Macedonia.

12. Bisitun relief and inscription, in situ

At the strategically placed Bisitun in Media, Darius I (r. c.520–486) had himself depicted in crowned majesty under the divine protection of Ahura Mazda, great Zoroastrian god of Light. The text, in three languages (Elamite, Babylonian and Old Persian), gives his versions of how he saved Persia from a usurper and re-established Persian control over the subject peoples. The image shows him with his foot on his main rival, while the other rebels, their hands bound and a noose around their necks, await their turn.

13. Persepolis palace relief

The Great Staircase leading up to the audience-chamber (Apadana) of the great palace at Persepolis, where the Great King received tokens of tribute and submission from his subjects during the annual spring festival ceremony. Altogether twenty-three pairs of delegates from different parts of the empire are depicted, each in national costume. The lion-and-bull motif may symbolize the arrival of the new year. The palace was built originally by Darius I and embellished by his successors.

14. Gold coin, obverse
(Money Museum, Teheran)

Great King Darius I made this gold coin the coin of the Achaemenid realm and gave it his own name, 'daric'. Archery in Greek eyes was a sub-elite activity, but bowmen in Persia were counted among the most honoured functionaries and soldiers. On the Bisitun relief (Fig. 12) Darius's bow is held by one of the six noblemen with whom he collaborated to seize back control.

15. Apadana Great Staircase, Persepolis

Another view of Fig. 13. The royal guard and officers of the court march in the background.

16. Illumination from *Le Livre du Trésor* by Brunetto Latini (1220–94) (MS 269, Folio 108, Bibliothèque Inguimbertine, Carpentras)

An excellent illustration of the way Alexander's legend penetrated to the furthest reaches of mediaeval Christendom (here, Carpentras in Provence). Alexander is shown being taught by Aristotle, a favoured motif.

17. Lion of Chaeronea, in situ

Philip II's decisive victory over Greeks at Chaeronea in Boeotia in 338 BCE is marked to this day by this huge reconstituted lion-monument, placed, it is thought, where the 300 members of the Theban Sacred Band (150 pairs of lovers) died to a man.

18. Gold funerary casket, 'Tomb of Philip', Vergina (Archaeological Museum)

Literally the star find from the 'Tomb of Philip', this gold casket is adorned with a sixteen-pointed sunburst, symbol of the Macedonian kingdom, and contained cremated bones and remains of the fancy purple cloth in which they had been wrapped. This could be the actual coffin of Philip II.

19. Gold Scythian *gorytos* (quiver-case), 'Tomb of Philip', Vergina (Archaeological Museum)

This magnificent quiver-case was either a gift or a commissioned item, or simply plunder. It reminds us that one of Philip's seven wives was a Scythian, for it was fashioned by Scythian craftsmen from north of the Black Sea.

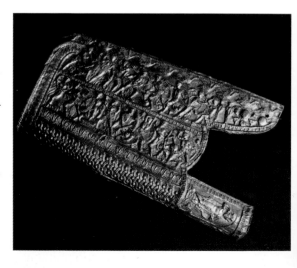

ander to cross the Hellespont at his leisure and to unite with the bridgehead force commanded by Parmenion at Abydus unimpeded. Alexander is said to have made a point of being the first to leap on to Asiatic soil, in full armour, after having discharged his spear into the ground. The point of the symbolism was to claim Asia prospectively as his very own spear-won territory. A different sort of symbolism was put into effect by a role-playing visit to Homer's Troy, or what was then taken to be such. Here Alexander is reported to have placed a commemorative wreath on the supposed tomb of Achilles, while Hephaestion (see Figure 29) did the same on that of Achilles's dearest friend, Patroclus. In Homer, there is no explicit mention of any sexual dimension to the deeply intimate relationship between the older Patroclus and Achilles. But classical Greeks from at least Aeschylus onwards unhesitatingly interpreted their friendship as actively homoerotic.

The same, almost certainly, may be inferred for the relationship between Alexander and the slightly older Hephaestion, though it is not absolutely certain that it continued to be so much if at all after they had passed beyond adolescence. The point is that in classical Greece homoeroticism among males during adolescence was considered perfectly compatible with an actively heterosexual adult lifestyle later on. Nor was there any stigma of a religious or other nature attaching to homosexuality in itself: what mattered was how it was expressed, with whom, and in what contexts. The Theban Sacred Band of 150 homosexual couples formed as an elite military strike force in 378 is the most spectacular illustration of this cardinal social fact about ancient Greece. Persian attitudes to homosexuality are harder to discern, though the practice undoubtedly existed in various forms. But the Greeks at any rate thought that all oriental 'barbarians' were incapable of appreciating its finer points, not least because their culture forbade the display of the naked male body and so the cult of the gymnasium.

The Persians' second big error was to lose the Battle of the Granicus river, in late May 334, the first of the three major pitched battles between Alexander and the prime forces of the Persian Empire.

The Persian troops, not yet led in person by Darius, were encamped at Zeleia. To meet them Alexander had to cross the terrain of the Troad which was intersected by rivers flowing north into the Propontis, or Sea of Marmara, among them the Granicus. This was by no means a major river, but it was swift and deep, and to the Persian defenders it had the further tactical advantage of a steep bank on the far side from Alexander. So he would have the twofold obstacle of the river itself and the bank to surmount before he could engage the Persian forces on something like equal ground.

Before the battle, at least as Arrian reports it, Parmenion allegedly advised Alexander to wait until the light of the next day's dawn to advance into conflict across the river. But Alexander is said to have replied that delay would merely increase the Persian side's confidence, adding that the Hellespont would surely blush for shame if Alexander hesitated before crossing the much less significant Granicus. He therefore, in this account, went straight into the attack. There is a good case for thinking that many such exchanges and differences of opinion were written up by Callisthenes with a view, prospectively, to discrediting Parmenion. But this story does also illustrate a key aspect of Alexander's generalship: his constant emphasis on the factor of morale. For this reason, I prefer Arrian's version to that of Diodorus, who says that Alexander did delay the attack until the next morning.

This is how Plutarch, some four hundred years later, describes part of the battle itself:

> Alexander plunged into the river with thirteen cavalry squadrons. He was now advancing through a hail of enemy missiles towards a steep and heavily defended bank, while negotiating a current that swept his men off their feet and pulled them under. His leadership seemed foolhardy and reckless rather than prudent. Yet he persisted and with great effort and hardship reached the opposite bank of the river, which was wet and slippery with mud. He was at once forced into a chaotic battle and obliged to engage, man against man, the enemies who came bearing down on

them. This was before the troops making the crossing could get into any sort of formation. The Persians came charging at these with a roar. Alexander's men lined up their horses against the enemy's and fought with their spears until they were shattered and then with their swords. A large number closed in on Alexander, who was easily recognizable because of his shield and the crest on his helmet, on each side of which there was a strikingly tall, white plume of horsehair. Alexander was hit by a spear in the joint of his breastplate but not wounded. Then the Persian commanders Rhoesaces and Spithridates came against him in unison. Alexander sidestepped Spithridates and struck Rhoesaces, who was wearing a breastplate, with his spear. But when his spear shattered, he resorted to his sword. While the two were engaged in hand-to-hand combat, Spithridates halted his horse beside them and, raising himself up sharply in his saddle, struck Alexander a blow with his barbarian battle-axe. The crest of Alr's helmet was broken off, along with one of its plumes. The helmet itself only just withstood the blow, which actually grazed the top of the king's hair. Spithridates then raised the axe and was about to deliver a second blow when Cleitus the Black intervened and ran him through with his spear. At the same moment Rhoesaces, too, was felled by a stroke of Alexander's sword.

What if Cleitus had not got there first? Such is the unpredictability of history.

The Granicus battle was a relatively small-scale but also tricky affair, and as always it was Alexander's Macedonian cavalry that eventually delivered the hammer blow. Sir Walter Raleigh, something of a commander himself, put his finger on the victory's true significance (in the fourth Book of his *The History of the World*):

It was therefore wisely done of Alexander, to pass the River of Granick in face of the enemy; not marching higher to seek an easier way, nor labouring to convey his men over it by some safer means. For having beaten them upon their own ground, he did thereby cut off no less their reputation, than of their strength, leaving no hope of succour to the partakers and followers of such unable Protectors.

Only after this victory, be it noted, did Alexander officially proclaim his support for democracies among the Greek cities that were now, or in the future, to be liberated from Persian control. He himself was no ideological democrat, of course, but practicality and pragmatism were dictating his support for democracy at this stage. For Persia, like most imperial powers in history, had imposed or propped up various forms of oligarchy among its subject Greek people. As noted in Chapter Five it is still quite hotly debated whether Alexander incorporated the liberated cities into the League of Corinth on the same terms as its original members. Undoubtedly he was entitled to do so, without consulting the existing allies. But the question is whether he would have wished to bind himself by religious oaths to recognize and preserve their freedom and autonomy, rather than treat them as subjects of his empire in the Persian manner. The available evidence is indecisive, but I think on balance that he did. In practice, however, it mattered little either way, since Alexander did more or less what he wanted, as the relationship between him and the Greek cities depended not on legal agreements but on power.

For the time being, though, he was prepared to keep up his public adherence to the Panhellenic myth. In 334 he sent back to Athens as spoils of the Granicus victory three hundred suits of armour, for dedication to Athena on the acropolis. The point of the accompanying inscription (p. 96) was to remind the Greek world that it was the Spartans who had sold out the Greeks of Asia to Persia in 386, and that they were now not only in more or less active opposition to Macedon, outside the framework of the League of Corinth, but actually in treasonous contact with Persia.

Having appointed a Macedonian to govern the former Persian satrapy of Lesser (Hellespontine) Phrygia, Alexander moved on south into Lydia. Its capital Sardis, though fortified, fell nevertheless without a blow. A brother of Parmenion, Asandrus, was appointed satrap. In Greek Ionia, further south, Alexander on the whole enjoyed an enthusiastic reception. For example, the cities of Ephesus (perhaps after a democratic revolution) and Priene both welcomed him as a liberator. The region of Caria, on the other hand, in both its Greek and its non-Greek components, was a different proposition. Here, the still oligarchic city of Miletus was determined to resist the would-be liberator, and Alexander was therefore obliged to undertake his first siege. Siege warfare was generally underdeveloped in the Greek world, where the typical method of approach was to try to blockade and starve the enemy out rather than take his city by storm. But this was a branch of warfare in which Philip had made giant strides, and in which Alexander showed perhaps his greatest determination and resourcefulness.

The siege of Miletus also revealed a characteristic change in Alexander's policy towards the many thousands of Greek mercenaries who still thought it profitable – and perhaps ideologically preferable – to fight against him rather than for him. As we saw earlier, after the Granicus river battle Alexander had treated the captured mercenaries on the Persian side as traitors to Greece and sent them to work the gold and silver mines of Mount Pangaeum in Thrace. This ostensibly Panhellenist ploy had, however, proved counterproductive, since thereafter Greek mercenaries on the Persian side were opting to fight to the death rather than give themselves up or be taken alive. So, when during the siege of Miletus some Greek mercenaries found themselves trapped, Alexander offered instead to take them into his service – an offer they found they could not refuse. Alexander rarely made the same mistake twice.

The siege of Miletus proved relatively painless for Alexander. His next siege, at Halicarnassus (the strongly Hellenized capital of the sub-satrapy of Caria), proved the reverse. Despite his skilful deployment of the latest refinements in long-range artillery, he was only partially successful in dislodging the Persians' garrison. One reason for this lack of total success was that he was not master of the sea. His suspicious refusal to make use of his Athenian fleet had led him to utter the famously defiant oxymoron that he would defeat the Persian – mainly Phoenician – fleet by land: that is, by capturing its bases. But this was a strategy that by rights should have failed, and Alexander very nearly came unstuck in the Levant in 332. For the time being, though, he continued to progress without major hitch.

In the autumn of 334, for the first time he reappointed a native oriental ruler to the same post he – or rather, in this case, she – had held under Darius. The ruler in question was not just a woman, though, but a self-styled queen: Ada of Halicarnassus. She was the younger sister of the Mausolus who (thanks to the extraordinary tomb built for him at Halicarnassus by his sister–widow Artemisia) has given his name to the 'mausoleum'. The Hecatomnids, as the dynasty is known, were strongly Hellenized in culture but by no means entirely Greek in their political or familial practices. Ada, though, was certainly not unknown to Alexander. Towards the end of Philip's reign Alexander seems to have entered into negotiations to marry a daughter of Ada's younger brother Pixodarus, much to Philip's intense annoyance, since he too had politico-diplomatic designs on the lady.

Those negotiations had inevitably proved abortive, and led to a serious breakdown in relations between Philip and Alexander, affecting also a number of the prince's closest comrades. But relations between Alexander and Ada were not damaged, and three years later they were clearly prepared to do business with each other. Indeed, much more than that, for perhaps the most extraordinary single episode of Alexander's campaign in autumn 334 was his formal acceptance of Ada as his honorary (or surrogate) mother. The mind can only boggle at what his real mother Olympias thought. We are told that Alexander could find her antics burdensome. He is even said to have quipped that she charged him a high rent for the nine months she had housed him in her womb. But having to put up with competition for maternal status and services from a foreign queen would not have either improved

Olympias's temper or lessened her importunities. Worse, possibly, was to come, when in 333 Alexander struck up an amicable relationship with Darius's mother too.

From a still not wholly occupied or pacified Halicarnassus Alexander nevertheless moved east along the coast of Lycia, and then inland again through upland Anatolia to Gordium in Phrygia, which he reached by the spring of 333. The Phrygian kingdom had been founded in the eighth century BCE by one Gordius, and consolidated by his son Midas. This was the Midas of Greek myth whose alchemical touch turned everything – unfortunately for him, including food – to gold. The site of Gordius's burial had been marked by a ceremonial wagon, the yoke of which was fastened to its pole by a peculiarly complex knot. The legend was that whoever unloosed the knot would obtain the dominion of all Asia. In the sixth century Phrygia like the rest of Anatolia became subsumed in the new Achaemenid Persian Empire, but the legend lived on intact, as did the Gordian knot. Until 333, that is: when Alexander reportedly somehow dissipated it, either by untying it or – more in character, probably – simply by slashing through it with a sword. Sceptical scholars have suspected that the whole story of the Gordian knot incident was a pious fabrication, but most students of Alexander believe that he did somehow unhitch – or cut – the knot whereby the wagon of Gordius had been secured.

The true significance of this incident, if Aristoboulus is to be believed, is that it was only after abolishing the knot that Alexander made his first public claim to the overlordship of Asia in so many words. Much hard fighting, however, lay ahead. Forcing the Cilician Gates with great elan, Alexander reached Tarsus in Cilicia (future birthplace of St Paul) by early July. Plutarch speaks of a long delay in Cilicia, which he claims was due to Alexander's contracting an illness after bathing in a freezing-cold river. It seems clear that he was in any case intending to wait there for the arrival from Iran of the vast army that was being raised and commanded in person by Great King Darius III. It always took a very long time to raise any serious Persian force, so far-flung and so multi-ethnic was the Empire. The point of Alexander's waiting at Tarsus was to lure Darius down into the narrow coastal strip where his overwhelming superiority of numbers would be nullified.

Ironically, just as the ploy was succeeding, Alexander decided to wait no longer and proceeded south towards the Levant. Hence his astonishment to find Darius's army actually in his rear. Plutarch claims that (good) fortune provided Alexander with a suitable battle site, near the town of Issus by the Pinarus river. But it took all of his military genius to extricate himself from this potential mess and to win comprehensively the battle which, of all his set pieces, he should properly have lost. Here is a modern description, in suitably clipped military style, of the forces ranged on either side:

> [Alexander's] infantry line (right to left) was: three units of
> hypaspists under Nicanor; phalanx units under Coenus,
> Perdiccas, Meleager, Ptolemy, and Amyntas respectively; left-
> wing infantry was commanded by Craterus; Parmenio was in
> overall command of the left wing. Thessalian and Paeonian (?)
> cavalry was now posted on the right; Greek mercenary troops
> were sent to the left. These included Cretan archers with
> Thracian cavalry, both under Sitalces. The left-wing cavalry was
> mainly allied (Greek). The Thessalians were now brought round
> the rear to strengthen the left-wing cavalry. On the right were
> Protomachus' scouts with Paeonians under Ariston and archers
> under Antiochus. Attalus with archers and some cavalry drove off
> the flanking threat in the mountains. Last-minute moves: two
> squadrons of horse, under Peroedas and Pantordanus
> respectively, were moved out from centre to right. A line of
> Agrianes and Greek mercenaries was used to outflank the Persian
> left. Persian positions during Alexander's advance: a screen of
> 30,000 cavalry and 20,000 light infantry was thrown forward,
> south of the River Pinarus, to protect Darius's main body while it
> was being deployed for battle. When deployment was complete,

this advanced line was withdrawn and used mostly to reinforce
the Persian right wing, now confronting Parmenio. Darius's
front thus consisted of 30,000 Greek mercenaries and 60,000
'Kardakes' [probably lightly armed Persian infantry]; the latter
were posted on either wing of the Greeks. Behind these forces
were ranged the multinational contingents of Darius's imperial
army. He himself rode in his war-chariot in the centre.

– Sekunda and Warry, *Alexander the Great. His Armies and*
Campaigns 334–323 BC, p. 79

The actual course of the battle is uncertain. Despite his over-whelming numerical superiority and initial advantage of surprise, Darius grew so demoralized and fearful for his life that he fled the battlefield, thereby ensuring the immediate collapse of his side's cause. He even left behind among the camp followers who fell into Alexander's hands his own mother, a wife and two of his unmarried daughters. Pro-Alexander sources made a very big deal of the extreme courtesy with which he allegedly treated these royal Persian ladies. This picture of his behaviour is literally reproduced in a famous painting by Paolo Veronese now hanging prominently in London's National Gallery (Figure 27, although it is not quite clear which figure Veronese meant to be Alexander, and which Hephaestion). But more scurrilous modern interpreters have been prepared, or even anxious, to believe that an Oedipal, mother-fixated Alexander actually slept with Darius's mother.

At any rate, the Battle of Issus in Cilicia in November 333 was quite certainly significant from the point of view of the morale of Alexander and his troops. Indeed, if Arrian or his source is to be trusted, it emboldened him to lay claim to being the legitimate heir to the Persian throne and Empire and, somewhat perversely, to denounce Darius (whose title was admittedly not impeccable) as a mere usurper.

Darius had sent his baggage train on ahead to Damascus in Syria. It was captured there by Parmenion, and this enabled Alexander to persevere with his paradoxical policy of attempting to defeat the Persian navy from the land. Since 525, the backbone of any Achaemenid Persian fleet in the Mediterranean had been provided by the Phoenicians living mostly in what is now Lebanon but also on Cyprus. In their defeat, therefore, lay the key to Alexander's land-based strategy. All the more crucially so, since during the couple of years that included the Issus battle, between 334 and 332, the Persians embarked on the strategy most likely to defeat Alexander.

Under the inspired leadership of a Rhodian Greek called Memnon, who had married into the high Persian aristocracy, the Persians aimed to wrest control with their navy of the most important Aegean islands. Using these as forward bases, they would send over ships, men and gold to mainland Greece in order to stir up rebellion behind Alexander's back. This would not have been by any means the first time that Persian gold had played a key role in destabilizing mainland Greek interstate relations. Memnon had also rightly seen that a scorched-earth policy ahead of Alexander's advance was more likely to be effective than a pitched encounter such as the one at the Granicus. It was he too who ordered three separate Persian forces to be sent behind Alexander's back into Anatolia, leaving the one-eyed Macedonian general Antigonus to save Alexander's bacon three times over.

If Memnon had not fortuitously died in 333, and had his amphibious strategy been steadfastly pursued, it is arguable that Alexander's Macedonian regent Antipater would have been unable to resist and Alexander would have had to return. As it was, aided crucially by those three victories won in Anatolia by Antigonus (who thereby served notice of the major role that he would play in post-Alexander affairs), Alexander was permitted the luxury of conducting his longest-ever siege. This was directed at the Phoenician city of Old Tyre during the first seven months of 332, with only relatively minor embarrassment from the rest of the Phoenician and Cypriot fleets. Indeed, the sternest resistance by far came from the Tyrians themselves. Their heavily fortified city, built on an offshore island, was nigh-on impregnable, and it was only the defection of the main body of the Phoenician fleet that eventually gave Alexander the sort of unimpeded access to the island he required. None the less, if Alexander deserves permanent commemoration as a general, then it is above all in his capacity as a besieger, and of all his sieges Tyre was his masterpiece (see Chapter Seven).

Tyre eventually fell. Alexander is said to have vented his wrath at the Tyrians' all too successful resistance by crucifying a very large number of them along the shore. The Athenians too had been accused of a similar atrocity after their exceptionally prolonged siege of Samos conducted by Pericles in 440/39. Alexander was now able to proceed south to yet another siege, this time of Gaza. Yet although this was an altogether more minor affair, the very fact of Batis the Arab governor's resistance so incensed him that he inflicted on him the cruellest of exemplary punishments. Achilles had notoriously tied Hector to his chariot and dragged him three times round the walls of Troy. But at least Hector was dead before being attached and dragged. Alexander ordered that Batis be attached to a chariot while still alive and driven round and round the walls of Gaza until he died an excruciatingly painful and ignominious death. The aim was the deterrence of resistance in the cases of both Tyre and Gaza, but the means verged on the sadistic.

Now, at last, Alexander's strategy for gaining mastery of the sea had succeeded, against all probability. The way was finally open to the major prize of Egypt, vital both for its strategic position and for its economic wealth, not least in grain. Here Alexander found himself gifted with an advantage only rarely on offer in other parts of the Persian Empire: a friendly native upper class. Egypt had been conquered by Cyrus the Great's son Cambyses and annexed to the Persian Empire in the 520s. Darius I had taken an intelligent interest in Egyptian affairs, but his son Xerxes had offended the priestly caste.

In Egypt's theocratic state and society they were close to the apex of power, both centrally and locally, and they served as a focus for national longings for self-determination.

The first major Egyptian revolt against Persia occurred in the mid fifth century. But that was a mere blip compared with the fact that between 405 and 344/3 Egypt was in practice independent of Persian rule. In retribution for this gross disloyalty Darius III's predecessor Artaxerxes III had targeted the priesthood for persecution, who were therefore prepared to tolerate Alexander as the lesser of two evils. Alexander in any case always showed exaggerated but not necessarily insincere respect for local gods and religious observances. In Egypt he ingratiated himself with the priesthood particularly by sacrificing to the sacred Apis bull at the old capital of Memphis. He may indeed even have had himself formally crowned Pharaoh at Memphis on or about 14 November 332.

From Memphis Alexander sailed northwards down the Nile to its delta. At one of the delta's mouths, the Canopic, he is said to have personally selected the site for the future Alexandria (the officially recognized date of Alexandria's foundation appears to have been 7 April 331). This was to become the greatest of his several Alexandria city-foundations, the capital of the Successor dynasty founded by Ptolemy, and a major centre for the dissemination of Hellenic civilization and culture throughout the Middle East and, later, the Roman world. It was for the Jews of Egyptian Alexandria, for example, that their Hebrew Bible was translated into Greek as the Septuagint.

It was following the designation of a site for Egyptian Alexandria that Alexander chose to make the somewhat puzzling and decidedly risky detour to the oracle of Ammon (Amun) at the Siwah oasis, in the western desert of Egypt bordering on Libya.* The ancient sources for this visit are not exactly unimpeachable, and modern scholars have produced a wide variety of explanations for its objective and outcome.

---

* See Appendix, pp. 266–70.

These fall into three broad categories: pragmatic, mystical, and a combination of those two. I personally favour the last of the three. For whatever practical advantages the Siwah trip might have seemed to Alexander to afford, they were surely outweighed by the personal dangers involved and by the strategic precedence it temporarily surrendered to Darius. The Persian Great King, still smarting from the Issus humiliation, was given ample time to regroup his forces for a further major and – as it turned out – decisive battle.

That encounter took place at Gaugamela not far from Nineveh (in modern Iraq), the old capital of the Assyrian Empire whose destruction by the Medes in 612 had paved the way for the rise of the Empire of their Persian cousins in about 550. The Battle of Gaugamela in effect witnessed that latter Empire's demise. After retracing his steps from Siwah to the Lebanon, Alexander had reached the Euphrates river by way of Syrian Damascus by early August 331. The Tigris was crossed about 18 September, and the Gaugamela battle took place nearly two weeks later, on 1 October. Most agree that this was Alexander's greatest set-piece battle. It at any rate gave him mastery, in effect, of the Persian Empire from western Iran westwards.

When the Battle of Gaugamela was over, the major agreed objective had been to capture Darius alive. A large part of the reason for the Persians' defeat at Gaugamela, as at Issus, was the Great King's incontinent flight. The weakness as well as the strength of the old Persian monarchy was its intensely personal character. Alexander already had in his possession some of Darius's closest female relatives. But to make his propaganda coup of legitimate succession as oriental emperor truly effective, he needed also Darius himself, alive and in person. Then, and only then, could the transfer of power be seen to be done, physically as well as symbolically. The efforts he made to achieve Darius's capture were prodigious. He covered some 450 miles (720 kilometres) in three weeks, the 250 miles (400 kilometres) from Ecbatana (Hamadan in Media) to Rhagae (near modern Teheran) in eleven days, the remaining 200 miles (320 kilometres) in five days after a rest of five. In one eighteen-hour period he covered perhaps as many as fifty miles (80 kilometres).

Alas, all to no avail. Darius's distant relative Bessus, satrap of Bactria (northern Afghanistan), had other ideas. Given that so much depended on the character and skill of the Great King, there was no further hope of the Persians defeating Alexander under Darius's leadership. In 330 Bessus therefore deposed and murdered Darius and assumed the tiara for himself. Alexander reached Darius only as a still warm corpse. After burying him with all due honours, he sent a detail including Ptolemy after Bessus, who was eventually caught, tortured, mutilated and executed (see Chapter Four).

THEREAFTER Alexander regarded himself – and behaved – as the legitimate successor of the Persian royal dynasts. He did not seek, that is, to transplant a Macedonian-style monarchy to his Asiatic domain but rather represented himself as the King of Asia according to a pattern closely modelled on that of the old Persian Kings. The first concrete sign of this orientalist policy was delivered at Babylon. He entered the city in triumph through the ceremonial gate devoted to the goddess Ishtar, as if he were the newly installed king of Babylon conducting the New Year ritual. Appropriately enough, since, like some of his Persian predecessors, he had himself crowned king of Babylon, as he had perhaps already had himself crowned Pharaoh of Egypt. Even more revealing of his future intentions was the fact that he confirmed in office as satrap of Babylonia the high-ranking Persian noble Mazaeus. Alexander had in other words decided that, if he was to perpetuate his and his successors' rule over the conquered Empire, he must tap the talents and secure the allegiance of the traditional Iranian governing class. That he should have inaugurated this policy in Babylon was doubly significant. Not only was Mesopotamia geographically central, but with its sophisticated system of irrigation canals and complex economic administration it was also the richest and most fertile province of the Empire. Only Egypt ran it at all close.

What were the implications of this orientalizing policy of Alexander's for the original Panhellenic crusade? The straight answer is that the two were mutually incompatible, indeed diametrically opposed. A nice token of the contradictions Alexander was landing himself in was the torching of the old Persian ceremonial palace at Persepolis in southern Iran in May 330 (Chapter Five). On the one hand, this was, perhaps, symbolic retaliation for the burning of Greek temples in 480/79 and a bonfire of the vanities of the old Achaemenid regime. On the other hand, it was hardly an act likely to promote the desired loyalty of the Iranian upper class. We are reminded a little of the contradiction involved in his destruction of Greek Thebes five years earlier. Nor did Alexander's contradictions end there.

In his new role as King of Asia he established, inevitably, in parallel to his Macedonian and Greek court an oriental, chiefly Persian court. This allegedly included a harem of 365 concubines, one for every day of the year (a practice imitated more recently by a certain Moroccan pasha). He adopted a version of the Great King's regalia and began to incorporate western Iranian recruits into his hitherto exclusively Macedonian Companion Cavalry (see further, Chapter Eight). Of the three national groups most centrally concerned with Alexander's interpretation of the governance and symbolism of the new Empire – the Macedonians, the Iranians and the Greeks – the last were the most dispensable. Thus, when he arrived in early June 330 at the Median capital of Ecbatana, he cashiered his Greek contingents – those supplied by the League of Corinth allies – and thereby implied that the Panhellenic crusade was formally at an end. His major administrative problem, however, the reconciliation of the Macedonian with the Iranian ruling class, was to dog him to the end of his life and was never satisfactorily resolved.

Alexander therefore had no choice but to start acting as King of

Asia without the talisman of Darius's captured person to launch him on his way. He did so at Zadracarta in Hyrcania in northern Iran. From there Alexander moved on east in August 330 towards Bactria. The aim, as well as to capture and kill the pretender Bessus, was chiefly to secure the north-eastern approaches to the Iranian nerve centre of his entire new imperial operation. For, paradoxically, it was not from the west that the Achaemenids had found their Empire's integrity constantly threatened but rather from the central Asian steppelands. A revolt by the satrap of the province of Aria necessitated a diversion to Artacoana (modern Herat, just inside Afghanistan), and it was at Artacoana that the first flare-up between Alexander and his senior Macedonian officers occurred.

FROM the deaths – or rather murders – of Philotas and his father Parmenion in August 330 to the death (or murder) of the official historian Callisthenes in late 327, stretches a continuous web of alleged plotting against Alexander countered by utterly ruthless suppression by the king. What was mainly at issue was his seemingly excessively favourable treatment of the Iranian upper class. As already in 336, after the assassination of Philip, he showed himself at his most formidable always when he felt seriously insecure.

Perhaps early in October 330 Alexander proceeded south from Artacoana. Over the next three years he passed through Drangiana, Arachosia and Paropamisadae, then over the Hindu Kush mountains to Bactria and Sogdiana and back again to his new foundation of Alexandria-by-the-Caucasus (near modern Begram and Charikar). These vital years saw him adapting brilliantly to meet and overcome unprecedented political and military conditions: vigorous local nationalism, rugged and often appallingly difficult mountainous terrain, plus all the uncertainties of guerrilla warfare. Even when severely pressed as here, though, Alexander considered the needs of his officers and troops and made time for some light relief. The slaughtering of four thousand wild animals, including lions, in a safari park near Samarkand during an organized hunting party following the particularly exhausting capture of the Sogdian Rock deserves a special mention.

For some connoisseurs of Alexander's generalship, the campaign of 'pacification' in what is now Afghanistan and central Asia most entitles him to be labelled a military genius. Certainly, the achievement does become even more astonishing against the background of major cultural and political discontent simmering and occasionally boiling over at the very heart of his Macedonian court. His father Philip had used marriage alliances opportunistically as a politico-diplomatic tool to avert or facilitate warfare. Alexander, as so often, borrowed this leaf from Philip's book. But his strategically desirable marriage in 327 to Roxane, daughter of a major Sogdian baron, was not calculated to allay such discontent. Philip too had married 'barbarian' (not just non-Macedonian but non-Greek) women, but they had been part of the solution. Roxane, an oriental, was precisely part of the problem: namely, Alexander's problem in winning over the hearts and minds of his most trusted Macedonian followers to his orientalist policy of imperial governance. Not coincidentally, the defeat of the last Iranian military opposition in 327 was very soon followed by the so-called Pages' Conspiracy (see Chapter Four) and the arrest (and execution) of his official historian Callisthenes.

It is fitting that a difference in cultural interpretation of body language should have lain at the core of the issue. Especially in a situation of verbal incomprehension, body language and all outward symbolism become vital media of communication and authority. The fact that Alexander failed to achieve universal and willing compliance from his Macedonian and Greek courtiers in performing ritual obeisance to him is a telling comment on the overall success of his new imperial project as a whole.

SEVEN

THE GENERALSHIP
OF ALEXANDER

I had been much more interested in entering northern Iraq direct from Turkey and following the Tigris down to Gaugamela, scene of Alexander's great battle with Darius. But in Mersin I heard rumours that Iraq was now using chemical weapons in the north against the Kurds and so I was finally reconciled to abandoning that project. Politics preventing me from following Alexander overland from Turkey, I booked a flight to Karachi, to meet him again in Pakistan.

– Anne Mustoe, *A Bike Ride: Twelve Thousand Miles around the World* (1992)

THERE have been many modern Alexanders, a multiplicity due ultimately to the failings of the ancient sources. Two things, however, at least are tolerably clear about any Alexander you care to mention, or invent. First, he was one of the most extraordinary individuals ever to have walked the earth. He above all others deserves to be called 'the Great'. Second, his ancient greatness and his present claim to remembrance alike rest primarily and ultimately on his generalship, his leadership of men in war. It has been said of him that a list of his field successes reads like the logbook of a military Midas – everything that that legendary king of Phrygia touched turned to gold. That is a judgement from which Alexander would have been the last to dissent.

Yet Alexander the all-conquering general has also had his stern detractors: here again is Sir Walter Raleigh (in the fourth Book of his *The History of the World*):

> *it seemeth, Fortune and Destinies (if we may use those terms) had*
> *found out and prepared for him, both heaps of Men, that*
> *willingly offered their necks to the yoke, and Kingdoms that*
> *invited and called in their own Conquerors.*

This, I shall hope to demonstrate, is a monstrously unfair judgement. It is nevertheless a sobering thought that, as one of Alexander's greatest admirers (Napoleon Bonaparte) once said, with understandable hyperbole, 'To conquer is nothing, one must profit from one's success.'

Let us therefore begin by putting Alexander on the spot, as his mutinous Macedonians finally did at Opis near modern Baghdad in the summer of 324. In response to those mutineers Alexander delivered a shaming harangue. He contrasted the greatness of their achievements under his leadership with their intended, thoroughly ignoble, desertion of him and dereliction of their duty. This is what he said – or rather, what Arrian makes him say:

> *You all wish to leave me – well, get going then! And when you*
> *get back home, tell them that your king, Alexander, conqueror of*
> *Persians and Medes and Bactrians and Sacae, destroyer of Uxii*
> *and Arachotians and Drangians, who added to his empire*
> *Parthians and Chorasmians and Hyrcanians as far as the Caspian*
> *Sea, who crossed over the Caucasus beyond the Caspian Gates,*
> *and over the Oxus and Tanais and Indus, which none but*
> *Dionysus had crossed before him, and the Hydaspes and Acesines*
> *and Hydraotes – yes, and the Hyphasis too, if you hadn't shrunk*
> *back in fear; who broke through to the great Ocean beyond by*
> *both mouths of the Indus, and traversed the desert of Gedrosia,*
> *where no one had previously been with an army, and acquired in*
> *addition Carmania and the land of the Oreitae as he passed*
> *through, while the fleet had already sailed along the coast from*
> *the land of the Indians to Persia; who was brought back by you*
> *to Susa – tell them it was him you deserted and left to the mercy*
> *of the barbarians . . .*

There is a real sting in that 'barbarians' (though as a rule Alexander was far less contemptuous of barbarians than his ordinary Macedonian troops habitually were).

This rhetorical passage is useful to us in two main ways. It conveys impressionistically but also most impressively the sheer geographical vastness of Alexander's military–political achievement. Second, it reminds us that we are all at the mercy of the available sources, such as Arrian here. This is not so crucial, perhaps, when they disagree over numbers of troops, casualties and so on (though these discrepancies can be telling enough). It is crucial when the discrepancies are like those regarding the accounts of the Battle of Granicus in 334. Did Alexander, as Arrian says, advance at once to the attack? Or did he, as Diodorus reports, pitch camp for the night and steal across the river at dawn? To decide on such issues of basic fact we have to ask further questions, such as: would Arrian's or Diodorus's ultimate source(s) be the more likely to invent, suppress or distort the truth? In the long run, the answer often comes down to our subjective judgement of the kind of behaviour we would predict of Alexander on the basis of our overall conception of his outlook and pattern of conduct. But, as that conception must itself be to some extent drawn from those very same sources, the risk of a vicious circle of argument is always shadowing us.

One further caveat. Even (especially?) participant eyewitnesses, alas, are notoriously unable to agree afterwards on exactly how any given battle went. Partiality – of vision, recollection and self interest – rules. Any modern account, therefore, that seems to present an uncontroversial narrative of what precisely happened, how and when in any particular engagement – let alone a bullishly confident explanation of why – merits the greatest possible suspicion, even disbelief. But with those provisos firmly in mind and eye, I shall advance to the fray. As a plan of historiographical campaign I shall adopt Major General J. F. C. Fuller's 'method of inherent probabilities'. This holds that, 'once the character and talents of a general have been assessed, his aim and problem fathomed, and the conditions in which he was called upon to wage war appraised, it is possible to arrive at a highly probable picture of what happened in a given set of circumstances'. Or fairly probable, anyhow.

Alexander's good fortune was proverbial, as we have noted. Plutarch in an early rhetorical work even felt obliged to defend him against the charge that his success was due *merely* to good luck. It was, however, fortunate to say the least for Alexander's future as a general that he should have been born the son of Philip II of Macedon and inherited (just . . .) the best army yet created in Europe – though Alexander himself was to regard this as a mixed blessing. Philip of course, we must add, was heir to earlier military developments, which he brilliantly exploited, and what he achieved would not have been achievable much before the mid fourth century BCE.

Money, it has rightly been said (by Cicero and others), is the sinews of war. Philip conquered and annexed land that yielded lavish amounts of minable precious metals. In 356 he acquired the gold and silver mines of Mount Pangaeum, which were said to yield him an annual revenue of one thousand silver talents. He made his ownership abundantly obvious by renaming the town of Crenides in the mining district as 'Philippi'. This money he used in the form of coined cash in several ways: partly to bribe foreign politicians – Diodorus not implausibly believed that his diplomatic triumphs gave him as much or more satisfaction than his or his generals' military successes; partly to hire Greek mercenaries and distribute largesse to his Macedonian troops. But he also used it to patronize Greek technological specialists such as the Thessalian engineer who designed for him the first workable arrow-firing torsion catapult. It can also safely be assumed that this money contributed to improvements in arms, armour and other equipment – though only a royal, presumably, like one of the occupants of the Great Tumulus at Vergina (see Figure 1), could have afforded the luxury of an iron breastplate tricked out with gold.

Right down to the end of the fifth century BCE, Macedon had remained something of a backwater – economically, politically, culturally, and so militarily. In Philip's Macedon, too, the relations of production remained almost what we might call 'feudal'. Like the rest of Greece, the kingdom was fundamentally an agrarian society. But instead of the predominant free peasant smallholders of Attica, or the chattel slaves owned by the more affluent Athenians, the Macedonian primary workforce consisted of serf-like dependent labourers of Thracian origin, more akin in status and treatment to the Helots of Sparta or the Penestae of Thessaly (though both those groups were ethnically Greek). The analogy with the Penestae is especially apposite, since, like these, the Macedonians' serfs provided the economic basis for a governing aristocracy of opulent cavalrymen.

It was not until the very last decade of the fifth century that King Archelaus from his new capital of Pella in Lower Macedonia began the process of unifying Lower with Upper (western) Macedonia. He also introduced, albeit partially, the type of infantry force that the settled, relatively urbanized Greek cities to the south had had since the seventh century – that is, the heavy-armed hoplite infantry phalanx. But the nature of the Macedonian terrain and the quasi-feudal economic structure ensured that here cavalry would continue to play a far more significant, indeed decisive, role than in any other region of mainland Greece except neighbouring Thessaly immediately to the south.

This, as Alexander above all was to make plain, was a blessing disguised from most Greeks. For them, cavalry served mainly for carrying out reconnaissance, ravaging the enemy's crops or protecting their own from being ravaged, pursuing or covering a retreating army, or for harassing a hoplite line with missiles – in other words, for almost anything except delivering the knock-out blow in a set-piece battle. That role the Greeks entrusted to their hoplite militias, with their semi-ritualized and relatively immobile shovings and head-on collisions. This type of warfare was quintessentially conservative and, indeed, amateur in the full sense of that term – in strategy, tactics and equipment alike. It has been well observed that a shield found by the

American excavators in the destruction debris of Olynthus, a major city in Chalcidice that Philip razed to the ground in 348, would not have looked out of place on the left arm of the soldier-poet Archilochus – who had flourished three centuries earlier. However, in warfare as in so much else the Atheno-Peloponnesian War of 431 to 404 proved to be something of a watershed.

Fought by land and sea over the span of an entire generation in a wide range of terrains and in situations demanding improvisatory strategic responses, this war had forced the Greeks to rethink their entrenched military attitudes. As far as tactics were concerned, mobility in attack came to seem more important than absolute rigidity in defence. Strategically, Athens's naval power made a mockery of the Spartans' annual invasions of Attica just before the grain (mainly barley) harvest. Yet even the arch-conservative Spartans were able to adopt a wholly new strategy for this war's decisive phase. More important even than these developments was the fact that a whole generation grew up knowing little more than active military service, or at least life lived under wartime conditions. What the Greeks called *stasis* – that is, internal class-based strife or outright civil war – increased exponentially in the course of the Atheno-Peloponnesian War, as its historian, Thucydides of Athens, pointedly remarked.

As a direct result, large numbers of young Greek displaced persons were thrown up. These the Persian pretender Cyrus the Younger was only too keen to recruit as mercenaries in 402/1 in his unsuccessful attempt to seize the throne from his older brother Artaxerxes II (r. 404–359). The subsequent fate of the so-called Ten Thousand Greek mercenaries was immortalized by Xenophon in his *Anabasis*, the work that Arrian took as the model for his account of Alexander. As the fourth century progressed, it became the norm rather than the exception for Greek cities to hire mercenaries to help them fight their wars and, correlatively, to hire out their citizens to others to help them fight theirs. Leading individuals were also hired or hired themselves out as 'advisers' to other cities or potentates. Charidemos of Athens advising

Darius III of Persia at Issus was one rather special case. Memnon of Rhodes was in a slightly different category, as he was half-oriental anyway and was appointed by Darius to the command of the very much junior Persian service, the navy.

One result of the prevalence of mercenaries was that warfare in the east Mediterranean world during the fourth century became ever more 'scientific', not only in the strategic and tactical sense but also in an intellectual sense. There was increased use of lighter-armed troops rather than hoplite infantrymen, troops such as the peltasts who originated in non-Greek Thrace and took their name from their much lighter shield. Mechanical inventions such as the arrow-firing torsion catapult were harnessed to military purposes. Moreover, manuals of warcraft were now being written and circulated. One well-known example was a treatise on siege warfare by Aeneas the Tactician, who is probably to be identified with a member of Xenophon's Ten Thousand. Siegecraft was crucial to some of Alexander's greatest victories.

Philip's staple battlefield units were cavalry and infantry, named sooner or later the Companion Cavalry, the Shield Bearers and the Foot Companions. The Companion Cavalry were stationed somewhere on the right of the line and used to deliver the knockout blow. Starting with only six hundred in 358, Philip so built up the force that in 334 Alexander had 3,500 at his disposal. These cavalrymen, like all ancient cavalrymen, were hampered by the lack of stirrups and their horses' unshod hooves, but they more than compensated by being brought to a pitch of efficiency through training, especially in how to manipulate the horses' movements with their knees. What they missed in body armour or weight of lance they made up for by speed, cohesion, superb horsemanship and courage at close quarters. The wedge formation that Philip borrowed from the Scythians and Thracians was likened by an ancient writer to the familiar sight of a flock of cranes in flight; it encapsulated all their virtues.

Between the Foot Companions in the centre, and the Companion

Cavalry on the right, were stationed the Shield Bearers (*Hypaspistai*). An elite force picked for their height and strength, they were almost a body of professionals – the commandos of the army. In line of battle they covered the unshielded right side of the Foot Companions and provided a fluid link between them and the Cavalry. Outside the line of battle they were deployed as a special corps for operations demanding speed and endurance over long distances – though of this aspect of their work, as of all others, we learn virtually nothing until the reign of Alexander. The Foot Companions, like the Cavalry, were recruited on a territorial basis. Their distinguishing feature was the *sarissa* or iron-tipped pike up to eighteen feet (5.5 metres) in length, made of cornel wood in two jointed sections and wielded with both hands (Figure 23). The pikes of the men in the first three or four ranks projected beyond the front of the line and gave the phalanx the appearance of a metal porcupine. The swishing of their blades (smaller than those of the Cavalry, since they were designed to puncture the enemy's armour or flesh rather than give him a nasty upward jolt to the head) must have been a terrifying prospect, not alleviated by the Macedonian 'Alalalalalai!' battle cry. On occasion the Foot Companions could play a decisive offensive role on their own, but the *coup de grâce* would normally be delivered by the Companion Cavalry.

In other Greek states the majority of the adult male free citizens could not afford the equipment necessary to serve as hoplites or horsemen. So they became, *faute de mieux*, light-armed troops of very secondary importance. In Philip's army, in the sharpest contrast, it is remarkable that the light troops, mounted and on foot, were both very largely not Macedonian and yet, on the other hand, of great importance. Among the light infantry we might single out the Agrianians from an area to the north of Macedonia, who have been called the Gurkhas of Alexander's army, and the Greek archers from Crete (a very ancient tradition indeed, going back at least to the early first millennium).

Another and integral component of Philip's army, developed even further by his observant son, was the siege train. The invention of the torsion catapult under Philip's patronage has already been mentioned. These arrow-firing spring-powered crossbow-type *katapeltai* were used notably by Alexander at Tyre (of which more below). They could achieve an effective range of up to 330 yards (300 metres). Alexander also employed both wheeled and wheelless sling-type catapults, or mechanical rock-throwers. Moreover, under Philip and Alexander siege towers were made taller and more sturdy, mobile and adaptable. The connection between these mechanical developments and the fact that Philip's sieges were over in days and weeks rather than months or even years is easy to draw. Only twice, in fact, was Philip unsuccessful in a siege campaign, and in neither case disastrously so. Alexander's siegecraft masterpiece took him very much longer to complete, as we shall soon see, but that was due to geographical circumstances beyond his control.

These, then, were Philip's means to warfare, human and non-human. They were welded together into an – almost – unbeatable fighting force (unbeaten after 353, anyhow) by the factors of morale, discipline and training. For this Philip personally deserves a good deal of the credit, though external circumstances undoubtedly helped him. In 368 the fifteen-year-old prince was removed to Thebes, the greatest Greek military power of the day, as a hostage for his older brother the king's good behaviour. It can't, I think, reasonably be denied that a three-year enforced sojourn in the city of Epaminondas and Pelopidas, and in the house of another leading general, Pammenes, left its stamp on Philip's attitude to warfare in general and on his strategic and tactical thinking in particular. For example, one thinks immediately of his – and Alexander's – use of the oblique line of attack and the concentration of decisive force. Also influential on him were the circumstances in which he came to the Macedonian throne, following the death of a brother in a major defeat by the Illyrians to the west, and faced with enemies on all sides, Greek as well as non-Greek. The lessons he drew and applied were that unity was strength, safety lay in numbers, and military professionalism was power: banal enough to state, fiendishly difficult to accomplish.

Philip was a simply ferocious disciplinarian. He would station horsemen behind his lines to apprehend deserters. He once stripped a mercenary commander of his post for washing in warm water – a privilege permitted in Macedonia only to women who had just given birth. He trained and drilled his men constantly: in this area not just Thebes, but also Sparta, was inspirational, for intimate familiarity and repeated practice bred cohesion in the stress of battle. He reduced the allowance of service personnel from one per soldier (the Greek hoplite norm) to one between ten, and so compelled the men to fend for themselves by carrying their own provisions and equipment on long route marches. This was to prove a huge boon to Alexander, since it cut down the size of the baggage train (the Latin for which is *impedimenta*, in the plural, for the good reason that the multifarious paraphernalia of baggage trains impede an army's rapid progress). Philip rendered distance a negligible factor in Balkan warfare for the first time. He confounded Demosthenes by fighting at all times and seasons of the year – most unsportsmanlike, as it seemed to that admittedly not terribly warlike Athenian politician. In short, Philip turned warfare into a whole new ball game and made the Macedonian army supreme throughout mainland Greece.

If Philip had an obvious military weakness, it was not on land but at sea. He neither inherited nor developed a Macedonian navy, though after the conquest of Greek Amphipolis (357), Methone (354) and Olynthus (348) he had easy access to good and controllable harbours. It is this obviously deliberate lack that probably explains why he treated with kid gloves the one Greek state that could surely supply the deficiency for his projected invasion of the Persian Empire, namely Athens. Conversely, as we shall see, Alexander felt he could afford to be tougher than Philip on Athens, since he had decided, rightly as it turned out, that he could dispense with making serious use of their, or indeed any, fleet – a nice illustration of the dialectical relationship between military and political factors.

However, in the young Alexander's eyes the lack of an adequate navy was by no means the only, let alone the greatest, shortcoming of Philip's mighty armament. For along with Philip's army Alexander inherited his high command too. It takes conscious imaginative effort to remember that Alexander had no divine right to unquestioned authority. He was young and, inevitably, inexperienced in taking personal command. He had to win – or spin – his pre-eminence. Above all, he needed to assert himself against, and eventually over, the immense weight of influence wielded by the Upper Macedonian noble Parmenion, Philip's senior general since the very beginning of his reign in the early 350s.

In 336 Parmenion was about sixty-four, more than three times Alexander's age and almost two generations his senior. Philip had dispatched him in the spring of that year to Asia Minor to establish a bridgehead. In 334 he was still there, now as Alexander's second in command, as he was to remain until his death – or rather murder – in 330. Nor was he by any means the only member of his family or family circle to hold high military office under Alexander. As we noted in Chapter Four, one son of Parmenion's, Philotas, was commander-in-chief of the Companion Cavalry. Another, Asandrus, commanded the *Prodromoi*, or Mounted Scouts; yet another, Nicanor, the elite Shield Bearers. A son-in-law, Coenus, commanded one of the six infantry regiments of the Foot Companions, which recruited from the Upper Macedonian canton of Elimaea (or Elimiotis). A friend of Parmenion's, Hegelochus, commanded a squadron of the Companion Cavalry at Gaugamela. Another friend, Polyperchon, took over the command of another of the infantry regiments, that of Upper Macedonian Tymphaea, after the Battle of Issus. And the three sons of Andromenes, who were friends of Philotas, commanded at various times another of the six infantry regiments.

All in all, this constituted a formidable web of influence, if not control, within the higher commands, and at the centre of the web was Parmenion, who – to put it in factional terms – was a 'Philippian' rather than an 'Alexandrian'. A man of Alexander's temperament, with his massively ambitious plans for his personal role and rule in Asia, was bound to find the conservative and traditional Parmenion and his entrenched connections a gigantic obstacle. Setting the facts out baldly like this does, I think, help to explain why Alexander should have wished eventually, and sooner after the Battle of Gaugamela rather than later, to get Parmenion out of the way, permanently. And by murder if it was the only means of achieving that end.

This explains, too, why Parmenion was left behind at Ecbatana in 330, and why Philotas was spied on. And hence the stream of 'official' denigration of Parmenion that we find preserved in Arrian, originating no doubt with the official historian Callisthenes. The unhappy episode of the executions of Philotas and Parmenion in 330 reminds us also that, when appraising Alexander's meteoric career as a general, it is vital not to approach it anachronistically. We must not read back the position of unchallenged authority he had acquired over his general staff and higher commands by, say, 328 (when he manslaughtered Black Cleitus) into the situation in 336 at his accession, or in 334 at the start of the Asiatic campaign, or even in 331 when he fought the last of his set pieces against Darius III.

After the executions of Parmenion and his son, Alexander carried through a major shake-up in the higher commands. Right at the top there was no longer to be a single and obvious deputy commander-in-chief like Parmenion. Moreover, Philotas's overall command of the Companion Cavalry was now split, at first between two men each of whom acquired the title of Hipparch (Commander of Horse). One of these favoured two was Hephaestion, 'Alexandrian' par excellence. The other was Black Cleitus, brother of Alexander's wet nurse, the man who had saved Alexander's life at the Granicus river battle (Chapter Six). His appointment was surely designed to reassure the older Macedonians in the army that not all was being sweepingly changed, whereas had Alexander appointed Hephaestion, a man without a significant military track record, as sole commander, that would likely have given exactly the opposite impression.

Cleitus, however, unfortunately for him, was in a sense too conservative and traditional. In reminding Alexander at Maracanda in 328 of what he owed to Philip and others, and pointing out the perils of high-handed autocracy, he said the wrong things at the wrong time and paid for his words with his life. By late 327, if not before, there were eight, no longer just two, Hipparchs. It is striking that these were men of the highest distinction, whereas the former squadron commanders of the Companion Cavalry had generally been relatively undistinguished men – Cleitus himself being an exception to that rule. From the ranks of these new-style Hipparchs were to emerge what might aptly be called the marshals of Alexander's new Empire: Hephaestion, Coenus, Perdiccas and Craterus. In case it seems puzzling that Coenus, son-in-law of the late Parmenion and brother-in-law of the late Philotas, had managed to survive the cull of his relatives in 330, the simple explanation is that he turned his coat and declared himself a fervent 'Alexandrian'.

But was there perhaps more to the change from squadrons (*ilai*) to hipparchies in the Companion Cavalry than a mere change in the name of the principal subdivisions? Our ancient evidence unfortunately fails us at this point, typically enough. But the modern suggestion that it coincided with a radical change in the ethnic composition of the subdivisions is quite persuasive. By 324, at any rate, we know for sure that Alexander was brigading oriental lancers in the same units with Macedonians. The suggestion, therefore, has been made that this practice had been introduced many years before, perhaps even as early as 330, when he was certainly already using orientals as mounted archers and javelineers. If the change had indeed happened that early, this would further help to account for the fatal bust-up between Alexander and Cleitus in 328 and the objection to Alexander's attempted orientalization of Macedonian and Greek court ceremonial in 327 (the *proskynesis* affair). On the latter, Alexander was forced to back down. But nothing and no one were going to impede his policy of military fusion. The shake-up in the higher commands and the orientalization of the army after 330 should therefore be seen as two sides of the same coin, both equally reflecting Alexander's overwhelming desire for independence of thought and action (see further, Chapter Eight).

So much for the conditions in which Alexander was called upon to wage war. Now to what J. F. C. Fuller calls Alexander's 'aim and problem', with special reference to his 'operations in plan' (strategy). From the very start of the expedition he aimed to conquer and rule all 'Asia'. This was a conveniently fluid concept, which could be interpreted either politically to mean the existing Persian Empire or geographically to embrace some larger entity of Alexander's choosing. In the latter sense it might extend – at the limit, literally – to the edge of the world bounded by the engirdling Ocean. Alexander's problem was deciding what strategy he should adopt to achieve this aim of conquest. Consider the wise words of the nineteenth-century Prussian general Karl von Clausewitz, in his classic military manual *On War* (*Vom Kriege*): 'strategy forms the plan of the war' and, at its uppermost levels, it 'borders on political science, or rather . . . the two become one'. It's not often, perhaps, that one thinks of Alexander as a political scientist. But the policy of ethnic fusion in the army and his manipulation of the higher commands to further that policy certainly don't entirely discourage the thought.

As analysed by Fuller, strategy in its practical application consists of seven basic principles: maximization of forces and martial energy; concentration of forces at the decisive point; speed; surprise; consolidation of victory by immediate pursuit; establishment of secure bases; and, finally, secure communications. Alexander's brilliance on the field of battle illustrates his marvellously effective adherence to and exploitation of these strategic basics. Five episodes in particular stand out: the campaign of 335; the war at sea, 334–332; the siege of Tyre in 332; the Battle of Gaugamela, 331; and the Battle of the Hydaspes in 326.

ON LEARNING of the death of Philip in the autumn of 336 several Greek states, the most important being Thebes and Athens, revolted against Macedon. Alexander by a speedy march into central Greece cowed them into submission and a renewal of their oaths of allegiance at Corinth. The Greeks all now knew that Alexander was not, as Demosthenes liked to dismiss him, a mere 'boy'. (Some Romans similarly misprized the twenty-year-old Octavian three centuries later – he became Emperor Augustus by the age of thirty-six.) If the Greeks were to revolt against Macedon successfully, they could not do so when Alexander had his hands free to deal with them. The year 335, therefore, seemed to offer a more promising situation, happily reminiscent of the bad old, good old days of the Macedonian monarchy before Philip.

Alexander then found he had trouble on his eastern, northern and western frontiers simultaneously, from respectively the Triballi, the Paeonians and the Illyrians. In order to secure these frontiers a firm demonstration of his authority was called for, and this required forceful military intervention. But there was a further consideration in play, applying not only to these troublesome non-Greek neighbours in the north but also to the whole of the Greek peninsula. With a view to promoting the Persian expedition already under way, which he aimed to join just as soon as he could, Alexander had to secure his rear in Greece. And secure it so far that he could with confidence leave Greece behind in the care of a deputy, and not worry whether he would be required to return from Asia at any moment to settle southern Balkan affairs (as King Agesilaus of Sparta had been, in 394). This explains why he did not content himself with merely quelling the neighbouring tribesmen, but also pushed on as far north as the far bank of the Danube, which could be regarded as the 'natural' northern frontier of his kingdom of Greater Macedonia. It also explains the severity of his treatment of the southern Greeks – who once again, on hearing a false report of his death among the Illyrians, went into open revolt, led by Thebes.

Of course, in 340, when still only sixteen, he had already acted as regent for his father and, as such, conducted a successful operation in Thrace. He had, moreover, led the Companion Cavalry in the Macedonians' famous victory over Thebes, Athens and their allies at Chaeronea in 338. But the northern aspect of the campaign of 335 demanded the application of forward planning, keen anticipation, on-the-spot improvisation in the face of unexpected obstacles both meteorological and technological, and, above all perhaps, confident and inspiring leadership.

All these, and more, Alexander displayed as he avoided a torrent of wagons hurled down on his troops through the narrow Shipka pass, deployed long-range artillery to provide covering fire as he crossed the Danube on floats improvised from animal skins stuffed with straw, and terrified the Illyrians by a demonstration of Macedonian drill in marching and countermarching. Then, what surely was a stroke of luck intervened in his favour. He had just quelled the perennially trouble-some Illyrians when he learned of a second revolt against him by sadly misinformed Greeks. Within two weeks he marched his army south-wards some three hundred miles (five hundred kilometres) and by an unexpected route (avoiding the Thermopylae pass) to the walls of Thebes, an exercise of speed that entailed the achievement of surprise.

So great indeed was the beleaguered Thebans' surprise, or shock, that they refused at first to believe it was Alexander himself who had arrived. Militarily, the revolt was at an end within an extraordinarily short space of time, as Alexander demonstrated next his unique competence in siege warfare. What followed was no less a political than a military act, reminding us of von Clausewitz's most famous, if usually misinterpreted, dictum that war is 'the continuation of politics (or policy) with the admixture of other means'. The near-annihilation of Thebes in October 335 was above all else an act of political terrorism intended to deter any Greeks who might otherwise have entertained similar illusions of being able to escape at will from Macedonian control.

Within just six months, Alexander had both enhanced the security of his core Macedonian kingdom and secured his rear preparatory to joining the advance force for the invasion and conquest of Asia. In so doing, the twenty-one-year-old demonstrated that he had attained full maturity as a general at a remarkably early age.

GREEK sources always tended to inflate the size of Persian armaments, to make their own victories over them seem greater. We should not therefore leap to believe that in 480 Great King Xerxes had 1,207 ships on the water at Salamis. That figure can safely be halved, or even reduced by three-quarters. On the other hand, during the fifth and fourth centuries the Persian King – any Persian King – does seem to have been able normally to count on a fleet of three hundred or so ships to meet emergencies in the eastern Mediterranean. And this is probably the kind of figure that Alexander should have expected to have to contend with in 334. True, the chief areas from which Persian fleets were mustered, Phoenicia and Cyprus, had been in revolt as recently as a dozen years ago. But there was no good reason for Alexander to believe, or hope, that they would not produce their quota to counter him.

It was, therefore, another stroke of good luck for Alexander that the Persian fleet was not mobilized by Darius III in time to oppose his crossing of the Hellespont. The importance of this piece of good fortune was all the greater in that, although Athens alone had nearly four hundred ships on the stocks in 334 (we have the contemporary dockyard records) and was capable a dozen years later of manning 170 of them (in revolt against Macedon), Alexander's total fleet that same year was only somewhere in the order of 160-plus. The most convincing explanation of this glaring deficit is that he simply did not trust the Athenians enough to have confidence in using their fleet.

Proof of this would seem to come in 334 at Miletus in Ionia. Here Alexander disbanded even the navy he had, with the exception of twenty Athenian ships. That left him with a flotilla rather than a fleet, but this was not intended for offensive naval operations but rather to serve as a floating encampment for hostages, some four thousand Athenian citizens in all, the threat to whose lives would guarantee their city's good behaviour back home in mainland Greece. Alexander himself is said to have quipped that he would conquer the Persian fleet from the land, by capturing its bases. This sort of remark was necessary as morale-boosting propaganda. But it was necessary mainly because in fact this (non-)naval strategy of Alexander's was an act of folly or, on a more generous estimate, a highly risky gamble. That it did indeed pay off in the end was due to three factors, two of which were outside Alexander's control.

First, Memnon of Rhodes, the best of the Persian commanders, died conveniently in summer 333. He had advised the correct scorched-earth policy (rather than the failed Granicus pitched battle) against Alexander in Anatolia in 334, and had been responsible for preventing him from making his siege of Halicarnassus a complete success later that year. Above all, Memnon had conceived the potentially deadly strategy of using Persian naval supremacy in the Aegean so as to stab Alexander in the back through fomenting revolt in mainland Greece. What if a Persian fleet with ample supplies of cash had landed in the Peiraeus in 333 or, better still, 332? We can get somewhere towards answering this by considering what in fact did happen in the Lamian War of 323/2, given Persian money but no Persian fleet to back it up. Alexander, in other words, might well have had to return to Greece, if only temporarily, to shore up the situation on behalf of his regent Antipater. As it was, Memnon died, and his successors were far less effective. Darius recalled the Greek mercenary sailors and diverted his money to prepare for the Battle of Issus in November 333. This was a battle that he probably should have won, but, as we have seen, did not.

At this stage, the second factor outside Alexander's direct control came into play. Refugees from the Persian side at Issus tried to get through to the Aegean to link up with the Persian fleet. Three times they had to be defeated in heroic and desperate battles led by Antigonus the One-Eyed (Monophthalmus), commander of Greater Phrygia. Alexander, of course, deserves credit for having appointed the right man in the right place at the right time to prevent his communications being interrupted. But this was cutting things very fine indeed. On the other hand, the third factor redounds almost entirely to Alexander's credit. Defeating the Persian navy by land, in the sense of capturing their bases, involved a whole series of sieges. During the most daunting of them all, a siege that most generals would not even have contemplated, let alone concluded successfully, Alexander's outstanding qualities as a field commander were tested to the utmost.

'Genius', Napoleon said, 'is the inexplicable measure of a great commander.' It was at Tyre, if anywhere, between January and July of 332 that Alexander displayed this genius. New Tyre in Phoenicia (in modern Lebanon) was a walled island stronghold nearly three miles (4.5 kilometres) in circumference; it was separated from the Levantine mainland by about 870 yards (800 metres) of sea. The landward walls were tall and thick, the sea around the island some 100 fathoms (almost 600 feet, 185 metres) deep. Alexander had no fleet, as we know, and even his most efficient stone-throwing catapult could do no serious damage to such walls from a distance of more than about 160 yards (150 metres). Logically, therefore, but hazardously, he embarked upon the only possible course of attack. He ordered a mole, or pier, to be built out into the sea between the mainland and New Tyre to serve as a platform for his huge siege towers and his arrow-firing and stone-throwing catapults. He at least had a partial precedent to inspire him. In 398/7 the Sicilian Greek tyrant Dionysius I, after constructing a mole, had conducted a successful siege of Phoenician-founded Motya, a small island off the west coast of Sicily. But the sea around Tyre was deeper, and the Phoenicians of that city were of sterner mettle than their kinsmen of Motya. Even Alexander's skyscraper (twenty-level) siege towers with their improved grappling irons, their reinforced battering rams, their greater capacity for carrying warriors and their swathes of untreated animal skins to act as protective screens for the huddled besiegers, were largely ineffectual against the Tyrians' determined and ingenious resistance.

Arrian emphasizes the crucial importance of the episode by giving Alexander a rousing speech:

> Friends and fellow-soldiers, I do not see how we can safely
> advance upon Egypt so long as the Persians control the sea.
> To pursue Darius with the city of Tyre neutral in our rear, and
> Egypt and Cyprus still in enemy hands, would constitute a
> serious risk, especially in light of the situation in Greece. While
> our army was on the track of Darius far inland towards Babylon,
> the Persians might well regain control of the coast, and thus be
> enabled to transfer the war to Greece with more power behind
> them. There Sparta is already openly hostile to us, and Athens is
> only an unwilling ally whom fear, not goodwill, is keeping on our
> side for the moment. But with Tyre destroyed, all Phoenicia
> would be ours, and the Phoenician fleet, which is the
> predominant element in Persia's sea power both numerically and
> qualitatively, would very likely come over to us.

But not even Arrian could conceal Alexander's many setbacks, including the forced abandonment of the first mole, and appalling losses of manpower. The cause of the abandonment, in the words of an expert in the history of the use of fire in antiquity as a military weapon, was 'the most stupendous fire ship of all':

> The historians Arrian and Quintus Curtius described the ship as a
> floating chemical firebomb. The Phoenician engineers fitted a very

large transport ship (originally used for carrying cavalry horses)
with two masts and yardarms. From these they suspended four
cauldrons brimming with sulphur, bitumen, and 'every sort of
material apt to kindle and nourish flame'. The foredeck of the
ship was packd with cedar torches, pitch, and other flammables,
and the hold was filled with dry brush liberally laced with more
chemical combustibles. Waiting until the wind was favorable,
Phoenician rowers towed the great fire ship right up to the
offensive mole . . . The mole had two movable towers and many
ballistic engines behind its palisades, all protected with curtains of
raw hides in case of flaming arrows. But the Macedonians were
unprepared for the unstoppable ship of flames. The Phoenicians
ignited the transport and then rowed like mad to crash the
burning mass into the mole. They escaped by jumping overboard
and swimming to skiffs that returned them to safety. On impact
with the burning ship, the cauldrons on the burning ship spilled their
flammable contents, further accelerating the flames.

– Adrienne Mayor, *Greek Fire*

Romantic stories were spread to distract attention from Alexander's travails. For example, one of his old childhood tutors back in Pella, Lysimachus (who fancied himself as a latter-day Homeric Phoenix to Alexander's Achilles), allegedly insisted on joining Alexander in a diversionary raid on some neighbouring Arabs in the mountains of the anti-Lebanon. But Lysimachus was unable to keep up with the rest, and on one dark and bitterly cold night (as Plutarch tells the story) he would undoubtedly have perished had not Alexander remained with him until daybreak. Indeed, Alexander is even said to have stolen fire, Prometheus-like, from a couple of the Arabs encamped nearby in order to make a fire for Lysimachus. But this and other such morale-boosting stories fail to cover up the uncomfortable truth – that, without a proper fleet, the Tyrian enterprise was foolhardy, even madcap.

And yet Alexander did emerge, eventually and at great cost, the victor. The turning point came at last when 220 Phoenician and other ships in the Persians' service, influenced by the ever more likely prospect of Alexander's eventual victory over Darius, came over to join him. These turn-sail ships made it possible for him to take on the Tyrian navy and attack the city's weaker seaward walls, and to build a second mole. Even so, the victory required a testing combination of concentrated and diversionary tactics. Namely, battering ships, infantry assault by the Shield Bearer commandos, covering fire from the ship-mounted artillery, a fleet to attack both island harbours, and archers and catapults as diversions. And the attackers had also to run the gauntlet of yet more fiendish Phoenician incendiary devices that infiltrated particles of burning sand beneath their breastplates, searing their flesh and causing intolerable agony.

It speaks worlds for Alexander's leadership qualities, therefore, that he had not only not given up but had actually inspired his men with his own furious energy over so extended a period. One of the Macedonian so-called Successor monarchs, Demetrius, would earn the permanent title of 'the Besieger' (Poliorcetes) some three decades later, but in truth it was a title that Alexander could lay better claim to than anyone.

Success, however, had taken seven months. This would have been permissible perhaps for a siege that was the only item on that year's campaign menu, as in traditional Greek siege warfare. But here it constituted a major delay to a rolling campaign of conquest like Alexander's, and a major boon for Darius in the wake of his crushing defeat at Issus. It was also perhaps unfortunate that Alexander should have rather taken the gloss off his triumph by having two thousand of the Tyrian captives crucified in an act of savagely cruel revenge and exemplary punishment.

By the time 331 dawned, Alexander had two important set-piece victories under his belt – the Battles of the Granicus river and of Issus. He had reduced Tyre after a protracted and hard-won siege. He had liberated the subjects of most of the Achaemenid Persian Empire west of the Euphrates. In winter 332/1 he had made his mysterious visit to the Siwah oasis oracle of Ammon, and in April 331 he formally founded his new city of Alexandria on the Nile delta. Only in the late spring of that year did he return directly and fixedly to the main business in hand – the final defeat of Darius III. For the past six months Darius had been thinking along similar lines, and thinking all the harder because, since Issus, members of his immediate family including a wife and his mother had been captives and hostages of Alexander. The famous Issus mosaic from Pompeii, based probably on an earlier painting, well captures the interpersonal psychological dimension of the struggle: Alexander literally gives Darius the eye as the latter turns tail. Besides, it would have concentrated Darius's mind wonderfully to realize that another such major defeat would almost certainly be his last.

The Issus disaster had taught Darius several lessons. One of the most important was that he must ensure not only that his forces were vastly larger than those of Alexander (who had had the numerical advantage at the Granicus, but not at Issus), but also that the battlefield was entirely of his own choosing and suitable in every particular for exploiting this numerical superiority. This explains why he did not attempt to block Alexander's advance. The latter's route took him from Egypt through Syria and Assyria, across the Euphrates at Thapsacus (probably modern Meskene or possibly Jerablus), and then eastwards by way of Nisibis and across the Tigris (at modern Bezabde), until he finally reached Darius's chosen site of Gaugamela in what today is northern Iraq. This was not all that far from Nineveh, where an earlier empire, the Assyrian, had gone down in 612 to the Persians' kinsmen, the Medes.

It would be wrong, though, to say that Alexander was enticed by Darius to Gaugamela. For Alexander too needed and wanted one final, decisive encounter, with no holds barred. One of the several supposed verbal exchanges between him and Parmenion makes this point clearly enough. Parmenion allegedly advised, on the night before the battle, that in order to minimize Darius's numerical advantage Alexander should make a night attack. 'I will not', Alexander retorted hotly, 'demean myself by stealing victory like a thief.' (It is ironic, therefore, that in Iran today he is still slandered precisely as Iskander 'the thief'.) This was not because he was opposed on principle to the use of stealth. Far from it. But, like Napoleon, he was of the view that in warfare 'the morale [factor] is to the physical as three to one'. The morale value of defeating Darius on even terms in an open and fair fight was deemed to be of overriding importance, both militarily and politically.

On the day of the battle itself, either 30 September or 1 October, Alexander's 47,000 men lined up against Darius's perhaps quarter of a million. Darius had about 30,000 cavalry drawn from Media, Armenia, Afghanistan and, not least, Scythia. Alexander had only some 7,000 cavalry. Darius disposed his cavalry on his wings, intermingling them with infantry, while he himself occupied the dead centre, together with his bodyguard and fifteen tanks – or rather 'tanks', for these were Indian elephants. In front of the two wings he placed more cavalry, and in front of the line as a whole two hundred scythed chariots for which the ground had been specially levelled. As usual, the Great King was weak in heavy infantry, the more so now as he was down to only about 6,000 Greek mercenaries (compared with 30,000 at Issus). Alexander faced Darius with 10,000 *sarissa*-wielding Foot Companions in his centre. Their right flank was protected by 3,000 Shield Bearers, who formed the link to the Companion Cavalry on the right wing led by Alexander himself. In front of the Cavalry on his right he stationed some two thousand archers, slingers and javelineers. On the left, the Foot Companions were continuous with the Greek (Thessalian) and more Macedonian cavalry under Parmenion. So much larger were Darius's forces that Alexander's right lined up opposite Darius's centre. Therefore, in order to counter any outflanking manoeuvre, Alexander innovatively organized a second line of defence, some 20,000 Greek and non-Greek infantry. This would wheel face about should Darius's cavalry escape the flank guards of cavalry hidden within the infantry that Alexander posted like flaps at the very tip of each wing. These flank guards and the rear line were master strokes – unprecedented, probably, in all Greek warfare.

The evolution of the battle itself cannot be precisely reconstructed, any more than that of any other ancient – or, to some extent, modern – battle. To look no further, so to speak, there was the all-enveloping dust of a northern Iraqi plain at the end of a long hot summer. Only the main lineaments can be followed and described. Alexander, operating with his usual front-line order of battle, effected his usual oblique line of advance, refusing – that is, holding back – his left wing. This was a device learned via Philip from Epaminondas of Thebes. As the two sides approached each other, Alexander began to lead his whole line briskly to the right. This was partly to get his horses away from Darius's elephants, and partly to counter the outflanking on his right. As intended, a gap duly opened in Darius's centre, into which Alexander led the Companion Cavalry at the gallop in a flying wedge formation, cutting back sharply from the right. Darius ignominiously fled, even though Mazaeus on his right was almost certainly at least holding his own against Parmenion on Alexander's left, and the Foot Companions had been penetrated at several points. The battle was fought in four separate areas, but it was won by the concentration of some three thousand Companion Cavalrymen and eight thousand Shield Bearers and other infantry at a point of weakness for Darius.

Compare and contrast this minimalist and hopefully sober record with the following excerpt from Curtius, with its characteristic preference for doom-laden omens and rhetorical Grand Guignol:

> With the two main bodies almost in contact the two kings
> spurred on their men to battle. There were more Persian dead
> now, and the number of wounded on either side was about equal.
> Darius was riding in his chariot, Alexander on horseback, and
> both had a bodyguard of hand-picked men who had no regard
> for their own lives ... each man thought it a noble fate to meet

his end before the eyes of his king . . . Now whether their eyes
were deceiving them, or they really did see it, Alexander's guards
believed they saw an eagle gently hovering just above the king's
head, unaffrighted by either the clash of arms or the groans of the
dying. For a long time it was observed around Alexander's horse
[Bucephalas], apparently hanging in the air rather than flying.
The seer Aristander, dressed in white and holding a laurel branch
in his right hand, kept pointing out the bird to the soldiers even
as they were engaged in fighting, insisting that it was an infallible
omen of victory. The men who moments before had been terrified
were now fired with tremendous enthusiasm and confidence for
the fight . . . It is said that Darius drew his scimitar and
considered avoiding ignominious flight by an honourable death,
but . . . while he wavered between hope and despair, the Persians
gradually began to give ground and broke ranks, and . . . Darius
turned his chariot in flight.

Soon after, as we have seen, Darius was deposed by his distant relative
Bessus. But the change of monarch came too late. Gaugamela had
broken the camel's back of Persian resistance at its centre. Three years
of stiff guerrilla resistance in the far eastern satrapies lay ahead, and
Alexander's accomplishments as a guerrilla commander would reveal
an extraordinary capacity for adaptability (see Chapter Six). But he
had only one other set-piece engagement left to fight – in 'India'.

ONCE upon a time the Achaemenid Persian Empire had extended over
the Hindu Kush into Pakistan, Kashmir and the modern state of India
as far as the Indus river. But by 326 that was long past. Porus, as the
Greeks called the Rajah of the Pauravas, held his kingdom to the east
of the Indus but he had never owed allegiance to Darius III. Alexander's motives for attacking him were therefore necessarily different
from those that had impelled him against the Persian Great King.
Among them were the sheer desire to conquer and extend his dominion

as far as the world could be known and tamed; greed for fabled Indian wealth; and the need to establish some sort of defensible south-eastern frontier by eliminating hostile native rulers and/or co-opting friendly ones. Porus, it would turn out, was both – both hostile at first and friendly later. Alexander took no chances with him to begin with, then gave him every chance.

Again, as at the Granicus, Alexander was faced with an enemy occupying the far bank of a river, in this case the Hydaspes. But whereas he had outnumbered his enemies at the Granicus, at the Hydaspes the reverse was the case. Porus, moreover, controlled considerably more elephants (eighty-five) than Darius had deployed at Gaugamela – and these were fully trained war elephants. Porus himself, who was over 6 feet 6 inches (2 metres) tall, sat atop an especially fearsome beast. So Alexander resorted at once to guile. He divided his forces, leaving Craterus in charge of the troops drawn up directly opposite Porus, while he crossed the river further upstream under cover of darkness and of a usefully situated river island. Porus on the following day thus found himself pincered, and facing an Alexander who (according to Curtius) now turned to Coenus and other Macedonian commanders and delivered the following supremely confident and sententious pre-battle exhortation:

> *Together with Ptolemy, Perdiccas and Hephaestion I am going to attack the enemy's left wing. When you see me in the thick of it, set in motion our right wing and attack the enemy while they are in a state of confusion. Antigenes, Leonnatus, Tauron – you three will attack in the centre and put pressure on their front. Our spears are long and sturdy. They can never serve us better than against these elephants and their mahouts. Dislodge the mahouts and stab the beasts. They are of dubious value as a military force, since their ferocity is greater against their own side. They are driven by command against the enemy, but by fear against their own men.*

Once the Macedonians had seen off the pachydermous threat, and thanks chiefly, it seems, to the phalanx and light infantry, victory was quite soon theirs. Alexander lost perhaps 200 cavalry and 700 infantry. But Porus suffered some 12,000 dead, and 9,000 men and almost all his elephants were captured. Prudently, he surrendered unconditionally. Rather than executing him, Alexander decided to use him as a servant of his Empire. Not only was he reinstated as Rajah of the Pauravas, but Alexander even added further territory to his control. Nor was his trust in Porus's loyalty misplaced.

Unsurprisingly and not unjustly, Alexander made a huge song and dance about this great victory. He ordered a series of commemorative silver medals and medallions to be struck in two denominations, ten-drachma and four-drachma, both seriously large values. Their weights were erratic, and the quality of the carving and the striking by local Indian craftsmen was uneven. But their true significance has only recently been appreciated and fully explicated. The iconography consists mainly of Indian archers, chariots and elephants, obviously a reference to the Indian campaigns. One type of the larger medallions shows on the reverse a horseman fighting an Indian mounted on an elephant (Figure 21). This might naturally be interpreted as depicting Alexander (on Bucephalas) and Porus, especially as the obverse of the medallion features a mighty Macedonian warrior about to be crowned with a wreath by a small figure representing the goddess Victory (Nike) (Figure 22).

This was not just any Macedonian, surely, but Alexander himself. For who but Alexander could have been represented holding in his right hand a thunderbolt – figuratively stealing (or borrowing) the thunder of mighty Zeus? Of course, such elaborate interpretations as these would not have been necessary for the Macedonian veterans who were their original recipients. But the daring of Alexander in having himself represented like this would still have taken their breath away.

Soon after the battle Alexander lost Bucephalas, the Thessalian charger that he had tamed some twenty years ago and from which he had been more or less inseparable ever since. But Bucephalas did not die in vain. Further down the Indus valley Alexander founded two cities, one of which he named Bucephala in the old warhorse's eternal honour. (The other was called Nicaea – Victoryville.)

THAT Alexander was a military leader of genius is clear, but what of his character as a general? We are not privileged to know whether he, like the British commander Orde Wingate in Abyssinia (as it then was before the Second World War), ever gave his officers their battle orders lying in his tent stark naked and smoothing his pubic hair with someone else's toothbrush. Perhaps Macedonian generals did not use toothbrushes. What we do know, and can be absolutely certain of, is that there was something about Alexander that inspired extraordinary personal devotion. He gave his soldiers the sense that, with him, nothing was impossible. The dash of youthful brio helped. In the Second World War Field Marshal Lord Carver (as he became) was considered spectacularly young to be commanding an armoured regiment at the age of thirty. Alexander had won all his great victories before his twenty-sixth birthday.

Youthful dash, though, was only part of it. The late Lord Louis Mountbatten, the last Viceroy of India, was quoted as saying that he had a congenital weakness for thinking he could do anything. Alexander manifestly not only shared that 'weakness', but communicated it vividly to his men. At the siege of Gaza in 332, for example, he is said to have expressed the belief that, the greater the difficulty, the more necessary it was to take the city; for a success so far beyond reason and probability, he argued, would inflict a serious blow on the morale of the enemy. Once again, we note his scrupulous attention to the morale factor, though actually, as we have seen, the capture of Gaza was not a military necessity and his treatment of its governor, the Arab eunuch Batis, was unnecessarily savage.

Then there are his personal leadership and undaunted daring to be taken into account. Unlike Gilbert and Sullivan's Duke of Plazatoro in *The Gondoliers*, Alexander consistently led his men from the front. I can think of only one occasion on which he was not at the forefront when he might just conceivably have been, and that was at the Sogdian Rock in 327. Here three hundred volunteers with well-attested rock-climbing skills undertook an exceptionally hazardous mission that, though successful, cost the lives of a tenth of them. Normally, Alexander was right up there in the thick of things. And it is quite possible that he received more wounds even than any of his ordinary soldiers, and quite certain that he suffered more than any of his officers. At the Battle of the Granicus, famously, he came within seconds of being hacked to death. Among the Malli of the Indus valley, as we shall note shortly, he received a near-fatal wound in the chest that punctured a lung.

He fought in this life-on-the-line way for a number of reasons. Such engaged leadership and sharing of the hazards faced by the common soldiers were excellent vehicles for instilling and maintaining high morale. Another reason seems more viscerally personal: as Arrian perceptively observed, for Alexander 'the sheer pleasure of battle, as other pleasures are to other men, was irresistible'. Battle, in other words, gave him the kind of thrill that other men sought from – usually less tumultuous and certainly less life-threatening – sexual adventures or conquests. We might therefore want to apply to Alexander the words that Lord Macaulay used of his hero, William of Orange (King William III of England): 'It was remarked that his spirits were never so high and his manners never so gracious and easy as amidst the tumult and carnage of a battle. Even in his pastimes he liked the excitement of danger. Cards, chess and billiards gave him no pleasure. The chase was his favourite recreation, and he loved it most when it was most hazardous.' So also Alexander, as far as the chase, at least, was concerned.

Two individual incidents, in conclusion, perhaps most fully capture and sum up the character and talents of Alexander the general. Both occurred in 325.

Whatever the reasons, Alexander decided to march back from India to Iran through the generally waterless Gedrosian desert. All in his party, himself included, were tormented by thirst, and many died. One day, some men almost miraculously found a little water and, carefully scooping it into a helmet, brought it to Alexander for him to drink. Ragingly thirsty though he was, he poured it out untouched on to the burning sand, as if to demonstrate that his life was no more valuable than those of his men. It was presumably because of this effacement of self and his manifest sharing of exactly the same conditions as those of his followers that Arrian adjudged this gesture 'the finest thing he ever did'. It must, however, be added that the context in which he performed it was a self-inflicted disaster, the outcome of something like a stroke of tactical insanity.

The other incident occurred earlier in 325, as Alexander was leading his men back down the Indus valley and leaving behind him a trail of native blood in what looks suspiciously like a fit of frustration at having been forced by his own troops (through their mutiny at the River Hyphasis) to turn back. Major General Fuller believed that 'Alexander's aim was to achieve, as far as it was possible, a bloodless conquest', but the less prejudiced ancient military historian Barry Strauss is much nearer the mark when he writes that 'Alexander was a great general but he was also a great killer of innocent people'. On the other hand, as A. K. Narain, himself an Indian historian, has sagely commented: 'If the Indian historian suffers from sentiment, the western historian suffers from guilt.'

In leading this assault on the principal town of the Mallians Alexander was, perhaps deservedly, gravely wounded in the chest. His men believed the wound to be fatal. He (as Arrian tells the story) set out to convince them otherwise:

> As soon as he was able, Alexander had himself conveyed to the banks of the River Hydraotes. He then sailed downstream, as the camp was at the confluence of the Hydraotes and Acesines;

Hephaestion was in charge of the land troops there, and Nearchus had the fleet. As the boat bearing the king approached the camp, Alexander ordered that the screen be removed from the stern, so that he might be clearly visible to everybody. But they still refused to believe their eyes, as they were convinced it was Alexander's corpse that was being conveyed. So, when the ship had actually put in to the shore, Alexander raised his hand in greeting to the crowd of onlookers. They roared back in return, some flinging their arms skywards, others extending them towards Alexander himself. Many had tears in their eyes at this unexpected turn of events. Some of the Shield Bearers then brought a litter to carry the king from the ship, but he refused it and ordered that his horse be brought alongside. When next he was seen, he was mounted on the horse, and at this the entire army applauded wildly over and over again, and the riverbanks and the nearby glens resounded with the noise. As Alexander drew near to his tent, he dismounted, so that he could also be seen walking. The crowd then pressed up against him on all sides, some touching his hands, knees or clothes, others just wanting a close sight of him, so that they could cast a blessing on him and go away. Some threw wreaths over him or just flowers that were in season.

EIGHT

ALEXANDER AND
THE PERSIANS

This . . . man [Calanus, a Brahman sage] . . . is . . . said to have
given Alexander a famous illustration of how to rule an empire.
He threw on the ground a dry and shrivelled hide and stood on
the edge of it. The hide was thus pressed down where he stood,
but rose up everywhere else. Calanus walked all around the edge
of the hide, flattening each spot in turn and showing what
happened. Finally, he stood right in the middle, which made the
whole hide lie still and flat. He thus demonstrated to Alexander
how important it was for him to concentrate his authority at the
middle of his empire and not travel far away from it.

– Plutarch, *Life of Alexander*

IN AUTUMN 1971 the imperial Iranian government, amid great
pomp and splendour, celebrated the 2,500th anniversary of the
founding of the Persian Empire by Cyrus II the Great. (To be more
precise, 1971 was the 2,500th anniversary of his death in 530 BCE.)
How are the mighty fallen . . . If I were a Herodotus or a Xenophon, I
might ascribe the overthrow of the late *Shahanshah* (King of Kings) to
tisis, divine retribution. But I can also think of perfectly good secular
reasons for his demise. This theme of retribution and usurpation has
its relevance to the history of Alexander.

In about December 333, soon after the Battle of Issus in Cilicia,
Alexander allegedly sent a letter to his defeated Persian opponent,
Great King Darius III. Among much else it said:

You assassinated Arses [Artaxerxes IV] in conspiracy with
Bagoas [the chief eunuch and kingmaker] and unjustly and

> *illegally seized the throne, thereby wronging the Persians . . .*
> *Through the gift of the gods I now am in possession of the*
> *country . . . and now that I am lord and master of all Asia,*
> *come to me . . .*

Nothing, it seems, is new under the oriental sun. But did Alexander make any important innovations in either the administrative structure or the ideological apparatus of the Empire he had conquered, or significantly alter its dominant culture?

The invasion of the Persian Empire was Alexander's inescapable legacy. But Philip had done more than just bequeath the project of Persian conquest to his son and successor. He had already applied ideas derived from Persia to the remaking of Macedon. In his effort to modernize the patriarchal Macedonian monarchy that he had inherited in 359 and transform it into a large and complex state, he had palpably sought to imitate aspects of the Persian military machine and administrative structure. Fortunately, apart from the general knowledge of Persia that he could obtain through intermediaries, he was also able to get the most direct and intimate information available from such high-ranking Persians as the ex-satrap Artabazus, to whom he gave sanctuary at his court as a refugee.

Thus the new Macedonian imperial province of Thrace, which was placed under the control of a Macedonian general in 343, looked much like a Persian satrapy. The Greek Eumenes from Cardia on the Hellespont reorganized the Macedonian chancellery along Persian lines (and continued in post throughout Alexander's reign). Philip's Companions in the narrow sense were not unlike the Persian King's 'Friends'. As for the Macedonian Royal Pages, they are said to have assisted Philip to mount his horse 'in the Persian manner'. This all lends weight to the view that Philip had the conquest of the Persian Empire in mind well before the invasion was launched in 336 – perhaps, indeed, as early as 346. This Persianizing of Macedon is surely also an important clue to the nature of Alexander's motivations and aims. We may fairly suspect that his Panhellenic propaganda of a crusade to avenge impious injuries inflicted on the Greeks by the Persians in 480/79 was just that: merely a propagandistic smokescreen to cover his real – personal and Macedonian – motives.

There are further clues. We cannot ever know for sure how far Alexander intended to go when he set off from Macedonia in 334. But before leaving, he distributed among his Companions most of the land he personally possessed in Macedonia, and after crossing the Hellespont in full armour he cast his spear symbolically on to Asian soil to claim Asia as his own spear-won land. These gestures probably indicate two things – that he aimed from the start to conquer at least the existing Achaemenid Empire as a whole, and that he was intending to rule his vastly enlarged kingdom and Empire from Asia. The earliest certain evidence of such ambitions and intentions was the Gordian knot episode in 333 (see Chapter Six), and it was not until 326 that he actually went beyond the existing limit of the Achaemenid Empire by invading 'India' – that is, the Punjab.

Under Darius I, in about 500 BCE, the eastern limit of the Empire had been the River Indus. Under Darius III it was the Hindu Kush mountains, what the Greeks called the Indian Caucasus. This loss of territory is a sign of the Achaemenid Empire's relative enfeeblement by Alexander's time, though even the powerful Darius I's rule over this bit of India was hardly tight. Another, and much more immediately crucial, sign of its weakness was Darius III's failure to prevent Alexander from crossing the Hellespont in 334, or indeed even to try to prevent him. The explanation for that failure is very revealing of the nature of the opposition that Alexander faced.

The core of the Persians' navy had been provided from about 525 by the city-states and petty kingdoms of Phoenicia, together with the Greeks and Phoenicians who lived on Persian-controlled Cyprus. The very largest Persian fleet that could be mustered on paper seems to have been about six hundred ships, but the less glorious reality on the water was three hundred or fewer. Besides, within the decade immediately prior to Alexander's invasion both the Phoenicians and the Cypriot Greeks had been in active revolt against the Great King. This was by no means unprecedented. Persian subjects had periodically revolted ever since the massive and widespread outbreak of the late 520s that Darius I had successfully quelled. But during the course of the fourth century revolts had become alarmingly frequent and permanent. Egypt, most conspicuously, was actually able to maintain its independence for some sixty years after revolting in 405, despite three major Persian invasions designed to restore it to the Empire. Nor had revolts been limited to foreign subjects, either. From the late 370s, and especially between 362 and 358, Artaxerxes II (r. 404–359) and then Artaxerxes III (r. 359–338) had had to face revolts by their own satraps in Asia Minor.

Thus a combination of factors operating between about 400 and 336 – less real than apparent power, disaffection from above and below, palace intrigues and assassinations – encouraged Alexander to attempt the conquest of the whole of the Achaemenid Empire. This he achieved through his decisive victories at the Granicus river, Issus and Gaugamela. Less obvious, however, is what he made of the Achaemenid Empire once he had conquered it. Was he an innovator, seeking to create new organs and institutions of governance and administration? Was he, on the contrary, a traditionalist, merely wishing to substitute himself for Darius and to give jobs to some of his Macedonian and Greek trusties, alongside cooperative members of the old Iranian ruling class, and within the old Achaemenid framework? Or did he aim to walk a middle way, combining tradition with serious innovation? Finally, was Alexander merely a conqueror – or did he entertain a higher vision of what he wished to achieve through and after his conquests? This in a way is the biggest question of all, though it is dangerous to attempt a definitive judgement on a work that was necessarily incomplete at the time of his early death.

It seems that, like most of the Achaemenids, Alexander sought in general to act on the principle of invisibility. This secret of empire (as

Tacitus might have called it) was most succinctly expressed by a British Viceroy of India in 1879: 'It may not be flattering to our *amour propre* but I feel sure I am right when I say that the less the Afghans see of us, the less they dislike us.' This is probably applicable universally to empires. In other words, so long as efficient tribute collection and secure political control were not impaired, Alexander did not interfere with local systems of law, religion or culture. Indeed, as we have seen, he seems positively to have respected the customs of other peoples, quite unlike most of his fellow-countrymen.

Official religion, for example, was a highly sensitive issue. The Persian Kings had consciously and openly placed themselves under the special protection of the Iranian divinity Ahura Mazda, following the lead of his prophet Zoroaster. But they had not imposed Zoroastrianism outside Iran. Likewise, Alexander thought of himself as a follower, even a son, of Ammon or Zeus, but he did not try to convert the Iranians to Graeco-Macedonian polytheistic beliefs. Indeed, he was able to make political capital out of his proclaimed toleration and respect for local religious beliefs and practices in two vital satrapies, Egypt and Babylonia. Here, some at least of the Achaemenids had been uncharacteristically intolerant. In Egypt and Babylonia, therefore, he was welcomed as something of a saviour figure rather than abhorred as a conquering desecrator. What cannot, unfortunately, be determined is how far this policy was a matter of practical politics, how far a product of sincere religious and cultural belief. On the other hand, Alexander was certainly not a confirmed believer in some abstract concept of 'the unity of mankind'. Nor was he a high-minded humanitarian philosopher with a mission to ladle the milk of human kindness throughout the known inhabited world.

What, then, did he set out to achieve, and how successful was he, through the administration and management of his Empire? In areas as diverse as the lush valleys of Mesopotamia and the desert of Gedrosia he may have made some effort to restrict the satraps' military independence. Yet there are several pieces of evidence that he did not do so systematically. Despite the imposed presence of Macedonian or Greek garrison commanders, the mainly Iranian satraps were still left in charge of levying local troops for Alexander's army and were still permitted to recruit Greek mercenaries, at least until 325/4. In that year, though, the practice was forbidden, as part of the sweeping changes of satrapal personnel whereby Iranians were by and large replaced by obscure Macedonians.

An early test case of Alexander's administrative vision is Egypt, which at first was not organized as a satrapy at all. Here, the Persian satrap appointed by Darius had surrendered to Alexander without a blow in late 332, and Alexander was seemingly welcomed. He initially introduced a canny and original division of administration and control – or so it must have seemed. Two native Egyptians were appointed as the equivalent of joint satraps. Under them were two Greek governors, one for Libya in the west, the other for 'Arabia towards Heroöpolis' in the east. The latter appointee was Cleomenes, a native of Naucratis, the Greek port of trade established in the Nile delta over two and half centuries earlier. He was given tax-raising authority in the area under the Egyptian governors' jurisdiction as well as within his own designated area. But the odium of physically collecting the taxes fell at first on the two native Egyptian rulers. In addition, two Macedonians were put in charge of the army of occupation, and a third was appointed admiral of the Egyptian fleet. Besides these, there were Macedonian garrison commanders stationed at the old capital, Memphis, and at the crucial eastern frontier fort of Pelusium. There was also, finally, a Greek mercenary commander, assisted by a Greek second in command, but he was supervised by two Macedonians.

This was, on the surface, a sophisticated and egalitarian system of checks and balances. The hard reality, however, was that by 324 Cleomenes had in effect enlarged his own role and sphere of competence to those of a satrap – and had been recognized as such officially by Alexander. He had certainly not earned this recognition through just treatment of Alexander's allies and provincial subjects in Egypt. He had extorted a large amount of treasure from the priests whom Alexander had been so anxious to conciliate in 332. He had, moreover, aggravated a widespread and lasting food shortage in mainland Greece (330–326) by monopolizing the export of wheat from Egypt and selling it at high prices. A major part of the explanation of Alexander's tolerance of him must be that Cleomenes had succeeded in maintaining order in the province and, above all, in raising the required tribute and having it conveyed to where Alexander needed it. But there may be more to it than this – possibly collusion by Cleomenes in a sensitive matter very dear to Alexander's heart (rather than his head).

In a letter to Cleomenes reported by Arrian, Alexander says he will pardon Cleomenes's acknowledged crimes provided that he erects shrines in honour of the deceased Hephaestion (died 324) in Alexandria and on the offshore island of Pharos. In other words, loyalty to Alexander and faithful execution of his most personal demands might have counted for more than upright provincial government and administration – if, at any rate, that letter is authentic. In any event, loyalty to Alexander does seem, hardly surprisingly, to have been crucial to his making and maintaining of satrapal appointments. In short, the separation of military and administrative powers should probably be seen chiefly as a device whereby Alexander secured personal loyalty rather than as a positive mechanism for beneficial government.

On his return from Egypt to Phoenicia in 331 Alexander reorganized the financial machinery of his oriental Empire, which then consisted of part of Asia Minor, the Levant and Egypt. Following the capture in 334 of Sardis, the satrapal capital of Lydia, he had left behind Nicias (probably a Greek) to take charge of the collection and dispatch of tribute. Cleomenes was appointed to the same position in Egypt in late 332. But then, in spring 331, Alexander transferred two Macedonians from his central treasury and gave them wide-ranging spheres of competence not corresponding to those of any Achaemenid satrap. Coeranus was put in charge of Phoenicia; and Philoxenus of Asia west of the Taurus mountains (which may mean just Cilicia or the whole strip along the west and south coasts of Asia Minor).

Their task was presumably to collect what Alexander, following an Athenian precedent, tactfully called 'contributions' (*syntaxeis*). This was because their areas included city-states without satrapal supervision and, in the case of Philoxenus, Greek *poleis* that Alexander had ostensibly come to liberate. Coeranus apparently did not hold his post for much more than six months, but Philoxenus rose from being a glorified tax-collector to a position of general supervision, in virtue of which he controlled troops and made arrests. The change in his status perhaps came in 330, when 'contributions' lapsed at the same time as Alexander abandoned the Panhellenic crusade. A parallel development occurred in the career of Cleomenes of Naucratis, so presumably Philoxenus too was being rewarded not only for efficiency but also for conspicuous personal loyalty to Alexander.

In 331 the central treasury was placed once more under the control of Harpalus, even though shortly before the Battle of Issus in 333 he had deserted to Megara in mainland Greece. Alexander's exceptional toleration and leniency towards him were probably owed to the fact that Harpalus had been an intimate friend of his from boyhood. When in 330 Alexander took possession of Darius's various treasuries – at Arbela, Babylon, Susa, Persepolis and Pasargadae – Harpalus found himself in charge of a stupendous amount of bullion worth at least 180,000 silver talents. This was initially brought together in one place at Ecbatana in Media. Later, anticipating Alexander, Harpalus removed himself to the more agreeable environment of Babylon. As light relief from his heavy financial responsibilities, he amused himself here with a couple of Greek mistresses (one of whom he literally worshipped – at any rate after her death) and a garden. Even this relief proved inadequate, however, and in 324 he decided that Babylon was after all too hot for him and absconded back to Greece, taking with him the vast sum of 5,000 talents.

It would seem that in the case of Harpalus Alexander's trust was seriously misplaced. He may perhaps be adjudged guilty of favouritism towards a boyhood friend brought on by the 'loneliness of power' (Ernst Badian's phrase). Yet even Harpalus's fandangoes did nothing to diminish the overall roaring success of Alexander's public finances. He was reported to have invaded Asia with a paltry sum of cash in the official Macedonian war kitty and a huge outstanding debt caused by Philip's over-lavish military expenditure and diplomatic largesse. The vast quantity of Alexander's coinages, in gold as well as silver, is alone sufficient to demonstrate the positive effect of 'liberating' the bullion that had been merely stored up by the Achaemenids. Though coinage is not synonymous with commercial exchange in the ancient world, Alexander's post-conquest monetization unquestionably promoted massive economic change and development, both in the short and in the longer term.

The chief interest of Alexander's Empire for us, however, lies less in satrapal organization or imperial finance than in his own position as ruler of it, and his attitude to its administration. His methods, abilities and character are alike on exhibition here. The Macedonian monarchy to which Alexander was heir was in practice an autocracy, whatever customary limitations and quasi-egalitarian restraints there may have been in theory. Not even autocrats, however, are automatically omnipotent. As we saw earlier, even Alexander was forced ultimately to turn back at the Hyphasis river by the mutiny of his Macedonian soldiers in 326, and earlier, in 327, to abandon the attempt to impose obeisance on his Macedonian and Greek courtiers. Yet these two failures do stand out starkly by their very rarity. In all other major areas of policy his will was done. Politically speaking, therefore, from the point of view of his capacity to act as King–Emperor, there was no practical need for Alexander to ordain divine worship for himself and demand recognition of his living godhead. Nonetheless, he would later take that extraordinary and controversial extra step.

Is there any evidence – despite the powerful counter-examples of Cleomenes and Harpalus – that Alexander showed care and concern for his subjects' well-being? There is, although here too he was probably motivated chiefly by considerations of political utility. The prime evidence, or test case, concerns his wide-ranging overhaul of satrapal personnel in the winter of 325/4. Of the twenty to twenty-two satraps then functioning, eight were deposed, six of these being put to death. Four more died at about this time, of causes unknown, and five more were summoned to Alexander's court. Of those deposed, five were Iranians, of whom four had been appointed originally by Darius III and kept in post by Alexander.

There are two possible ways of looking at this surely extraordinary turnover of high-ranking personnel as a test of Alexander's quality as imperial ruler. According to the less favourable construction, what took place at this time was nothing short of a reign of terror, and the charges of maladministration made against the satraps were merely a smokescreen. Really, Alexander wished to prevent them, especially the Iranian ones, from developing independent power bases. This he did by frequent changes of personnel and also, in this instance, by promoting relatively humble Macedonians who would owe everything to him. Hostile critics of Alexander suggest that he was using the cover of a spuriously necessary administrative measure to vent his spleen after the Hyphasis mutiny and the terrible rigours of the march back to Iran through the Gedrosian desert. The more favourable version argues that the satraps who were sacked and/or executed in 325/4 were indeed guilty as charged of high crimes and misdemeanours, which had inflicted undue suffering on the Empire's subjects. A turnover even as high as 35 per cent would still not have constituted a 'reign of terror'. Of course, there was an element of personal advantage to Alexander involved too, since suffering could lead subjects to undertake rebellion. But overall, goes this argument, Alexander should be given the benefit of the doubt.

My own view inclines more towards the less favourable interpretation. The flight in 324 of Harpalus, to whom Alexander had shown himself if anything over-indulgent, seems to me to signal that he had perceived a change in Alexander's temper. It was in the same winter of 325/4, too, that Alexander ordered the deaths of the men who had carried out the murder of Parmenion in 330. There does, in other words, seem to be a pattern here: of Alexander seeking to wipe clean the inherited administrative and executive personnel ledgers and to make a fresh start with his own men, just as he had wiped the slate clean in organizing his high military command in 330. Loyalty to him was all. The threat of the emergence of serious rivals for his power must be pre-empted at all costs.

But what was the precise nature of his power as it had developed to this point? Catching up with the already murdered Darius in 330, Alexander bestowed on him a burial appropriate to his status as the last generally recognized Achaemenid sovereign. This was partly done to allay the Iranian nobility's fear that Alexander as a Macedonian would not understand or respect Iranian cultural usages. It might also help to smooth the handover of the succession from Darius to Alexander. But what was Alexander succeeding to, exactly? He did not simply become the next Great King, occupying precisely the same throne, literally and symbolically, as Darius. That position remained vacant after Darius's death; or rather it was, in Alexander's eyes, rendered obsolete. Some high-ranking Iranian nobles – Bessus in 331–329 and a Mede called Baryaxes in 324 – might still present their opposition to Alexander's conquests as a claim to the Achaemenid throne, out of nostalgia for the old symbolic order. But they were, as we say, history.

Instead, Alexander became 'Lord of Asia', cleverly verbalizing the Achaemenids' claim to being the rulers of all Asia while sidestepping the obstacle that they had been first and foremost ethnic Persian rulers, under the aegis of their god Ahura Mazda. It was this new throne of Asia that he occupied in majesty. And it was now, entirely aptly, that he took to wearing a modified form of oriental regalia. He did not wear the Achaemenids' purple and gold cloak or the scarlet panta-loons. He did, though, wear the purple and white tunic, the gold belt, the purple mantle and the diadem (a strip of cloth) – though he had the latter bound around the traditional Macedonian broad-brimmed hat (the *kausia*). He also encouraged his Companions to adopt Persian dress, as had been the practice among the Achaemenids' oriental subjects (for example, the Phoenician kings of Byblos and Sidon). But only his Hephaestion and Peucestas, the Macedonian who had cru-cially shielded Alexander after his near-fatal wound among the Indian Malli, seem to have been conspicuous in doing so. This wearing of basically oriental regalia was a natural move for Alexander to make, since otherwise his oriental subjects, used to the show of imperial pageantry, would have doubted his legitimacy as supreme ruler. But the fact that he adopted a mixed version is also highly significant. It implies that he was seeking either to forestall or at any rate to minimize anticipated Macedonian opposition.

From his new position as oriental potentate Alexander attempted to implement a policy of 'fusion' between, on the one hand, the Macedonian and Iranian ruling classes in respect of court ceremonial, and, on the other, ordinary Macedonians and Iranians within the context of the army. The immediate preconditions of any fusion policy were satisfied by the victory at Gaugamela in October 331 and the capture and death of Darius III in July 330. Now that Persian military resistance was clearly broken, Alexander had to consider how best the post-Achaemenid Empire – his Empire – was to be governed. His first, momentous step, noted earlier, was to appoint the high-ranking Iranian noble, Mazaeus, who had been satrap of Cilicia and later Syria and Mesopotamia under Artaxerxes III and commanded the right wing under Darius III at Gaugamela, as satrap of the key province of Babylonia. Just how key it was is shown by the fact that after Alexander had begun to settle down it was to Babylon, not Susa, that he gravitated. Babylon, perhaps, was 'the middle of his empire' where

Calanus had advised him to stay firmly put (see the epigraph to this chapter).

Mazaeus may well have betrayed his master Darius at Gaugamela by pre-arrangement with Alexander. Also, he seems to have taken a Babylonian wife, since he gave his children names derived from that of the Babylonians' chief god Bel. He was therefore the perfect sort of person for Alexander to retain as satrap of an economically vital province whose important native priestly hierarchy nurtured no great love for Persian rule. Mazaeus was also being used as a propaganda weapon. The message from Alexander to other such high-ranking Iranians was that, if they came over to him without making trouble, there was a good possibility that they could do business together. Altogether some twenty oriental satraps were in fact appointed or reappointed by Alexander, most of them Iranian nobles like Mazaeus. If the policy apparently broke down in 325/4 when he replaced them, this was due less to its intrinsic unworkability or to the depravity of the individuals concerned than to Alexander's overriding anxiety to ensure personal loyalty and prevent the emergence of possible rivals, especially Macedonian ones.

The Macedonian opposition to the fusion policy erupted most visibly in Bactria in 327 over the issue of *proskynesis*. In Persia obeisance was a social gesture performed, in different ways according to caste and class perhaps, by an inferior to a superior, and so by all Persians to the Great King. For the Greeks, however, it was a religious gesture, performed by mortal men in honour only of the immortal gods, and many Greeks crudely misinterpreted the meaning of the Persian gesture by illegitimate cultural transference. Callisthenes, Alexander's official historian and learned relative of Aristotle, led the opposition to Alexander's imposition of obeisance on Greeks and Macedonians. What he did not like, he claimed, was not the requirement to signify publicly obedience to a supreme ruler but the implicit command to treat Alexander as if he were a living god.

As for the Macedonians who followed Callisthenes's lead, they would have been objecting mainly to being required to perform a gesture that was perhaps suitable for the Persians as an inferior and defeated people, but utterly inappropriate for members of a master race like the Macedonians. The requirement was all the more unpalatable for them, because they saw the Macedonian king as a first among equals. In face-to-face contact between the king and his Macedonian courtiers a degree of social equality was the unspoken rule. For three years, since 330, the Macedonians had had to put up with the existence of a parallel oriental court, with its lavish paraphernalia of cup-bearers, spear-bearers, eunuchs, concubines and so forth. What they were not prepared to put up with now was the forced amalgamation of the two courts by means of this imposed common gesture of obeisance. I suspect that what really outraged them was that they, the victors, were being compelled to make the major public concession by adopting a key custom of the generally despised 'slavish' orientals.

Alexander may perhaps have repeated his attempt to introduce a universal obeisance, but it was never successfully carried through. Far more successful, as we shall see, was the mass marriage ceremony at Susa in perhaps April 324. No less pragmatic and unromantic was Alexander's gesture in recognizing as legitimate the informal unions between his ordinary Macedonian soldiers and various nationalities of oriental women. His principal concern here was to recruit his future army from oriental, mainly Iranian, sources rather than have constantly to send back to Macedonia for manpower reinforcements.

Alexander's importation and integration of oriental troops into the Macedonian army was a crucial and controversial issue. By the end of 328 he had units of Sogdian and Bactrian cavalry, so presumably he was already drawing also upon the excellent cavalry of western and central Iran. In 327 he recruited more than thirty thousand young Iranians. Since Greek was to be the lingua franca of the new Empire, replacing the Achaemenids' use of Aramaic, he arranged for them to be taught the Greek language as well as the demonstrably superior

Macedonian infantry tactics. When they arrived at Susa in 324, he hailed them as the 'successors' – to the Macedonian soldiers' understandable consternation. These new recruits were probably also a modified continuation of an Achaemenid institution, designed to produce 'Macedonian' infantrymen regardless of their ethnic or regional backgrounds. By 324, moreover, Iranian cavalry had actually been incorporated in the regiments of the crack Macedonian Companion Cavalry. This was a measure perhaps as radical as incorporating Nepalese Gurkhas in a regiment of British Guardsmen would have been. In that same year, Persian infantrymen were incorporated in the Macedonian phalanx, though the commanders remained Macedonians. Finally, a new (fifth) mounted regiment of mixed Macedonians and orientals was formed under the command of an oriental, the Bactrian Hystaspes.

Here, then, was the policy of fusion with a vengeance. And, despite the Opis mutiny, which the policy had itself helped to engender, the traditionalist Macedonians were powerless to resist. Alexander was undoubtedly quite right to seek to place his military recruitment and organization on a new and fundamentally oriental basis. But his timing and methods were not calculated to win round his long-suffering Macedonian stalwarts. Like the Susa marriages, this idea too died the death with Alexander.

But this was the not the case, by any means, with his city foundations. These illustrate how far Alexander sought to use the spread of Greek culture and civilization as a tool of imperial administration. Plutarch, in his early rhetorical work on his fortune, claimed that Alexander himself personally founded more than seventy-two cities. Cooler and less apologetic modern criticism has whittled that down severely – to seventeen at the maximum, or a bare minimum of just six.

There seems to be no single or simple reason for the new foundations. The majority of those named Alexandria were located in eastern Iran, so they were probably just a development of the Achaemenids' system of imperial control through forts. Not that their control had been total and ubiquitous. Even within Iran itself there were still tribespeople such as the Uxii (south-east of Susa) and Cossaeans (of the Zagros mountains bordering Media) whom the Achaemenids had never completely subjugated. These people treated their supposed masters on sufferance: for example, by demanding – and receiving – 'tribute' in the form of transit tolls from imperial armies that passed through their territory. Alexander attacked them vigorously, but he too failed to subdue them permanently. Nevertheless, stations or forts such as the Iranian and some of the central Asian Alexandrias could have served as nodal points in a far-flung supply and communications network.

Purely military installations have to be distinguished from true *polis* foundations, Greek-style cities with a full panoply of self-governing civic and civilian structures. Many kept the name of the nearest native village, and in both cases the settlers were always the same: Macedonian veterans, often physically disabled, and Greek mercenaries. However, some Alexandrias, including the first and queen of them all, Alexandria in (or rather 'by') Egypt, were not only founded as *poleis* but also sited with an eye to peaceful civilian trade for the long-term future. With trade comes culture, and Alexander is said in one instance to have founded cities so as to encourage a nomad hill-people of Iran to adopt a settled and peaceful existence. Here he was following in his father's footsteps. As Arrian made Alexander say of Philip and the Macedonians in his post-mutiny speech at Opis:

> *He made you city-dwellers. He civilized you through the establishment of good laws and practices.*

Whether Alexander consciously intended it or not, many such foundations did become centres of Hellenization. This is evident both archaeologically and linguistically.

*

JUST beyond the oasis town of Sheberghan in northern Afghanistan (then in Soviet Central Asia) a tell, or man-made mound, known locally as the Hill of Gold, yielded a remarkable series of burials to the spades of Soviet archaeologists in the winter of 1978–9. The burial mound lay in ancient Bactria, on the plain running south to the Hindu Kush and north to the banks of the Amu-Darya (the ancient Oxus). The finds were simply stunning: twenty-one thousand pieces of gold in six burial chambers. They are datable to the later part of the last millennium BCE and were deposited by Kushan nomads. The cultural mixture of native Asian and borrowed Greek is particularly significant. In one chamber there was a horse skull, in another the skull of a young woman with a silver coin in her mouth, the fare to pay to Charon the ferryman of the Greek underworld (Hades). On a gold scabbard, turquoise-winged dragons are depicted mauling leopards; alongside this was an image of the Greek Aphrodite, represented according to local Bactrian ideas of female pulchritude (stern and plump, with small, jutting breasts).

In purely organizational, administrative terms, though, Alexander's new Empire left only a slight legacy. It was his name rather than his ideas or his achievements that the extraordinarily able – and no less extraordinarily ambitious – Successor dynasts sought to appropriate and perpetuate. And it was forms of Greek culture – religious, literary, artistic (theatre, music) – that provided such unity as the post-Alexander Hellenistic world was able to achieve.

NINE

THE FINAL YEARS
(327–323 BCE)

There is a wheel on which the affairs of men revolve, and its movement forbids the same man to be always fortunate.

– Herodotus's *Histories*, ex-King Croesus of Lydia speaking to Cyrus the Great of Persia

L ATE in 327 Alexander's greatest 'adventure' began. He invaded and partially conquered what the Greek sources patriotically call 'India', though Alexander did not in fact carry his arms much beyond the Punjab. The old Persian Empire did once stretch as far east as the Indus. But it had long since ceased to before Alexander arrived on the scene. Now, he was striking out into new territory, both geographically and politically. Since he was dealing with peoples who were hostile not only to him but also to each other, he had to tread exceptionally warily. The information he derived from the scouts he regularly sent ahead to provide advance intelligence was, correspondingly, an absolute necessity.

It was an adventure, too, in the sense that Alexander apparently had no intention of stopping even at the old Persian frontier. Rather, he was consumed with a desire to proceed ever further into the unknown, perhaps even – though this cannot be stated with any certainty – as far as what he conceived to be the very edge of the known inhabited world. Once again, as in 335 in Greece, 332 at Tyre and 330–327 in central Asia, Alexander's military genius was to be tested to near-destruction. He found himself having to contend with war elephants, the monsoon, and the equally unfamiliar phenomenon of a great river with strong currents. Nevertheless, he would triumph, eventually, over all these obstacles. The ultimate irony was that the one obstacle even he failed to surmount was the opposition of his utterly weary rank-and-file Macedonian troops.

Winter quarters were established in Assacene (Swat and Buner). After the capture of Massaga and the mighty Rock of Aornus (today Bar-sar ib Pir-Sar), Alexander advanced to the Indus river. In early spring 326 he crossed the Indus and advanced to Taxila in the Punjab (whose extensive remains were excavated and published a generation or two ago). The local ruler, whom the Greek sources name Taxiles, became his adherent and military adjutant. Alexander's path was next barred at the River Hydaspes by Taxiles's local rival and enemy, the powerful Porus. Thanks to a piece of cunning, Alexander succeeded in throwing his troops across the river under Porus's nose, but it took more than just cunning to defeat his huge army, equipped as it was with tank-like elephants. As we saw in Chapter Seven, it was mainly Alexander's phalanx and light infantry that won the day. But he was sufficiently impressed by Porus's performance – and perhaps by his immense stature – that (in Arrian's words):

> he restored to Porus his sovereignty over his subjects, adding to his realm other territory of even greater extent.

From the Hydaspes Alexander moved on across the Acesines and the Hydraotes rivers to the banks of the Hyphasis (the modern Beas). Here (see Chapter Four), for perfectly understandable reasons, the ordinary troops at last declared they would go not one single step further east. Disenchanted with their leader's seemingly unquenchable thirst for further exploration and conquest, they in effect mutinied. The many years of horrendously tough marching and campaigning, the appallingly dispiriting monsoon rains, chronic homesickness and a heightened fear of the unknown had taken their heavy toll. Alexander reluctantly – very reluctantly, and perhaps also seething with rage at having a burning ambition thwarted – turned back again to the

Hydaspes, having suffered what the sources call the only defeat of his career.

After some months spent constructing a fleet for the journey to the mouth of the Indus, Alexander apparently vented his frustrations in a bloodstained progress through the native villages and towns. Among the Malli he very nearly incurred the retribution he perhaps deserved, when he received that almost-fatal wound in the chest. But by mid July 325 he had reached Pattala (perhaps the site of modern Hyderabad) in the delta. From there his boyhood friend Nearchus was instructed to take the fleet down to the Indian Ocean and then west along the Arabian Gulf. Alexander himself, meanwhile, chose to lead the now severely depleted and campaign-weary army by land through the Gedrosian desert, the modern Makran in Baluchistan.

Arrian quotes the aged Aristoboulus on the many fragrant and unusually tall myrrh trees they found growing here, and other diverting flora and fauna. But that was just a prelude.

> Alexander took a difficult route through the land of the Gedrosians. Supplies were often lacking, especially fresh water for the army. They were forced to cover much terrain by night and rather far inland, even though Alexander was keen to proceed along the coast to see what harbours there were and to make as many preparations for the fleet as possible.

But all his hopes and preparations came to nothing; as Arrian notes:

> The majority of Alexander historians say that all the sufferings that the army endured for him in Asia put together were not comparable to the miseries experienced here.

Whatever may have been Alexander's true motivation for this desert march (one thinks back to the similar question mark over his detour to the Siwah oasis), the outcome was in this case unequivocally disastrous. His group failed to make their prearranged rendezvous with Nearchus's fleet. Supplies ran low – and then ran out. Many thousands of his troops, and their accompanying women, died en route from heat and thirst. This was surely a major error of military and perhaps political judgement on Alexander's part.

Once back in civilization again, in Carmania in southern Iran, Alexander indulged himself – or rather, his troops – in a kind of prolonged Dionysiac revel. The reference to Dionysus, the wine god of ecstasy and transformation, is utterly deliberate. In India Alexander had consciously sought to rival – and surpass – him. This Carmanian rout was a necessary release of the pressure that had built up on his ordinary troops over the past years of ever more gruelling marching and campaigning. It was during these celebrations that the almost unrecognizably bedraggled figures of Nearchus and his sailors, having docked at Hormozeia (Hormuz), were eventually reunited with Alexander. Their journey had covered a thousand miles (sixteen hundred kilometres) in two months, and, unlike Alexander's by land, had been in its way a great triumph. Only one ship had been lost, and Nearchus had a fund of traveller's tales to last him a lifetime. Alexander characteristically made yet more ritual sacrifices of thanksgiving to the gods – to Poseidon, of course, but also to another of his special favourites, Heracles, besides Zeus the Saviour, Apollo and others. Nearchus then left Hormozeia to sail on round into the Arabian Gulf.

But besides these joyous demonstrations of relief and release Alexander also, probably, exhibited the kind of response to near-disaster that we have come to expect of him. He instituted what has been called (rightly, I think) a reign of terror. A number of generals and satraps, both orientals and Macedonian, were executed. A clear sign of these very troubled times was that a boyhood friend of his, the Macedonian Harpalus, decided this was the moment to abscond to Greece, once again. Perhaps he feared, with good reason, that he would suffer the same fate as those executed generals and satraps. For as we know, he was Grand Imperial Treasurer of the entire Empire, and not averse to spending imperial funds on his own personal –

though not always private – pleasures. He had indeed gone native to the extent of creating in Babylon a 'paradise', a Persian-style garden of delights. But his true objects of desire, apart from himself, were a couple of Greek mistresses, Pythionice and Glycera. After Pythionice's death he worshipped her as a semi-divine heroine figure.

Rather less romantic, and far more unacceptable to Alexander if true, is the suggestion that Harpalus coined in his own name at Babylon. This makes him look a lot more like a rival to Alexander, rather than just an embarrassment. At all events, some time early in 324 Harpalus took fright and fled to Greece. This time he sought sanctuary in Athens, a city known to be perpetually hostile to Alexander and his cause. He compounded his offence in Alexander's eyes by handing over officially to the Athenians a huge sum of money, which they used in 323 to fund a serious anti-Macedonian rising among the Greeks of the League of Corinth.

After dismissing Nearchus Alexander continued his progress further into Iran, by way of Pasargadae and Persepolis. Pasargadae, Cyrus the Great's original administrative capital, was also the site of his monumental tomb (Figure 37). To Alexander's rage he was informed that the tomb had been desecrated, allegedly by Magi (Median priests), and he ordered the architect (and writer) Aristoboulus to see to its restoration. The reason for his concern was the same that had motivated him constantly since his capture and public burial of Darius in 330: namely, the desire to conciliate the old Persian upper class and make himself seem a worthy and legitimate successor to the Achaemenid rulers, albeit as ruler of a new Empire and not just of the old one continued. Likewise, when he moved on from Pasargadae to Persepolis, the old Achaemenid ceremonial capital, where he had made the ambivalent but probably inevitable decision to destroy the palace complex back in 330. But again the rivalry motif raised its head. The satrap of the province of Persis, Orxines, was a man of Achaemenid stock, but, thanks to Alexander's favourite eunuch Bagoas, he was accused of exceeding the limits of his rightful power and acting as a personal warlord. He was condemned to death by crucifixion, without trial, and his place was taken by Peucestas.

In 324 another episode of symbolic interest occurred at Persepolis – another very public funeral. This was of the Brahman Calanus who had accompanied Alexander since meeting him at Taxila in early 326. According to Arrian, it was impossible to write a history of Alexander without including Calanus. This is Arrian's account of the event, derived in whole or in large part from Nearchus:

> Calanus's body had grown enfeebled in Persia, though he had never previously been ill. Yet he absolutely refused to live the life of an invalid and informed Alexander that he would be happy to make an end of his life before he experienced any distress that might compel him to alter his regular regimen. Alexander remonstrated with him at length, but when he saw that Calanus would not back down, but would make an end of himself in some other way if thwarted in his intent, he himself gave the order for a pyre to be built for him, in accordance with Calanus's instructions. He appointed Ptolemy son of Lagos, one of his personal bodyguards, to take charge of the proceedings. Alexander reportedly had a procession of horses and men organized; some fully armed, others carrying all kinds of incense to be added to the pyre. According to other reports, they bore both gold and silver goblets and royal vestments. Since Calanus was incapacitated by illness, a horse was made ready for him, but he was too weak even to ride, so was borne on a litter, bedecked with garlands in the customary Indian manner and chanting Indian songs . . . He then mounted the pyre and, in full sight of the whole army, lay down with all due decorum. Alexander did not think it seemly for a friend of his to be thus publicly on display. The rest of the onlookers marvelled that even as the flames consumed him Calanus remained completely motionless. As the fire was lit by those charged with the task, Nearchus

20. Mosaic, House of the Faun, Pompeii (Archaeological Museum, Naples)

Hellenistic-period mosaic recovered from under the volcanic ash at Pompeii in a very good state of preservation; the original artist – a painter – has caught Darius in direct eye contact with Alexander at the Battle of Issus, the moment before he flees and concedes defeat.

21. Silver decadrachm medallion, reverse (British Museum, London)

Alexander wearing a plumed helmet and mounted on Bucephalas charges against Porus, the Paurava Raja, presumably at the River Hydaspes battle in 326. Latest research suggests this was one of a small series of such medallions struck soon after to commemorate the great victory and to reward his troops for facing up to such fearsome war-elephants.

22. Silver decadrachm medallion, obverse (British Museum, London)

In the same series as Fig. 21, Alexander is depicted on a silver decadrachm (ten-drachma coin) in the guise of a 'King of Asia'. He is being crowned by Victory, a reference to the Hydaspes battle, and in his right hand carries a thunderbolt, normally the property of Zeus.

23. (RIGHT) Iron sarissa points, 'Tomb of Philip', Vergina (Archaeological Museum)

Blades such as these were pointed at or implanted in Macedon's foes by the Foot Companions, who wielded their over-5m-long sarissas with both hands.

24. (BELOW) Silver coin (British Museum, London)

On this near-contemporary silver coin Alexander is shown wearing the horns of Ammon, a brilliant pictorial image of the king's identification with, and as, an Egyptian cultural icon.

25. Bas relief, temple, Luxor

Alexander is depicted as Pharaoh paying homage to the native god Min. It is not certain whether he had himself crowned Pharaoh at Memphis, but an image like this proves he aimed to be worshipped as such.

26. (LEFT) Marble statue from Pella (Pella Museum)

Alexander is represented a little satirically or mischievously as the goaty god Pan in this Hellenistic-period masterpiece. Pan was the eponym of panic in battle.

28. (ABOVE) Marble head of Alexander, from Giannitsa (Pella Museum)

A local, and near-contemporary (end of fourth century), depiction: a chance find from near the Macedonian capital, Pella.

27. (BELOW) Paolo Veronese, *The Family of Darius before Alexander* (National Gallery, London)

Veronese famously depicts Sisygambis, the Persian Queen Mother, in captivity after the Battle of Issus and kneeling before Hephaestion, the taller figure whom she mistakes for Alexander. Alexander is courteously putting her right.

29. Votive relief (Archaeological Museum, Thessaloniki)

A votive relief dedicated 'to Hephaestion the hero' by one Diogenes. Alexander had reportedly wanted Hephaestion to be accorded divine status after his death, but Ammon had sanctioned only the lesser status of hero. This dedication shows that Hephaestion remained a local as well as an imperial hero.

30. Marble herm of Alexander, from Hadrian's Villa at Tivoli (Musée du Louvre, Paris)

So-called 'Azara bust', because obtained by the eighteenth-century Spanish ambassador Jose Nicolas Azara, who presented it to Napoleon. Modelled after an original by Lysippus, this herm-bust carries the following label: 'Alexander son of Philip, Macedonian'.

31. Silver coin of Ptolemy I, obverse (Fitzwilliam Museum, Cambridge)

Alexander is depicted on this coin of his Successor, Ptolemy I of Egypt, wearing an elephant-scalp headdress, recalling the adventurous Indian campaign of 326/5 in which both men had participated.

32. Marble statue (Musée du Louvre, Paris)

If Alexander could be represented even as Pan (Fig. 26), how much easier it was to represent him as the Roman god of War, Mars.

33. Illumination from the *Alexander Romance* (MS Bodl. 264, fol. 50r., Bodleian Library, Oxford)

The Hellenistic-period and later *Alexander Romance* took Alexander to all the places that he had perhaps wished to visit but was prevented by either time or the limits of technology. Here, in a fourteenth-century French illuminated manuscript, he descends to the floor of the ocean in a glass bathyscape.

34. Illumination from the *Alexander Romance*
(MS 651/1486, Musée Condé, Chantilly)

What goes down must go up: here is a fifteenth-century French illustration of Alexander aboard a flying machine – a basket drawn by mythical creatures called griffins.

35. Albrecht Altdorfer, *The Battle of Alexander* (Alte Pinakothek, Munich)

Painted in 1529 by a leading German Renaissance artist. The 'label' included as if floating in the sky tells viewers (among other things) that it shows a victory of Alexander after which Darius's mother, wife and children were captured – making certain the identification of the scene as the Battle of Issus. W. G. Sebald, the contemporary German novelist and poet, was moved to make mention of the painting in his poem *After Nature*.

36. Silver octodrachm of Ptolemy I (Jan Vinchon, Numismatist, Paris)

Ptolemy I (r. 305–285), founder of the Ptolemaic dynasty, had himself represented on large eight-drachma coins like these struck at his capital, Alexandria – a far cry from the commemorative and propagandistic images of Alexander that he also issued (Fig. 31).

37. Tomb of Cyrus the Great, Pasargadae

The founder of the Achaemenid Persian Empire, Cyrus II the Great, established his capital at Pasargadae and was buried there, in this relatively modest stepped tomb. Alexander heard in 324 that it had been robbed of everything except the sarcophagus and bed, and ordered Aristoboulus to see to its reverent restoration.

> *records, the trumpets sounded – just as Alexander had ordered –*
> *and the entire army roared the battle cry they habitually raised*
> *when advancing to engage. Even the elephants echoed the shrill*
> *war cry, in honour of Calanus.*

What a way to go. That detail of Alexander's alleged scruples about
the public display of a friend would ring a bit hollow later in the year,
as he buried Hephaestion with the maximum of publicity. But there is
no doubting his genuine respect for his stoical 'barbarian' companion
and the manner of his dying.

IN MARCH 324 Alexander's fleet and army were reunited again at
Susa in Elam. It was the right occasion, Alexander judged, for another
grand gesture to mark the next stage in the orientalization of his
Empire, and it was in the April that the famous mass wedding was
staged. Well over eighty of his officially designated personal Companions took Iranian wives. Alexander himself took two – or rather
two more, given that he was already married to Roxane. One was a
daughter of his defeated enemy Darius, whose son-in-law Alexander
now posthumously became. This was a dynastic marriage in the
strictest and fullest sense. The other wife was a daughter of Artaxerxes
III, who had been assassinated in a palace coup in 338. Simultaneously,
Alexander gave his blessing to the de facto unions of some ten
thousand of his ordinary troops with oriental women, and added a
monetary wedding gift. But there was nothing merely sentimental
about this gesture. His overriding aim, as we have seen, was to create
an Irano-Macedonian ruling class and to perpetuate his army of empire
by tapping the fertility of oriental women.

In June of 324, however, as in India nearly two years earlier,
Alexander transgressed the limits of his soldiers' tolerance. He had
taken his army north of Babylon to Opis, there to greet a specially
trained infantry force of no fewer than thirty thousand young Iranians

whom he tactlessly called 'the successors'. They had been recruited in 327 and trained up since then in the Macedonian fashion so that they could be seamlessly integrated into the ranks of the Macedonian infantry phalanx – from which Alexander now demobbed ten thousand as no longer fit for service. Hardly surprisingly, the rank and file did not relish being 'succeeded' in this seemingly brutal manner. Again they mutinied. But Alexander had taken their measure, and was ready for them this time. Indeed, it is entirely possible that they acted precisely as he had anticipated and even wished. He quite simply told them to go home.

Faced with this fait accompli, the troops backed down, sensibly enough, and Alexander was thus enabled to make yet one more grand gesture. All his Macedonian troops, he announced, were henceforth to be known by the honorific – Persian – title of 'Kinsmen'. But the gesture was a hollow one. Alexander had had his way, and at the sumptuous banquet of reconciliation he made explicit his overriding political objective for the future. He prayed that 'Persians and Macedonians might rule together in harmony as an imperial power'. This was a far cry from what some sentimentalists have interpreted as a profession of the brotherhood of man or the unity of all mankind. What about the Greeks, for example? Where did they fit into Alexander's scheme of things? For the most part, they did not, except as cultural models and, he hoped, loyal subjects.

Craterus, one of the four Macedonian marshals of Alexander's Empire, and himself a Susa bridegroom, was put in charge of the ten thousand or so demobbed veterans and sent back home to Macedon in 324. It is possible that with him went an unannounced brief to supersede Regent Antipater (a known opponent of Alexander's orientalization policies). Perhaps spontaneously, or perhaps at Alexander's behest, the Greek states of the League of Corinth now sent out sacred ambassadors to him as to a living god. They arrived in early summer of 323 in Babylon, where Alexander was holding court. His claims to godhead had been advanced on several fronts since the visit to

Ammon's oracle at Siwah in 331. Resistance had been demonstrated at Alexander's own court, but many Greek cities were prepared to concede that his superhuman achievements merited supernatural recognition. On the other hand, just as many had been deeply discountenanced by the imperial decree he had had promulgated to the thousands gathered at the Olympic Games in late summer 324. This required all Greek cities within the League of Corinth to receive back their exiles, in flagrant breach of the supposed charter of autonomy. Hereby were sown the seeds of the great Hellenic revolt known as the Lamian War (see Chapter Five) that broke out in 323 immediately after Alexander's untimely death.

IN RETROSPECT, the last year of Alexander's life has to be accounted a considerable anticlimax. It was shadowed above all by the loss of Hephaestion, his closest friend and by then Grand Vizier of the empire, who died at Ecbatana in about October 324. No amount of bloodstained campaigning, such as that against the unsubdued Iranian people, the Cossaeans, in the winter of 324/3, could compensate for the loss of his lifelong companion. Nothing daunted, it was while at an advanced stage of planning yet another major campaign, this time against the Arabs, that Alexander was taken ill at Babylon. On 10 June 323, he died there. Soon after his burial, various of his alleged projects, the so-called 'last plans' – many grandiose in the extreme – were published. Whether or not they were genuinely conceived by him in precisely those terms, they are at least not inconsistent with the larger-than-life scale and character of the schemes he took to completion (see Chapter Ten).

The suggestion, or accusation, that Alexander met his death by poison – a low-level dose of strychnine would fit with his reported symptoms – was in the circumstances almost inevitable. His secretariat even published a document, known as the *Ephemerides* ('Journals'), in order to refute it. But it cannot be dismissed out of hand. To some of the leading Macedonians, especially those who hoped to step into his shoes, there may have seemed no other way of halting the orientalizing megalomania of their now uncomfortably remote king. As for the fate of his corpse, this is one of the great – and still unsolved – mysteries of the ancient world. To begin with it was embalmed and kept in state at Babylon. Some two years later it was decided to repatriate it to Macedonia, for burial in the old royal burial ground at Aegae (Vergina). But en route there it was hijacked by the satrap of Egypt, Ptolemy, one of Alexander's boyhood companions and a fellow-student of Aristotle at Mieza, who had risen to become a marshal of Alexander's new Empire.

Ptolemy had the corpse entombed first at Memphis, the old capital of the Pharaohs, and possibly even in the stone sarcophagus that had once held the remains of the last king of independent Egypt, Nectanebo (or Nectanebis) II. (The *Alexander Romance*, which evolved in Egypt, fancifully makes Nectanebo Alexander's natural father – but that is another story.) Later, Ptolemy had the corpse transferred from Memphis to his own capital, Alexandria, where from 306 he ruled as king of Egypt. The splendid mausoleum and tomb were still visible in the time of Octavian, better known as Augustus, the first Roman emperor; and there are some later references implying that their whereabouts were still known. But since late antiquity, though local tradition confidently claims to know the true original site they have vanished without trace.

The Greeks had a saying 'Look to the end', meaning that only then can the true value of a life be determined. A final assessment of Alexander's extraordinary achievement during a reign of just under thirteen years is impossible to reach. All too clearly, his life was hugely incomplete and unfulfilled. His reputation remains as contradictory and controversial in death as it was in life. The negative view has been well expressed by Ernst Badian, an unusually acute and acerbic historian of Alexander: 'After fighting, scheming and murdering in pursuit of the secure tenure of absolute power, Alexander found himself at last on a lonely pinnacle over an abyss, with no use for his power and security unattainable.' Besides, the united Empire of east and west died with its thirty-two-year-old founder. None of Alexander's marshals, who fought so bitterly among themselves in a prolonged orgy of funeral games during the next twenty years and more, had any realistic hope or expectation of keeping it intact.

The positive view of Alexander is more compelling. He was one of the supreme fertilizing forces in history, in a key cultural respect. The dissemination of Greek culture in visual and verbal forms to non-Greeks had, of course, been going on for centuries and had recently been given a further boost by Philip. But Alexander so speeded up the process, and spread Hellenism so far and wide, that he made it virtually irreversible. It was thus ultimately thanks to him that the Hebrew Bible was translated into Greek at Egyptian Alexandria, and that St Paul, a Hellenized Jew from Tarsus in Cilicia, wrote in *koine*, common Greek, to convert the city-dwelling Gentiles of the eastern Roman Empire to his new religion of Christianity. He was exploiting a ready-made cultural catchment area so large that it could be regarded as ecumenical – or global, as we might now say.

An eloquent modern illustration of that formidable Hellenizing achievement is contained in these deceptively simple lines by the poet Constantine Cavafy of Egyptian Alexandria:

> *We: the Alexandrians, the Antiochenes,*
> *the Seleucians, and the numerous*
> *other Hellenes of Egypt and Syria,*
> *and those in Media, and those in Persia, and so many others.*
> *With their extended dominions,*
> *and the diverse endeavours toward judicious adaptations.*
> *And the Greek* koine *language –*
> *all the way in to Bactria we carried it, to the peoples of India.*

> – Cavafy, 'In the Year 200 BC'

As graphic in its way is the carved decoration on what is probably the tomb of the Phoenician Abdalonymus of Sidon (Figures 2, 8). Appointed ruler by Alexander in the late 330s, he remained loyal to him to the end. At his death his body was interred in a stone sarcophagus bearing scenes that would have gladdened his mentor and emperor's eye and heart. Two outstanding themes dominate, as they were intended to: war and hunting. The hunt – for Alexander – very properly continues in the afterlife.

TEN

ALEXANDER
THE MAN

THE SCENE of Alexander's recovery from the near-fatal wounding in India in 325, and his troops' fanatical reaction to it, prove that he was nothing if not extraordinary. But just what sort of a man was he, in so far as he *was* a man (and not a god or hero)? Was he the reasonable Alexander of Ulrich Wilcken? the gentlemanly and visionary Alexander of W. W. Tarn? the titanic and Führer-like Alexander of Fritz Schachermeyr? the homerically heroic Alexander of Robin Lane Fox? or the amoral and ruthlessly pragmatic Alexander of Ernst Badian and Brian Bosworth?* Or was he none of these, or something of all, or some, of them? *Faites vos jeux, mesdames et messieurs.*

Following Alexander's death at Babylon in early June 323, in the somewhat murky circumstances described in the last chapter, there was inevitably a period of confusion and uncertainty. Perdiccas, who had emerged as a marshal of the empire and one of the leading Macedonian power brokers, produced what he claimed were Alexander's very own drafts for his 'last plans' (the last that he would have been able to draw up, anyhow). These were written down allegedly in the *Hypomnemata*, or 'Notebooks', but the only preserved evidence for them is in Diodorus's far from wholly reliable *Library of History*. We cannot, therefore, be sure that any one item in the list of plans is accurate and authentic, though none of them is demonstrably a forgery.

There were, as reported by Diodorus, five main projects. The most important, politically and militarily, was one to construct a thousand warships for a campaign against Carthage (in modern Tunisia) and

---

* See the Bibliography for full details.

other inhabitants of the western Mediterranean (Libya, Sicily, Iberia). This campaign was, of course, to follow that against the Arabs of the Arabian peninsula, for which Alexander had already launched serious preparations before he died (or was killed). The other four major projects were, first, the erection of temples – three in Greece, three in Macedonia (including one to Zeus at Dium, the Macedonians' sacred city at the foot of Mount Olympus), and a particularly lavish one to Athena at Ilium (New Troy). Second, a gigantic pyre to be completed at enormous cost (ten to twelve talents?) at Babylon as a memorial to Hephaestion, who had died at Ecbatana in the winter of 324/3 and been buried there with astonishing ceremony. Third, a pyramid to be constructed in honour of Alexander's human father, Philip. Fourth, significant population movements, including a transfer of peoples between Europe and Asia, and, finally, the formation of cities out of separate villages by the process the Greeks called 'synoecism'.

Perdiccas, though, presented the supposed document to the army in order for the Macedonian soldiers to reject it as the sort of extreme projects they had been objecting to ever since their successful refusal to advance beyond the Hyphasis river in 325. In other words, even though the *Hypomnemata* may not have been drafted or dictated by Alexander, they contained projects that his soldiers believed he would or could have drafted. In their way, then, they can be said to bring us as close to Alexander the man, at a particular point in his career, as – in the absence of a truthful autobiography – it is possible for us to get.

Whatever we make of the authenticity or realism of these plans, Arrian's authorial comment at the start of the seventh and final book of the *Anabasis* is salutary:

> For my part I cannot determine with certainty what sort of plans Alexander had in mind, and I do not care to make guesses, but I can say one thing without fear of contradiction, and that is that none was small and petty, and he would not have stopped conquering even if he'd added Europe to Asia and the Britannic

> *Islands to Europe. On the contrary, he would have continued to*
> *seek beyond them for unknown lands, as it was ever his nature, if*
> *he had no rival, to strive to better the best.*

To 'seek . . . for unknown lands', 'to strive to better the best': Arrian was clearly on to something here. It may be possible to detect in spiritual terms a progression in Alexander's choice of rivals. He started with Achilles the Homeric hero, went on to Heracles the universal hero who becomes a god, and climaxed with Dionysus the universal god of wine, transformation and spiritual release. Perhaps all that was left was to compete with himself as a god presiding over a universal empire? That would certainly have been 'striving to better the best', a thoroughly modern version of the age-old Homeric aristocratic ideal.

Throughout Arrian's historical account the word *pothos* – meaning a craving, yearning, longing or powerful desire – recurs in connection with Alexander's more adventurous undertakings. Thus in 335 he has such a craving to land on the further side of the Danube. In 333 he has a craving to visit the palace of the long-dead Phrygian king Gordius and his son Midas and to loosen the knot with which the yoke of Gordius's funeral wagon was fixed to its pole. In 332 he has a craving to found a city at the Canobic mouth of the Nile, the city that was to become the most famous and influential of his several Alexandrias. In 332/1 he has a craving to visit the oracular shrine of Ammon in Libya. In winter 327/6 he has a craving to capture the mighty Rock of Aornus overlooking the River Indus. In 326 he has a craving to visit Mount Merus near Nysa not far south of Aornus. In 324 he has a craving to sail down the Euphrates and Tigris out into the Persian Gulf. In 323, finally, he has a craving to explore the Caspian Sea.

This is a somewhat heterogeneous list, and it cannot be proved that the *pothos* motif is original to Alexander himself (as opposed to Arrian or one of his sources). The temptation to identify the dreamy look in the eyes of statues alleged to represent Alexander as an aesthetic visualization of this *pothos* should therefore be resisted. Yet there does seem to be the common element of seeking to do or to see the unusual, the daunting, that which is beyond the normal ken of most ordinary mortals. And in three of the eight instances cited, Arrian explicitly links the *pothos* motif to the motif of rivalry with Heracles and/or Dionysus. This does not mean that there were not also perfectly good secular or humanly rational motives for the various actions. But it does suggest or hint that such motives were not found entirely satisfying by Alexander himself. Or at least that he sought to project a persona of which a *pothos* for the out-of-the-ordinary was an integral component. That, to me, is the framework within which Alexander seems to have wanted and expected his personality to be assessed; an essentially larger-than-life framework.

Much is usually made of Alexander's physical, genetic inheritance from his parents, Philip and Olympias. His personal courage, outstanding generalship, quickness of decision and intellectual perceptiveness are qualities he shared with and so perhaps inherited from his father. To his mother's genes are attributed his strong will and passionate nature, stronger and more passionate even than Philip's, and his religiosity. But all this is mere speculation, since we are told so little in the surviving sources about Alexander's early life. In fact, more or less all we know is contained in the first ten chapters of Plutarch's *Life of Alexander*, which deal with his first twenty years. Still, there are embedded in these few chapters one or two bits of evidence that may give some clues as to the future course of his development:

> Alexander seems actually to have despised the whole tribe of professional athletes. At any rate he founded a great many contests of other than athletic type: in tragic drama, in playing the *aulos* and lyre, in the recitation of poetry, in fighting with staves, and in various forms of hunting.

For all elite Macedonian men, the hunting of wild animals, especially the wild boar and the mountain lion, was more than just an excuse for an invigorating workout or a pleasant diversion from more serious pursuits. It was itself a deadly serious calling. It made a man of a Macedonian youth, in the full social as opposed to the merely physical sense. In order to wear a distinguishing sort of belt, in order to be able to recline rather than sit at the symposium (the semi-formal elite male drinking party), one had to have killed a man and a boar in fair and open combat. Alexander triumphantly passed these manhood tests – so triumphantly, indeed, that it was as a huntsman that he was represented in eye-catching central position on the fresco adorning the front of the tomb at Vergina that has plausibly been identified as that of his father Philip (see Figure 1). In choosing its iconographic repertoire, Alexander's known wishes would have been followed to the letter by the painter or painters.

Two famous hunting incidents became staple ingredients of Alexander lore. In one, the less creditable perhaps, he is saved by Craterus from a possibly fatal mauling by a lion in Syria. It is thought that this very scene is depicted in a beautiful pebble mosaic of the late fourth century from Pella (see Figure 3). In the other, Alexander is enraged when a close companion, Lysimachus (not to be confused with the tutor, below), interposes himself during a hunt near Maracanda (Samarkand in Uzbekistan) and dispatches the imposing lion that he had selected as his own kill. This is how the Roman author Curtius tells the story:

> In that part of the world there are no better indicators of the barbarians' wealth than the herds of fine animals that they enclose within spacious tracts of wooded grazing-land . . . Alexander entered one such wood . . . , and ordered that the animals be beaten from their lairs throughout the area. Among these was an unusually large lion which came charging forward to pounce on the king himself. Lysimachus . . . happened to be standing near by and started to aim his hunting spear at the beast. But Alexander pushed him aside, told him to get out of

the way, and added that he was as capable as Lysimachus of
dispatching a lion single-handed.

From all the evidence a consistent picture emerges of an Alexander passionately attached, almost addicted, to the thrills and spills of the chase. Butchering wild animals was by no means irrelevant to the career of a man moved on more than one occasion to treat 'untamed' human enemies, such as the Cossaeans in 324/3, with unrestrained savagery.

Plutarch tells us that a great number of teachers were appointed to supervise Alexander's upbringing, but that in overall charge was one Leonidas, a relative of Olympias from Greek Epirus. Leonidas is said to have been a stern disciplinarian, but that he was much more than this is indicated by his being referred to as Alexander's foster-father and mentor. 'Foster-father' is wholly appropriate, since his real father was away from home so often during Alexander's formative years that he is unlikely to have had the chance to develop any warmer or more intimate feelings for him than admiration and respect – unless we count jealousy as a warm and intimate feeling. Alexander's other main boyhood tutor, apparently his favourite, was another Greek, Lysimachus from Acarnania to the south of Epirus. Plutarch dismisses him loftily as 'neither an educated nor a cultivated man' and refers with disapproval to his trick of likening the trio of Philip, Alexander and himself to the heroic Homeric trinity of Peleus, Achilles and Chiron (the half-man, half-horse centaur who tutored Achilles in Thessaly). But Lysimachus would appear to have tapped into a rich vein of symbolism and romance here, one that Alexander himself would mine to near-exhaustion in later life.

For Alexander, Achilles does seem to have been a hero in our sense of that word. And though it is possible to push the idea too hard or too far, Alexander frequently does appear to have acted in accordance with the aristocratic–heroic values of Homer. We note, for example, right at the end of his life, the 'last plan' to build a temple for Athena at Ilium. This was Alexander's peculiar take on the general Greek notion of *philotimia*, or competitive seeking for honour and fame, that motivated figures in the public eye. Homer by himself, however, would have been an inadequate guide for a future king of Macedon, especially one who like Alexander was not naturally bookish. Besides the textual education provided by Leonidas and perhaps by Lysimachus, we must make full allowance for the education and self-education of Alexander outside the classroom, especially on the hunting field.

But not even a diet of Homer and hunting was considered wholesome enough by Philip for the prince who by the time he emerged into his teens was the only serious candidate for heir. So in about 343, when Alexander was thirteen or so, Philip decided to broaden his son's mind by appointing Aristotle his tutor. This choice reflects as well on Philip's discriminating judgement as it does on Aristotle's intellectual equipment. Philip might, after all, have selected Speusippus, Plato's nephew and chosen successor as head of the Academy at Athens, or Isocrates, founder of his own rhetorical school at Athens and a correspondent of Philip.

Aristotle was primarily a scientist, who specialized in zoology and botany, and there is no reason to doubt Alexander's genuinely scientific fascination with exotic flora and fauna, or the stories of his having specimens sent back from Asia to Aristotle at Athens (where he established his Lyceum institute for advanced study in the mid 330s). It was also Aristotle, so Plutarch believed, who did more than anyone to inspire the young prince's interest in the art of healing. But here Alexander typically combined a scientific approach with traditional piety. Among the countless local legends the religious traveller–scholar Pausanias picked up in the mid second century CE is one concerning Gortys in Arcadia. Here, he was told, Alexander had dedicated a breastplate and spear to Asclepius, the universal Greek hero–god of medicine. Alexander, who was so often wounded or otherwise in need of medical attention, might well have thought it worthwhile to secure Asclepius's favour, even in this remote shrine.

Aristotle is also said to have instructed Alexander in the principles of politics and ethics, as well as in more secret, esoteric doctrines. We may, though, doubt just how deeply the political–philosophical teachings of the master sank into the pupil's consciousness. Not even he could lure Alexander very far away from Homer or tame his overriding passion for the *Iliad*, whose practical utility was strictly limited. So, resignedly, Aristotle gifted Alexander with a text of the poem that he himself had annotated – it would have been a very long papyrus scroll, or rather set of scrolls. Alexander is said to have carried this *Iliad* with him on the expedition to Asia, where it became known as the 'casket copy'. For among Darius III's personal effects captured after the Battle of Issus in 333 was a golden casket, and it was in this that Alexander stored the precious Aristotle-annotated text. Indeed, he was so attached to it that at night he allegedly slept with it – and a dagger – under his pillow. But, despite this parade of book-learning, it is doubtful whether Alexander ever thought the stylus was mightier than the sword.

Aristotle's pedagogical patch was located at Mieza, to the west of Pella and Aegae, probably near modern Lefkadia, where a suitable site – including a couple of caves, handy for retreat from the frequent winter rains – has been identified. This was far enough from the court for Alexander to escape the immediate control of Philip, Olympias or his boyhood tutors, and yet near enough for him to be recalled at need. In 340 the need was such, and the education he had received deemed sufficiently effective, that he was summoned to assume the role of regent while Philip campaigned at his Empire's eastern limits.

Almost as interesting as the relationship between Alexander and Aristotle, and as pregnant with future possibility, were his bonds with his hand-picked fellow-pupils. These proved remarkably long-lasting and significant. As we have seen, far and away the most important was with the Macedonian Hephaestion, a rather colourless individual who basked in Alexander's reflected glory. He never – so far as we know – opposed Alexander's will on a major issue. Indeed, he was instrumental in arranging for his wishes to be carried out in such ticklish matters as the trial (and execution) of Philotas in 330, the abortive attempt in 327 to procure *proskynesis* routinely from Macedonian and Greek as well as Persian courtiers, and the successfully enforced mixed marriage ceremony at Susa in 324. Alexander came to regard Hephaestion, and even perhaps to refer to him, as his alter ego. Depending on one's view of Alexander, therefore, Hephaestion was either a mere cipher or a rather sinister henchman.

Almost certainly, at one or more stages (early adulthood, possibly, as well as adolescence) the love between them was physically expressed. Efforts to expunge all trace, or taint, of homosexuality from their relationship are in any case seriously misguided. There was no stigma attached to homoerotic relations as such in ancient Greece, and homosexual and heterosexual experiences were not felt to be either emotionally or socially incompatible. If, however, Hephaestion really was Alexander's 'catamite', as a recent biographer of Oscar Wilde has casually alleged, that would not have been something of which Hephaestion would have wished to boast.

Of much greater moment than the precise physical character of the Alexander–Hephaestion partnership was its affective significance for Alexander and his behaviour patterns. One of his 'last plans' was allegedly for the construction of a huge funeral monument for Hephaestion at Babylon: for Hephaestion the hero, more precisely. At the news of his death, which was brought on by excessive drinking of alcohol, Alexander had suffered a truly Homeric paroxysm of grief. This was assuaged only by the news that Ammon had approved the posthumous hero cult of Hephaestion. Although Alexander had apparently hoped that he could be worshipped as a god, publicly he declared himself satisfied with Ammon's decision. Perhaps the really sobering thought is that Hephaestion alone had been able to fill the well of the loneliness of Alexander's power.

Other pedagogical friendships contracted or strengthened under Aristotle's tutelage were equally lasting, if rather less earth-shatteringly important. An incident that occurred in 337, when Alexander was nineteen, brings this home particularly vividly. Philip in that year contracted his seventh and, as it proved, final marriage, to a woman who was the first of his wives to be a high-ranking noble Macedonian. The marriage carried obvious dynastic implications, most unwelcome to Alexander and perhaps above all to his mother. At the inevitably drunken and uninhibited wedding feast Alexander was drawn into a vicious public argument with the bride's uncle and guardian. This provoked his father into lunging at Alexander drunkenly with his sword but falling over before he could reach him. Wisely, Alexander left Macedonia with Olympias to allow time and space for both himself and Philip to cool off.

This exile did not satisfy the enraged Philip, however. He expelled five of Alexander's most intimate friends – apart, interestingly, from Hephaestion. Harpalus, Ptolemy, Nearchus, Erigyius and Laomedon were all from outside the old Macedonian nobility. Alexander's friendship with them shows that he was from the start an outsider and a 'loner', keen to create his own circle of loyal adherents. It is equally noticeable – and to his credit Arrian does notice it – that all five were subsequently raised by Alexander to important offices.

It was possibly just before his teens that Alexander acquired another intimate personal friend, the famous four-footed one. It is tempting, indeed, to say that the two greatest loves of Alexander's life were both dumb brutes. Hephaestion we have already considered. The four-footed friend, Bucephalas, was offered to Philip by a dealer who demanded the astronomical sum of thirteen silver talents (several largish individual fortunes), even though the highly strung animal was not yet broken. Philip was all for rejecting the offer, but at that moment, so legend has it, Alexander took a hand. He tamed the horse by turning him away from the sun's shadow and mounting him – and then had the shaming effrontery to offer to pay the thirteen talents himself. The pair were thereafter inseparable. The Roman emperor Caligula is said to have made a horse of his a consul; our good English king Richard III would allegedly have given his kingdom for such an equine. But Alexander went further even than they. Not only did he personally lead a magnificent funeral procession for his trusty steed after he had died in ripe old age. He actually named one of his city foundations after him.

Boys, men and a horse: what about the women in Alexander's life? Possibly, he did not place sex – that is, sexual activity with members of the opposite sex – very high in his scale of values. 'Sex and sleep', he is supposed to have remarked, 'alone make me conscious that I am mortal.' One knows, or thinks one knows, what he meant. Why he should have taken this attitude to heterosex we can only speculate. It is at least worth considering the hypothesis – graphically depicted by the novelist Mary Renault – that he was put off the act by the sight of his hirsute, battle-scarred, one-eyed father making violent love to his mother. Alternatively, as already suggested, Alexander – appropriately for one who modelled himself on the Greek heroes of the mythical past – may have suffered from a repressed Oedipus complex. This is of course unprovable, though his complaints about his mother's importunities, his willingness to be 'adopted' symbolically by the Carian Queen Ada, and the exaggerated respect he showed towards Darius III's captive mother after the Battle of Issus, do point to ambiguous feelings towards his real mother.

On the other hand, there is equally no proof that Alexander was impotent, or a preferred homosexual. There are his marriages to consider. His first, to Roxane in 327, undoubtedly produced a child (born posthumously, and known as Alexander IV). He then married both a daughter of Darius and a daughter of Artaxerxes III, as his contribution to the Susa mass weddings of 324, but these may have been purely formal affairs of state. Hardly a formality, if true, are his alleged liaison with Barsine, the widow of his opponent Memnon, and the child he is said to have fathered on her (rather startlingly named Heracles). It has even been suggested that he had a sexual relationship with Darius III's mother, not to mention with an Amazon queen.

So it would better fit the facts to say that Alexander for the most part abjured heterosex, indulging in it mainly for political, or/and procreative, purposes. An excellent article by E. J. Baynham addressing this aspect of his personality and career is wittily entitled 'Why didn't Alexander marry a nice Macedonian girl before leaving home?' The author answers, rightly I believe, in terms of factional politics at Alexander's court between 336 and 334 BCE. As we have seen, he rarely allowed sentiment to take precedence over prudence.

If sex did not thrill Alexander, religion certainly did. This facet of his character may well have been, in significant part, an inheritance from Olympias. In ancient Greek terms, Alexander was monumentally pious, verging on the superstitious. It was perhaps no mere coincidence that the Greek term meaning superstition, *deisidaimonia* (literally, a fear of demonic or supernatural phenomena), was coined in Alexander's own lifetime. And Aristotle's best pupil, Theophrastus, made the Superstitious Man one of his gallery of thirty shrewdly observed caricatures that together formed his famous and much-imitated *Characters*.

In order to discover or test the will of the gods or other supernatural powers, Alexander had with him constantly his own seer (*mantis*), Aristander. He came from Telmissus in a rough highland area of south-west Anatolia, a fertile breeding ground of diviners. No major undertaking would be embarked upon without consulting Aristander, and there were occasions when his interpretation of an alleged omen or portent was decisive, directly affecting Alexander's course of action.

For example, when in 334/3 a plot against his life was reported to Alexander, he was undecided as to whether to give it credence. Then, while he was taking a nap during the siege of Halicarnassus, a swallow perched on his head and refused to budge. When Aristander declared that this portended a friend's treachery, Alexander acted to have that friend killed. Perhaps, as often was the case with omens and oracles in ancient Greece, the consultant did what he or she wanted to do anyway. But the support provided by an authoritative interpreter was vital for the course of action to be undertaken.

Alternatively, Aristander might merely make comforting predictions that would not affect Alexander's behaviour one way or another. For instance, when he was in camp on the River Oxus in the upper satrapies of central Asia in spring 328, a spring of water and a spring of oil (a gush of petroleum) rose up near each other close by his tent. Aristander duly declared that the spring of oil – the first certain mention of petroleum in all ancient Greek literature, incidentally – portended difficulties to come followed by eventual victory. Again, there are occasions on record when Alexander disregarded Aristander's interpretations, only for them to be proven correct in the event. It is quite remarkable that even the normally sceptical Arrian seems to have been convinced that Aristander had something special going for him, whatever exactly that rationally indefinable something may have been.

Nor was Alexander just monumentally superstitious. There was also a powerful streak of the religious mystic in him. This comes out most clearly during his visit to the Siwah oasis in 332/1. After it, he regarded himself as not merely descended from Zeus but actually in some sense Zeus's son. Yet it is important to stress that it was with Ammon, a non-Greek god, rather than with Zeus that Alexander contracted what we might call a 'special relationship' of filiation. When he made his curious detour to Ammon's oracular shrine at Siwah, he asked a question of the god and – so he said – was given the answer his heart desired. The exact nature of this answer he never divulged. Plutarch's report that Alexander wrote to tell Olympias that on his return he would reveal certain prophecies to her alone has, alas, to be treated with extreme scepticism. Undoubtedly, though, Ammon thereafter occupied a special place in Alexander's heart – hence in 328 Cleitus the Black's fatal accusation that Alexander had disowned Philip in favour of Ammon. For this, and other unfortunate suggestions, Alexander instantly killed the man who had saved his life at the Granicus river.

Arrian's reporting of Alexander's attitude to Ammon is impressively discriminating. He accepts that Alexander did indeed come to believe that he was a quasi-natural or naturalized son of Ammon, yet he does not include Ammon among the ancestral gods to whom Alexander was habitually disposed to offer sacrifice. Thus in November 326 at the River Indus he poured 'a libation to Heracles his ancestor and to Ammon and to the other gods it was his custom to honour'. Later on, in 325, he 'offered sacrifice to those gods whom he liked to say Ammon had instructed him to honour' – perhaps a coded reference to instructions he had (he said) received in person from Ammon at Siwah. The clearest proof of Alexander's special attachment to this exotic god was his accepting Ammon's response that Hephaestion should be worshipped as a hero rather than a god.

For his ancient contemporaries Alexander was, like Hephaestion, a hero in the precise technical sense that after his death he was worshipped as such, privately, in Pella and doubtless elsewhere. But as we know, he also saw himself, famously or notoriously, as a Homeric hero in the mould of his alleged ancestor Achilles or, even better, of his alleged ancestor Heracles. For Heracles was both a Homeric-style hero, a super-achiever, and the son of a god (Zeus) and a mortal woman, who achieved the status of full divinity after accomplishing his famous twelve Labours. Alexander's heroic self-estimate has evoked widely varying reactions among historians and analysts both ancient and modern. Our current view of heroes, at any rate, is very different from that of Alexander and his contemporaries. For a view much closer to that of the ancients we would probably have to track back as far as Thomas Carlyle's nineteenth-century *Heroes and Hero-Worship*. But not even that Victorian paean can quite capture the full range and flavour of ancient hero worship.

Alexander's extreme reaction to the death of his best comrade raises the further issue of his character and its evolution. In ancient Greek a 'character' meant a stamp; it was something innate, not socially constructed. At most, a person's natural birth character might be somewhat restrained or modified by education and experience. Otherwise the events of a person's life served only to reveal what that aboriginal stamped-on character truly was underneath the surface. The ancient literary sources for Alexander are unanimous that, in so far as his character changed, it underwent a change for the worse during the eleven years of his campaigning and rule in Asia.

This view was echoed by the great eighteenth-century Scottish Enlightenment historian William Robertson, who in his *History of India* noted 'the wild sallies of passion, the indecent excesses of intemperance, and the ostentatious displays of vanity too frequent in the conduct of this extraordinary man'. But Robertson also very properly added that these features 'have so degraded his character, that the pre-eminence of his merit, either as a conqueror, a politician, or a legislator has seldom been justly estimated'. We historians today, in our quest for that just estimate, are less overtly moralistic than Robertson, but we are no less passionately committed, both for and against.

Among the 'anti' camp is Ian Worthington, who has argued that:

> the 'greatness' of Alexander must be questioned, and the
> historical Alexander divorced from the mythical, despite the cost
> to the legend.

To which the American historian of Alexander, Frank Holt, has replied:

> The danger now . . . is that the new orthodoxy a reprehensible
> Alexander beset by paranoia, megalomania, alcoholism, and
> violence – may gather a deleterious momentum of its own.

My own view falls somewhere between these two and takes account of Lord Acton's dictum that 'Power tends to corrupt, and absolute power corrupts absolutely.' On top of the hugely self-indulgent mourning for Hephaestion, the following episodes seem to bespeak a diminishing self-restraint: the campaign of blood against native Indians such as the Mallian people after the mutiny at the Hyphasis in 326; the unnecessary forced march through the Gedrosian desert; the reign of terror (if that is really what it was) on his return to Iran in 324; and his severe, even callous reaction to his Macedonians after the Opis mutiny. But on the whole, historically rather than moralistically speaking, my Alexander is something of a contradiction – a pragmatist with a streak of ruthlessness, but also an enthusiast with a streak of passionate romanticism.

The finely balanced judgement of the French historian Claude Mossé, one of the sagest historians of all things ancient Greek, offers a fitting conclusion:

> He was no doubt neither the political and military genius that some have described nor the sage who derived total self-control from Aristotle's teaching. Nor was he the drunkard incapable of mastering his temper, nor the 'savage' barbarian who razed Thebes and burned down Persepolis. He was a man of his times, no doubt affected by the contradictions implied by a Greek education, the extent of his conquests and the servility of part of his entourage. But perhaps, in the end, that is not what matters most. Should we not rather judge Alexander by his achievements and by the evolution of the empire that he conquered in just over one decade?

We surely should – but does Alexander's legacy (or legacies) permit us the luxury of objective and rational judgement (see Chapter Twelve)?

ELEVEN

THE DIVINITY OF
ALEXANDER

A LEXANDER was one of the first Greeks – though not quite the very first – to be worshipped as a god in his lifetime. This striking fact excites many questions. How did the idea of the deification of living mortals originate, and how did it fit within the context of Greek religion generally? Did Alexander consider himself to be actually and genuinely divine? Did he order his own deification? If so, why? Religion is, too, an area of life where his world view and the very nature of his personality were most deeply at stake. Indeed, it might even be claimed that intense religious belief was the mainspring of all or most of his most important activity. The precise nature of Alexander's religious belief and behaviour, apart from the question of his divinization, has therefore already been explored in detail for the light it can shed on Alexander the man. Paradoxically, the issue before us now – of Alexander as hero and god – may well bring us to an even deeper understanding of our subject's humanity.

There is probably nothing harder to grasp, for those of us brought up within a monotheistic tradition of religion and spirituality, than the mental world of paganism. Its two most important features were that religion – for which the Greeks had no one-word equivalent – was a matter of cult acts rather than of dogma, faith or belief; and that the whole world was full of gods. More specifically, the worship of a (pagan, pre-Christian) Greek god or goddess involved some or all of the following: a temple, a cult statue (*agalma*) and a sacred precinct (*temenos*); sacrifice (typically, and most distinctively, animal blood sacrifice) on an altar; athletic and/or musical games; and the singing of the paean (a hymn sung usually to the Olympian gods such as Apollo or Poseidon). A 'basic' and ubiquitous goddess like

Zeus's daughter Athena, for example, could be almost indefinitely multiplied by adding the appropriate epithets: thus, Athena of Craftsmanship, Athena of Wisdom, Athena the Virgin (Parthenos – hence the Parthenon on the Athenian acropolis), Athena the City-holder (as at Sparta), Athena of Lindos (or wherever), and so on. Though represented anthropomorphically, a god(dess) was not exactly a person in the human sense. She or he was, rather, an embodiment of certain powers and forces.

The anthropomorphic character of Greek divinities could cut more than one way. Their powers were immensely greater than those of mere mortals, and yet there could be no absolutely hard and fast dividing line between men and gods. It therefore came quite naturally to the ancient Greeks to envisage a kind of halfway status between gods and men. This was the status they allocated to semi-divine heroes, who could be of various kinds. At one extreme were those who had supposedly lived in the dim and distant past and were of divine parentage on one side. The classic case is Heracles, who is also a direct part of the Alexander story, as we have noted. At the other end of the spectrum were the wholly human beings of the historical era who were granted heroic status posthumously on account of their extraordinary lifetime achievements and benefactions: men such as the Spartan Brasidas. After his death in 422 at Amphipolis in the Chalcidice, which he had just liberated from Athenian control, Brasidas was awarded the status of founder–hero by the Amphipolitans and given the appropriate religious veneration. His worship thereby displaced the cult of the city's actual founder, an Athenian, even though it had been founded only fifteen years earlier. This is a particularly clear illustration of the interpenetration of secularly political and transcendently pious factors within traditional pagan Greek religion.

Heracles had a head start over Brasidas, since he was divine on his father Zeus's side and so a hero from birth. No less relevantly so far as Alexander was concerned, he had achieved the unique feat of passing from heroic to fully divine status. Thanks to his enormous labours of benefaction on earth, he had been formally received among the immortal gods on the peak of Mount Olympus, Greece's highest mountain, which lay at the southern border of Macedonia. But Brasidas's hero cult also has its twofold relevance to Alexander. First, it was the highest that a wholly mortal man without a scintilla of divine parentage or even ancestry could normally hope to achieve. Second, in under twenty years it would be another wholly mortal Spartan, Lysander, who unprecedentedly went one better. Admittedly, Lysander – like Alexander – could claim direct descent on his father's side from Heracles. Yet there had been no reason to expect that he, unlike all other Spartans who claimed descent from Heracles (including the two Spartan kings) before him, would achieve a form of divinity – and in his own lifetime too.

Lysander was the naval commander who brought the Atheno-Peloponnesian War (431–404) to a triumphant conclusion for his city. Sparta's reaction to Lysander personally in his hour of triumph was characteristically restrained. Not so that of the returned oligarchic (fiercely anti-democratic) exiles of the island–city of Samos just off the Anatolian coast, who saw no reason for restraint whatsoever. To honour and thank their very present helper and benefactor, in or after 404 they set up altars, sang paeans, and rededicated and renamed their main annual religious festival. Instead of the Heraea (in honour of the city's patron goddess Hera) this now became the Lysandrea, as an official inscription from Samos datable to about 400 BCE explicitly states.

There was nothing remotely blasphemous about Lysander's deification. The Greeks did have a notion of blasphemy (the word is itself Greek). And they did, as a general rule, try to separate the human sphere quite sharply from the divine. For example, it was a standard rebuke to overweening power figures to remind them to 'think mortal thoughts' – that is, remember they were human beings, not gods. But since Greek religion, as noted, was precisely political, it was for a Greek city to decide what religious honours were appropriate to whom. There was no pontifical academy or other vocational hierarchy of experts to rule on such an issue as a matter of doctrine or dogma. And the flattering epithet 'godlike', used to convey the highest possible praise, went all the way back to Homer.

It was not, therefore, such a huge step to deem a man worthy of honours 'equal to those appropriate to the gods'. But why, then, was Lysander the first? One factor is the very personal and political bond between him and the restored exiles, forged by his restoring them to power after a particularly sharp episode of factional bloodletting. But the little extra something that may have tipped the balance in favour of a lifetime divine cult rather than just extraordinary secular honours or posthumous heroization was probably Lysander's own outlook and personality – in a word, his charisma.

In 404 Lysander had commissioned a huge group of bronze statues to be erected at Delphi, oracular seat of the god Apollo and the holiest single space in all Greece. This was a monument to his, rather than just Sparta's, final victory over the Athenians, and Lysander was cleverly exploiting the fact that in ancient Greece statues carried a peculiar numinous charge. They were set up, too, in a most prominent position, at the entrance to the Sacred Way leading up to Apollo's temple. The group included statues of the dozen Olympian gods, honorific rather than strictly cultic in nature. Most importantly, there was a statue of Poseidon, lord of the sea, depicted in the act of crowning Lysander with a wreath of victory. Lysander, in other words, clearly believed that his deeds entitled him figuratively to a place among the gods. The Samian oligarchs took the hint: they translated Lysander's self-estimate into literal reality.

After Lysander there is a marked trend during the course of the fourth century towards monarchy and monarchist thinking throughout the Greek world. An increasing number of personal or constitutional sole rulers is attested, and to accompany or buttress their rule there are the inklings of a theory justifying monarchy as the regime of a just benefactor. There are hints, too, of a changing conception of the ruler's place in the world. Consider the case of Clearchus of Heraclea on the western shore of the Black Sea. A former pupil of both Plato and Isocrates at Athens, he identified himself externally with Zeus both in his clothes and in his deportment. Furthermore, he called one of his sons 'Thunderbolt' (Ceraunus) after Zeus's most famous attribute – thereby anticipating one of the post-Alexander dynastic monarchs of Egypt, Ptolemy Ceraunus.

Yet more immediately relevant to Alexander than either Lysander or Clearchus was the example of his own father, Philip. At Olympia, the second most sacred site in the Greek world after Delphi and the home of the Panhellenic Olympic Games, Philip commissioned the erection of a structure immodestly named after himself, the Philippeum. In shape it was round, what the Greeks called a *tholos* ('beehive'). This shape was typically associated with sacred rather than secular structures, such as – most obviously – the Tholos at Marmaria in Delphi, a little way down the mountain from the main cluster of sacred buildings. Within it, moreover, Philip commissioned to be erected a set of chryselephantine (gold and ivory) statues depicting himself and members of his immediate family, including Alexander. Again, gold and ivory were the materials typically reserved for divine cult statues, such as – most famously (it became listed as one of the Seven Wonders of the Ancient World) and relevantly – the colossal cult statue of Zeus at Olympia fashioned in the 430s by Phidias of Athens.

Even more conspicuously, at Aegae in 336, Philip somewhat echoed Lysander in having a statue representing himself (presumably honorific rather than cultic, though we can't be absolutely sure of that) carried in procession together with those of the Twelve Olympians. This was on the occasion of his daughter Cleopatra's wedding – and his own assassination. To those literary and archaeological hints that Philip claimed more than merely human status we can now add clinching inscriptional evidence from Philippi, the town in Chalcidian Thrace that he had named, or rather renamed, after himself. This reveals that Philip's own Macedonians were prepared to treat him as a living god. Here, then, we have to deal with yet another area in which Alexander had his father as a model both to emulate and, if at all humanly (or rather, superhumanly) possible, to surpass. This puts the deification of Alexander in his lifetime in an entirely new light, in a context of both continuity and change, of both pious tradition and rivalrous innovation.

Two further written contemporary sources have a direct bearing on the changing climate of ideas of deification within which Alexander was moving. First, there is the *Third Letter to Philip* composed – and presumably in some sense 'sent' – by Isocrates, the arch-conservative Athenian pedagogue, rhetorician and pamphleteer. In this open *Letter* Isocrates wrote that, if Philip was to succeed in what was known to be his cherished project of conquering Asia, there would be nothing left for him to do but become a god. A fair paraphrase of this obsequious rhetoric would go something like this: 'If you conquer Asia, you will by then have achieved the limit of what is humanly possible.' But whether or not Philip read, let alone acted on, this advice, Alexander might well have chosen to take the hint more literally.

Another Greek writer, intimately connected to the king, has also been read as providing incitement for Alexander to claim divinity. Aristotle wrote in his *Politics*, composed in the 330s and 320s, that the man who is king in the fullest sense (literally, 'all-king') is 'as a god among men', and that it would be as wrong for others to rule over him as it would be for humans to claim to rule over Zeus. True, Aristotle does not actually say that the man who is in the fullest sense a king *is* a god, but only that he is *like* a god among men. And this king of Aristotle's is clearly only a theoretical construct, inconceivable in reality. But these remarks could easily have been interpreted more literally than their author intended. Quite possibly, too, Alexander had had similar views expressed to him directly at an impressionable age, when Aristotle was tutoring him at Mieza in the late 340s.

*

THREE key episodes are crucial in considering the question of Alexander's divinity, and each is hotly disputed, both in the ancient and in the modern literature. The first is his visit to the Siwah oasis in Libya in the winter of 332/1; the second, the attempted imposition of the Persian custom of obeisance at Bactra in 327; and the third, the order allegedly issued by Alexander from Susa in 324 commanding the Greeks to deify him.

There are three main difficulties concerning the Siwah trip. First, why did he undertake this detour to consult Ammon's oracle at this juncture? Second, what exactly happened at the oracle? Third, what effect or effects did the visit have on his subsequent behaviour, in terms both of his self-perception and of his self-presentation? Unfortunately, there is such a massive source problem, perhaps the trickiest in all Alexander scholarship, that we cannot know what actually happened at the oracle with any degree of certainty.*

There must have been unusually powerful reasons prompting Alexander to undertake such a long and dangerous journey, given that it necessarily meant surrendering the strategic initiative to Darius and his commanders in the west. These reasons could have been more or less pragmatic and rational, or more or less romantic and symbolic. One of them, surely, was Alexander's general urge to rival and outstrip even the very best of his predecessors. In this case, the rival in question was most likely Heracles, the ultimate ancestor (barring only Zeus) of the Macedonian royal house. A quarter stater gold coin issued by Alexander's Amphipolis mint in about 330 and buried in a rich man's tomb at Derveni in Macedonia provides telling confirmation. On the obverse it bears the head of Athena. On the reverse is the inscription 'ALEXANDROU' ('Of Alexander'), accompanied by three divine symbols: a thunderbolt (for Zeus), a bow (for Apollo) and a club (for Heracles). These are the four gods who, the sources suggest, were the

---

* See Appendix, pp. 266–70.

most meaningful to Alexander at this stage of his campaigns – and of his spiritual odyssey.

Another motive was probably a desire to find out (more) about his parentage – that is, if we are entitled to extrapolate backwards from later evidence, to obtain a satisfactory account of the nature of his superhuman, possibly even divine, origins. However, the evidence for exactly what story of his parentage Alexander was told, or proclaimed he learned, at Siwah is conflicting. At all events, it is absolutely clear that after the Siwah visit Alexander claimed a close relationship, possibly even physical filiation, with non-Greek Ammon, not with a syncretistic or hybrid Zeus–Ammon. A silver coin issued in Thrace after Alexander's own lifetime depicts him wearing the horns of Ammon (see Figure 24). Ptolemy I of Egypt went one better and issued a coin showing him wearing not only Ammon's horns but also an elephant-scalp headdress in token of his great victory over Porus at the Hydaspes river in 326 (see Figure 31). Clinchingly, it was to Ammon at Siwah that Alexander sent in 324 when he wanted to discover the answer to the most sensitive issue of the moment – how precisely should the recently deceased Hephaestion be posthumously venerated: as a god, or as a hero?

For Greeks and Macedonians, a claim to be the son of a god, whether Ammon or Zeus, was not at all the same thing as claiming actually to be a god. Yet to judge from Macedonian jibes against Alexander concerning his 'so-called father' (meaning Philip), his propaganda was far from totally successful. It was interpreted as a slap in the face to his late, natural father. In sharp contrast, the Egyptians – whose god Ammon was – did not bat an eyelid, any more than did the so-called 'Hellenomemphites' (intermarried Greeks and Egyptians living at Memphis) such as the lady attested on a contemporary papyrus from Saqqara called 'Artemisia [Greek name] daughter of Amasis [Hellenized version of an Egyptian name]'. These Egyptians simply assumed that, as Alexander was now their Pharaoh (whether or not he went through the formality of an official coronation at Memphis), he was to be worshipped as a living god. And in one of those local regal manifestations he would have been worshipped as the son of Amon-Ra. This explains, for example, the bas-relief from the Temple at Luxor depicting Alexander as Pharaoh in the traditional act of doing homage to Min (see Figure 25).

This obeisance *by* Alexander at Luxor was, in its Egyptian context, uncontentious and unequivocal. But the attempt to secure obeisance *to* Alexander at Bactra (Balkh) in 327 was markedly different. As we saw in Chapter Eight, what the Greeks called *proskynesis* was, for the Persians, a social custom, an obligatory mark of outward homage or respect to be paid to a social superior – and so by all Persians, no matter how elevated their rank, to the Great King. It was not, in Persian eyes, a religious manifestation. And the Great King, even though he was the vicar on earth of the great god Ahura Mazda, was not in himself considered a sacred being like the Egyptian Pharaoh. For Greeks, on the other hand, and perhaps Macedonians too, *proskynesis* was precisely that – an exclusively religious act, an act of worship, to be performed solely towards the gods.

Alexander was thus in something of a bind. In order to maintain the proper homage of his Persian courtiers that was due to his status as a Great King equivalent, he simply had to receive *proskynesis* from them. But to request it from, or impose it upon, his Macedonian and Greek courtiers would run the risk of an accusation that he was confusing the divine and the secular, and overstepping the limits of the human. This in turn would risk the wrath of the jealous gods. Yet Alexander decided that he did indeed wish to receive *proskynesis* from his Macedonian and Greek courtiers. This was in pursuance – as I have argued in Chapter Eight – of his orientalization policy, according to which a new elite of Persians together with Macedonians and Greeks was to be forged to rule the Empire jointly.

Perhaps, though, there was more to his request for *proskynesis* than a practical concern to oil the wheels of imperial administration. Given that the gesture for them did not carry implications of divinity, the position of the Persians would not be affected. But perhaps it was really a rather sneaky way of getting his own divinity tacitly acknowledged by the Greeks and Macedonians as well as by the Egyptians. This inference is not out of the question, as suggested earlier, although in 327 Alexander did not yet strictly need to concern himself with the political issue of establishing a theocratic basis for ruling over Greeks, Macedonians and Persians alike.

At any rate, it does seem that Callisthenes led the objection to Hephaestion's championing of *proskynesis* precisely on the ground that to perform it would have been, for him as a Greek, tantamount to recognizing Alexander as a living god. His real reason, of course, may have been that he did not wish to countenance the parity of esteem it would imply between Greek and Macedonian courtiers, on the one hand, and Persian courtiers, on the other, since that would mean a downgrading of the former's status to the benefit of the latter group. In either case, we cannot point with certainty to the obeisance episode at Bactra as unambiguous evidence of either a significant change in Alexander's perception of himself or a desire to be and worshipped by Macedonians and Greeks as a living god.

Precisely such a desire has been widely inferred, reasonably enough, from the order for his own deification that Alexander is supposed to have sent from Susa in 324. But the evidence for this order is admittedly not of the best. Only two ancient sources specifically mention it, and both are anecdotal and unreliable. Besides, divine pretensions in the ancient Greek (and Roman) world were often treated as a heaven-sent opportunity for a witty epigram. According to Plutarch, an otherwise unknown Spartan, Damis (possibly a mistranscription of 'Eudamidas' – that is, King Eudamidas I), said: 'We concede to Alexander that, if he so wishes, he may be called a god.' The very humour of the apophthegm requires that Alexander had sent an order to Sparta, but if the apophthegm is merely an invention, so too would be the alleged order. The other source is Aelian, a second-century CE Greek compiler of a *Varied History*, whose reliability is as various as his subject matter. In short, there is no unimpeachable positive evidence that Alexander ever ordered his own deification from anybody.

But can it be inferred that he did so, either indirectly from other evidence or from other general considerations affecting his overall position as supreme ruler? One passage does indeed suggest this; it comes from the seventh book of Arrian's *Anabasis* and relates to Alexander after his return to Babylon in summer 323:

> *successive official delegations from Greece also presented*
> *themselves, and the delegates, wearing ceremonial wreaths,*
> *solemnly approached Alexander and placed golden chaplets on*
> *his head, as if their crowning were a ritual in honour of a god.*

Arrian's language here is barbed: by writing 'as if' he may be implying that he, for one, was not convinced that Alexander had really become a god. He then virtually spells out this implication by adding: 'But, for all that, his end was near.' Gods, true gods, do not die; they are, by definition, immortal (*a-thanatos*, free from death). Yet Arrian, the accurate reporter of his sources, does not deny that the delegates were performing divine worship.

Strictly speaking, however, this does not prove that Alexander ordered his own deification, only that these Greeks were prepared to grant it. Nor, by any means, were they the only ones. Almost certainly, the Greeks of Asia – those whom Alexander had claimed to have come to liberate from Persian despotism – were also worshipping him as a god in his lifetime, and probably had been for several years already, before 323. The reasons in their case were precisely the same as those behind the divine worship granted to Lysander on Samos and, with added nationalistic considerations, to Philip at Philippi: a recognition of the honorand's supreme power coupled with a plea for his continued beneficence.

But not all the Greeks of old Greece shared their Asiatic cousins' positive motivation. Some indeed, like Athens and Sparta, had good reasons for not thinking of Alexander primarily – or indeed at all – as their benefactor. They had been more or less forcibly enrolled in the League of Corinth, either by Philip in 338 or under Alexander some years later, and the autonomy they had supposedly been guaranteed on oath had in practice been violated by Alexander. This, ultimately, is what makes me think that he probably did have to order his own deification by the Greeks of old Greece. This would also have brought them into line with most of the rest of his new Empire, the centre of gravity of which now lay far to the east of the Aegean. In all cases, though, the deification was equally and essentially a political rather than a spiritual manifestation and recognition.

If we grant, then, that Alexander did indeed order his own deification, the last question before us is why (apart from considerations of imperial harmonization) did he do so? Did he have other than political motives and goals? By 324 Alexander was master of the old Persian Empire and more, as well as being suzerain of Greece and the Aegean islands. He had, without question, begun to act more autocratically, even despotically. He had progressed, or at any rate changed, spiritually too, but in what direction? According to an intriguing suggestion of the late Austrian scholar Fritz Schachermeyr (who presented Alexander overall as a titanic, Führer-like figure), his spiritual progression can be measured in terms of his choices of ancestral heroes and gods to emulate or surpass at successive stages in his career. First, there was Achilles – that took him up to the first phase of Asiatic conquest, including the symbolic visit with Hephaestion to Troy. Then, before and after the Battle of Gaugamela, he took on Heracles, until it came to the invasion of India beyond the Achaemenid frontier, where Dionysus finally came into play. After successfully meeting all these challenges, and surpassing even these most powerful of gods, there was no one left, human, heroic or even divine, for Alexander to compete with. And therefore, Schachermeyr suggested, the way was clear for Alexander himself to become a god and be worshipped as such.

Perhaps so. Certainly the way had been well prepared. The visit to Ammon, the divine filiation, the flattering representations of Alexander on coins and medallions and in paintings with the attributes of Zeus, Heracles, Ammon and so on – all these pointed him in the direction of thinking of himself as more than merely human. Given his near-invincibility, such a thought was not in itself a sign merely of megalomania. Finally, one further, less idealistic and more deeply personal motive can be posited: the desire to exceed his father Philip's achievements and thereby to prove himself ultimately to his father's ghost.

THE DIVINE worship of Alexander in his lifetime would have been, on this reading, a happy coincidence of demand and supply. Odd though it may seem to us, it is also one of the greatest and most lasting of his successes. Alexander's posthumous cult has proved remarkably supple and durable. Unlike Lenin or Mao who, within formally atheistic state ideologies, were granted virtually divine status both during their lifetimes and for some time after their deaths, the cult of Alexander has had an immensely long run and, indeed, in some sense continues to this day. In Hellenistic Pella, the Macedonian capital, he could be depicted rather skittishly in marble, assimilated to the great god Pan – part man, part beast, all feisty sexuality (see Figure 26). Much later, he found his way, as a saint, into the Christian calendar of Coptic Egypt, and even later, as a prophet, into the Koran. But one of the most elevating images of him is to be found much further north and west: on a romanesque capital within Basle Cathedral, where he is shown ascending to heaven. This was a Christian reworking of an earlier, pagan representation developed in the fabulously fictional *Alexander Romance*, which we shall be looking at again in the next and final chapter.

TWELVE

THE LEGENDS
AND LEGACIES OF
ALEXANDER

The torch Alexander lit for long only smouldered; perhaps it still only smoulders to-day; but it never has been, and never can be, quite put out.

– W. W. Tarn, *Alexander the Great*

WALT WHITMAN, in his famously original poem sequence *Song of Myself*, sang that he was 'an acme of things accomplish'd', an 'encloser of things to be', and that he 'contain[ed] multitudes'. The same might equally be said of the career of Alexander the Great – as the actor Colin Farrell, who plays Alexander in Oliver Stone's feature film, rather nicely put it:

> *Everything is in it. There's greed, there's jealousy, there's love, there's pain, there's hope, there's desperation, there's pride, there's friendship, there's betrayal. It's an amazing, amazing story. There's so much in it – it's so dense that it nearly reads like bad fiction.*

There is no doubt that Alexander accomplished an extraordinary amount in his lifetime. But he also spawned multiple posthumous legacies that resonate to this day, including some not at all bad fiction. Here we are dealing not with the real Alexander – Alexander the man or god – but with Alexander the immortal hero of legend and folklore.

For getting a flavour of his multifarious heritage it would be hard to beat Diana Spencer's book, *The Roman Alexander. Reading a Cultural Myth*. The jacket comes adorned with an image of Andy

Warhol's Alexander series, which he did in the same mass-produced mode as his Marilyn Monroe series. Warhol, notoriously, claimed that in the modern world everyone would be famous for fifteen minutes. Spencer's index entry under 'Alexander–III of Macedon–the Great' confirms that Alexander has enjoyed many more than that. Here he appears as, among many things, 'Christian emblem', 'exemplar for British imperialism', 'exemplar for Roman imperialists', 'humanist Renaissance man', 'paragon of Hellenism in Second Sophistic [period]', 'Stoic cautionary tale', 'flower of chivalry', 'model for Kennedy presidency' and 'model for Lawrence of Arabia'. But not even Spencer's capacious index can find a place for Andrew Ducrow, the most famous of all early circus performers in Victorian England, who specialized in such 'hippodramatic' re-enactments as Alexander taming Bucephalas.

While Alexander's posthumous presence is ubiquitous, there are five areas of particular influence and contention. There was a politico-ethnic issue in his own day as to whether or not he counted, wholly or in part, as 'Greek' under the act. This aspect of his legacy exploded again very recently, in the early 1990s, with the dissolution of the former Yugoslavia and the establishment, on part of its ruins, of a new state: the Former Yugoslav Republic of Macedonia, but known unofficially (by its government) as just 'Macedonia'. This name is shared with the province of Macedonia within the contemporary Hellenic Republic, which was once part of the ancient Macedonia. The new, putative Macedonians compounded their heinous – in official and unofficial Greek eyes – offence by appropriating major symbols drawn from their namesake. For example, the (originally Venetian or Turkish) iconic White Tower of Thessaloniki, a city founded soon after Alexander's death, was pressed into iconic service, as was the sixteen-pointed star that appears conspicuously on the gold coffin found in the 'Tomb of Philip' at Vergina (see Figure 18).

The Greeks on their side responded in kind. A coin of the old drachma currency (superseded by the euro) showed on its obverse a head of Alexander. Here, as on near-contemporary ancient coins (see

Figure 24), he was depicted wearing the sacred horns of Ammon, and his image was accompanied by the superscriptions '*Megas Alexandros*' (Alexander the Great) and '*Basileus Makedonôn*' ('King of the Macedonians'). On the reverse was that very same sixteen-pointed sunburst, or star, accompanied by two more speaking legends: '*Ellênikê Dêmokratia*' ('Hellenic Democracy/Republic') and '*Vergina*'.

Here was just a modern variation on a very ancient theme – the use of coins as political propaganda. But whereas in antiquity coins were generally made of precious metals of high value, modern coins are cheaply struck from debased and composite materials and achieve a far wider circulation – or currency. The drachma coins, moreover, were only one of the media used by the Greek governmental agencies to promote their Hellenist message. For, as the American anthropologist Loring Danforth has rightly observed, 'From the Greek perspective Alexander is one of the most powerful symbols of the Greekness of Macedonia, both ancient and modern.' And relatively simple representations like this are believed to have a far wider and more immediate appeal than any more historically nuanced image, such as that of Alexander as (to quote Danforth again) 'the founder of a multiethnic empire inspired by dreams of different groups of people living peacefully together'.

Other no less politically potent legacies of Alexander include his inspiration to a motley crew of ancient kings, would-be kings and imperial generals. All borrowed some or all of Alexander's powers and symbolic attributes to bolster their own claims to unswerving devotion and submission. Ptolemy I (see Figure 36) and his fellow-Successors of Alexander, who ruled as dynastic kings over Egypt and other large territorial states in the post-Alexander Middle East, were one obvious group of imitators. Ptolemy, of course, had the added advantages – and disadvantages – of having known his model and exemplar very intimately. It was Ptolemy who inaugurated the widely imitated practice of issuing 'Alexanders', commemorative coins depicting Alexander with one or other distinguishing attribute – such as the ram's horns of

Ammon (particularly appropriate in an Egyptian context) or an elephant's scalp (to symbolize his famous victory over Porus the Indian rajah; see Figure 31).

In the very different circumstances of the death throes of the Roman Republic two centuries later, Pompey (Cnaeus Pompeius) was officially granted a Triumph in the late 80s BCE for his role in suppressing supposed enemies of the Roman state (in fact, factional rivals for supreme power). He thereafter added '*Magnus*' (the Great) to his two other names, as his cognomen or official distinguishing nickname. The allusion to Alexander was unmistakable. Pompey was then still a very young man, in his twenties, and he hoped to exploit the cachet of the dashing Macedonian world conqueror as an aid in his bid for supremacy within the imperial world of the Roman Republic. He very nearly succeeded, too – but found himself up against another Alexander-worshipper, one Caius Julius Caesar (with whose life, and *Life*, Plutarch paralleled those of Alexander).

It was only a matter of time before the bellicose and divinized Alexander was depicted for a Roman viewing public as Mars, the god of war, himself (see Figure 32). However, as is clear from our surviving Alexander histories of the Roman period (Trogus/Justin's, Diodorus's, Curtius's, Arrian's), the figure of Alexander was not an entirely unambiguous or uncontested one in either republican or imperial (post-Augustus) Rome. One of the standard questions set for practice in the Roman schools of rhetoric was 'Should Alexander the Great sail the Ocean?' This had no immediately burning political or military significance in itself. But it did implicitly touch on the issue of the overweening ambition of tyrants; and that might be as contemporary as anything.

In much later ages, both medieval and modern, powerful autocrats – tyrants to some – were conspicuously to fall under, and try to exploit, the spell of Alexander. For example, Charlemagne, who was crowned Holy Roman Emperor at Aachen on Christmas Day 800, betrays his debt to Alexander by his very name (in its French form) –

a compound of 'Charles' and *Magnus*. But for Alexander worship in post-antique times no one can come close to Napoleon Bonaparte. His official court painter Jacques-Louis David, well schooled in the classical tradition, knew that Alexander was the ultimate ancient reference point for a would-be world conqueror with a mission to remake that world in his own image. Napoleon on his rearing horse would instantly convey subliminal associations with Alexander and Bucephalas. Compare and contrast David's famous – and unofficial – portrait of Leonidas the Spartan king at Thermopylae (now in the Louvre): Napoleon simply could not understand why the painter had wasted so much of his valuable time on preparing this massive painting of such a failure.

In antiquity, visual imagery of Alexander achieved an enormously wide dissemination. He himself had allegedly 'authorized' only one sculptural image-maker, the Greek Lysippus – rather as he had authorized a single official historian, Callisthenes, and a single painter, Apelles. All subsequent versions of Alexander's facial image, and the 'Alexanderizing' images of other kings and commanders, were therefore somehow indebted to the prolific Lysippus's models (see Figure 30). The leonine hair, the tilted head, the upturned gaze: these were Alexander's – or rather Lysippus's – 'signature'. Copies of this and other images were produced in profusion for the purpose of creating suitably charismatic portraits of the kings and generals who wished to bask by reflected association in Alexander's aura.

One particularly fascinating Hellenistic-period icon of Alexander stood on a hill overlooking the city of Rhodes. The Colossus of Rhodes, nearly one hundred feet (over thirty metres) tall, was fashioned in bronze according to the design of Chares, a sculptor from Lindos on that same island. It was funded publicly by the city of Rhodes's selling off of surplus equipment left behind by Demetrius Poliorcetes ('the Besieger') after his failed siege in 305. The statue represented Helios, the sun god, who appeared also as the effigy adorning the city's exceptionally beautiful silver and gold coinage.

Coins of that series survive, and the head type chosen bears a striking resemblance to Alexander's. So too, it is thought, did the face of Helios atop the Colossus, which alas has failed to survive. Since Chares was a pupil of Lysippus, the suggestion is by no means implausible. If true, Alexander's gleaming facial features will have adorned one of the canonical Seven Wonders of the Ancient World.

In medieval times, representations of Alexander and/or his exploits multiplied prodigiously, in manuscript illumination, in stone carvings and in other media. Among the latter I single out invidiously a remarkable twelfth-century mosaic adorning the floor of Otranto Cathedral in the heel of Italy. Constructed from polychrome tesserae made of the local limestone and looking a bit like a richly embroidered prayer rug, it covers the nave and aisles almost up to the apse. The mosaic's theme is the Tree of Life, with 'life' being interpreted very liberally indeed, from the Christian point of view. For though it begins predictably enough with Adam and Eve from Genesis, it branches out fantastically thereafter to include not only the Jewish King Solomon but even the entirely non-biblical and indeed pagan hero, Alexander the Great.

Not everyone, though, has been equally enamoured of Alexander's image. One sober modern historian (Ian Worthington) is indeed so far proof against its charms that, relying mainly on Plutarch, he has described Alexander's appearance in the following highly unflattering terms:

> *He did not have the looks of a model: his neck inclined to the left so his face appeared lop-sided and his eyes were watery . . . he had a round chin, a long, thin nose, and his forehead bulged above the eyes . . . His skin was marred by patches of red on his face and chest . . . no doubt due to his excessive consumption of alcohol.*

There's no accounting for taste, clearly – but Worthington also takes a generally less than rosy view of Alexander's overall greatness, as we saw in Chapter Ten.

Another ancient visual image of Alexander with a remarkably long and colourful afterlife was the original Hellenistic-period painting after which the so-called Alexander Mosaic in the House of the Faun at Pompeii was created. This depicted imaginatively the face-to-face encounter between Alexander and Darius III at the Battle of Issus. The artist chose to portray the antagonists at the very moment that Darius was about to flee the battlefield in ignominy (see this book's jacket). A very much later pictorial representation of that battle takes us on almost nineteen centuries, from 333 BCE to CE 1529, when the German Renaissance master painter Albrecht Altdorfer devoted a large canvas to the subject (see Figure 35). Four and a half centuries further on, in 1988, another German master – the late novelist and poet W. G. Sebald – vividly described Altdorfer's painting in his long autobiographical poem *After Nature*. Here (in the English translation by Michael Hamburger) the poet–narrator 'dreamed that to see Alexander's battle/ I flew all the way to/ Munich . . .' – where Altdorfer's oil painting hangs, in the Alte Pinakothek.

In another literary tradition, an ancient one, Alexander himself became literally a caster of spells, a practitioner of magic. This was just one of the many guises in which the ever-questing Alexander was depicted in the *Alexander Romance*. Offering a hugely inflated and highly romantic literary vision of Alexander, this text probably had its origins as early as the third century BCE in Alexandria, but it was first given consolidated literary form only at the end of the first millennium BCE and beginning of the first CE, again probably in Alexandria. From there the original Greek version radiated out through the Middle East and became sufficiently established and popular to be translated much later into Armenian. Likewise, for distribution in what was then the western half of the Roman Empire, a version was circulated in Latin.

We have today modern versions of all major traditions of the *Romance*: the Greek, the Armenian and the Latin. Here is a passage from the Greek version (Chapter 14, in Richard Stoneman's excellent translation), which contains some major historical surprises:

*Alexander, meanwhile, was growing up, and when he was twelve
years old he accompanied his father to a review of the troops.
He wore armour, marched with the troops and leapt on to the
horses, prompting this remark from Philip: 'Alexander, child, I
love your character and your nobility, but not your appearance,
because you in no way resemble me.' All this was very irksome to
Olympias. She called Nectanebo to her and said, 'Find out what
Philip's intentions are concerning me.' Alexander was sitting by
them, and when Nectanebo took his tables and examined the
heavens, he said, 'Father, what you call the stars, are they not the
ones in heaven?' 'Of course, my child,' replied the wizard. 'Can I
not learn them?' asked Alexander. 'Yes, child,' came the reply,
'when evening comes, you can.' That evening, Nectanebo took
Alexander outside the city to a deserted place, where he looked
up into the sky and showed Alexander the stars of heaven. But
Alexander, seizing him by the hand, led him into a deep pit and
pushed him in. Nectanebo wounded his neck severely in the fall,
and cried out, 'Dear me, child Alexander, what possessed you to
do that?' 'Blame yourself, mathematician,' Alexander replied.
'Why, child?' 'Because, although you do not understand earthly
matters, you investigate those of heaven.' Then Nectanebo said,
'Child, I am fearfully wounded. But no mortal can overcome
destiny.' 'What do you mean?' asked Alexander. 'I myself',
replied Nectanebo, 'have read my own fate, that I was doomed to
be destroyed by my own child. And I have not escaped my fate,
but have been killed by you.' 'Am I then your son?' asked
Alexander. Then Nectanebo told him the whole story of his
kingdom in Egypt and his flight from there, his arrival in Pella
and his visit to Olympias to cast her horoscope, and how he
came to her disguised as the god Ammon and made love to her.
With these words, he breathed his last.*

We are already familiar, of course, with the idea of Alexander
having more than one father (or more than one type of father,

anyhow). But no seriously historical account had ever come anywhere near to even hinting what the *Romance* states here as a fact, that Alexander's real father was Nectanebo (or Nectanebis), the last Pharaoh of free Egypt. Stranger than fiction, indeed; though the purpose of the fiction is transparent enough. It is to provide both for native Egyptians and for Egyptians of Greek or Macedonian descent some direct political continuity between pre-conquest, native Pharaonic Egypt and the Egypt of the Graeco-Macedonian Alexander and his Ptolemaic Successors, cutting from the story altogether the period of Achaemenid occupation. A possible real source of this confusion, or confection, might be found in the tantalizing suggestion that Alexander's corpse spent some of its time at Alexandria in the coffin of Nectanebo. But that might be to dignify it overmuch.

It is thanks also to the *Alexander Romance* that Alexander achieved feats of fictional travel to which not even his own highly developed and better authenticated *pothos* could have aspired. In the *Romance* he both went up to heaven in some sort of basket (see Figure 34), and down, in a glass bathyscaphe, to the very bottom of the sea (Figure 33). A non-*Romance* story, but fabricated within the same sort of genre of fabulous tale, at least rivalled this: here Alexander is embarked upon a journey to Paradise, in a way aptly enough, since 'paradise' is in origin a Persian word. The latter story is included by Richard Stoneman in an appropriately marvellous collection of *Legends of Alexander the Great*, together with other such heterogeneous and heteroclite texts as a supposed 'Letter of Alexander' to Aristotle about India, and a supposed 'Letter of Pharasmanes' to the Roman emperor Hadrian (r. CE 117–38) on the Wonders of the East.

The modern equivalents of the ancient *Alexander Romance* and the ancient visual representations are, respectively, historical novels and feature films. Legion are the novels about Alexander, ranging in theme and tone from a deeply serious representation of him as a closet homosexual by Klaus Mann (son of Thomas) to a comic and absurdist effort by the classically educated Tom Holt. Holt invents as his leading character a grandson of the real Athenian comic poet Eupolis and credits him (as opposed to either of his tutors, Lysimachus or Aristotle) with instilling in Alexander the idea of emulating the exploits of Achilles and Agamemnon combined. The twist in Holt's tale is that this supposedly inspirational figure ends up himself as the very miserable founder of the most out-of-the-way of Alexander's several Alexandria foundations, Alexandria Eschate.

Mary Renault's trilogy of novels is a very good piece of imaginative literature in its own right. Valerio Massimo Manfredi's Alexander trilogy is by comparison with Renault's literalist and unimaginative. The difference in conception between the two may perhaps be summed up in a single pressure point. The middle novel of Renault's trilogy is entirely given over to Alexander's intimate, including sexual, relations with a Persian boy, who grows into a very powerful man indeed, though physically he is a eunuch. Manfredi, on the other hand, manages somehow to avoid mentioning the fact (as it undoubtedly was) that Alexander had sexual relations with persons other than sexually mature women.

Interestingly, though, Renault also wrote a 'straight' biography of Alexander revealingly entitled *The Nature of Alexander*. This was designed to exonerate her hero from some of the apparently more damning ancient and modern accusations, such as his alleged complicity in the assassination of his father. One thing at least rings particularly true:

> *Filtered and refracted by these layers of fable, history, tradition and emotion – a thing inseparable from him alive and dead – the image of Alexander has come down to us.*

Alexander's legacy to the thought-world of philosophy was prodigious. The conjunction of Aristotle and Alexander as teacher and pupil heralded a spate of philosophic exploitation of Alexander. This began actually in or near his lifetime among members of his immediate entourage such as Onesicritus, whose lost work portrayed his king as a Cynic philosopher in arms.* Such philosophic exploitation continued through antiquity down to the later Roman emperor Julian (r. 361–3), who tried to reverse Constantine's christianization of the Empire and recruited Alexander to his pagan-revivalist cause. The Cynics' and Julian's appropriations of Alexander were in their different ways favourable to the king and his image. But in this they were bucking the philosophical trend, which more predictably paraded Alexander as a classic exemplar of the absolute corruption caused by absolute power. That process, it was widely felt, was especially likely to occur, and particularly deadly, when contaminated by intimations of oriental despotism. This view is strongly echoed in the preserved history by Arrian. He was himself philosophically trained, having as a young man sat at the feet of the ex-slave Stoic philosopher Epictetus, who lived from about CE 55 to 135 and taught at Nicopolis in Epirus.

FINALLY, and in summary, we must try to answer one of the biggest historical questions of all: what difference did Alexander make – to his own world, or worlds, more or less immediately, and to subsequent worlds, including even – or especially – our own? The answer – any answer – can hardly be straightforward. Mine is double-edged. What became by conquest the eastern half of the mighty Roman Empire was, essentially, the Hellenized Middle East created in the wake of Alexander's conquests. Within the bounds of that eastern Roman Empire Christianity rose and was disseminated. Yet, from being an oriental religion by its origin, Christianity in some of its most politically potent forms became a Western one, indeed a pillar of Western civilization.

It is an image (possibly a mirage) of that Christian civilization, fatally coupled with the certainly distorted counter-image of Islam as an oriental 'Other', that has led directly to numerous conflicts between East and West – most recently, the so-called Iraq War of 2003. This

---

* See Appendix, pp. 251–2.

was a conflict waged both literally and metaphorically over the territory within which Alexander won his decisive land battle (at Gaugamela), and where he also died just under eight years later (at Babylon). The implications and reverberations of that conflict and its associated 'war on terror' will be with us all for a very long time to come. It is therefore worth recalling in closing that in its purely religious dimension Islam is, just like Christianity, a spiritual monotheism descended from Judaism.

The ancient Hebrews too wanted their share of Alexander's legacy – so badly, in fact, that they were prepared to invent a visit by Alexander to Jerusalem in order to pay his respects to the one true God. This pious fiction is memorably alluded to in a snatch of dialogue from Robert Byron's 1932 travelogue, *The Road to Oxiana*:

> 'Here', he [the guide] continued, 'is a picture of Alexander the
> Great visiting Jerusalem, and being received by one of the
> prophets – I can't remember which.'
> 'But did Alexander ever visit Jerusalem?'
> 'Certainly. I only tell you the truth.'
> 'I'm sorry. I thought it might be legend.'

But Islam went one better than Judaism, finding even for Alexander a hallowed place within its spiritual vision. Perhaps, then, this is the time for all of us – of whatever religious persuasion, or none – to recover an Alexander who can symbolize peaceful, multi-ethnic coexistence.

Appendix: Sources of Paradox

Our word 'sources' perpetuates the French metaphor of springs, as in springs of water. Sometimes the springs of the evidence for Alexander not only flowed rather brackishly but were tainted at their very origins. Alexander's meteoric career naturally provoked a spate of what might loosely be called 'historical' writings about him, beginning in his own lifetime. And he has preoccupied the brains, pens or keyboards of those interested in antiquity ever since. Alexander himself took unusual – though by no means entirely unprecedented, in Middle Eastern terms – steps to try to ensure that his own approved version of events was the one that was most widely and authoritatively disseminated. Yet the earliest surviving continuous narrative account not only is jejune and incomplete but dates from many centuries after his death. And it was produced in a very different cultural and historical context from that in which Alexander himself had lived and died. Hence:

> It is one of the paradoxes of history (and of historiography) that
> this King, who made arrangements unusual at that date for his
> doings to be recorded, and whose career was sensational enough
> to compel the attentions of historians who were his
> contemporaries and (some of them) his associates, to say nothing
> of many later historians who knew a good story when they saw it
> and could not resist this one, should have been handed down
> finally in history as an enigma.

– G. T. Griffith (ed.), *Alexander the Great: The Main Problems*

It is the full implications of this paradox and enigma, both in antiquity and in contemporary and indeed future times, that it has been the business of this book to hunt down. In this Appendix interested readers may find a more in-depth treatment of the sources – written and unwritten, documentary and literary, archaeological and art-historical – on which my hunt was based.

The extant source materials are principally in written form. They consist of literary accounts, whether histories or biographies, of Alexander's deeds written down very much later, and contemporary documentary sources such as official state decrees or private religious dedications. But there is also a wealth of contemporary and non-contemporary material evidence available, scattered throughout the huge world that Alexander's career embraced, from Epirus in north-west Greece to the Indus delta, from the Danube to the Nile. An important component of this evidence are the many images of Alexander in paintings, statues or coins that brought versions of his features, especially his head, to the immediate attention of many of his subjects who either could not read at all or could not read Greek. These were by no means the least important medium of Alexander's mission.

It has been well said that the search for the historical Alexander is something like the search for the historical Jesus. Many contemporaries had an interest in preserving a version of what he said and did, but none of the subject's actual words has been certainly preserved verbatim; and those writers whose words have survived all had an interest in recording, or creating, a particular image of their hero – or villain – for the edification of their contemporaries or posterity, with the result that the searches for both tend to be massively controversial. To get a modern-day flavour of what such ancient controversy might have been like, we could instance the Hollywood actor and director Mel Gibson's overriding passion to film the Gospels. This has deeply divided religious and other communities that have a vested interest in the depiction of the historical Jesus.

In other words, although the surviving evidence is quite ample in quantity, it is poor in quality, being contradictory, tendentious and mainly non-contemporary. In this respect, we can dismiss at once the *Alexander Romance*, which is known alternatively as the 'Pseudo-Callisthenes' (for a reason that we'll come to soon). This does contain some arguably factual material, but only by accident, since it is mostly and by design a fable and fantasy that bears as much – or rather as little – relation to the historical Alexander as does the *Chanson de Roland* to the historical Charlemagne. It is, though, as we saw in Chapter Twelve, irredeemably a part – and a major producer – of the legacy of Alexander.

The situation we are faced with can be summed up roughly as follows. Inspired by the example of Theopompus and his pioneering *Philippica* (a history of Greece written around the career of Philip II of Macedon, Alexander's father), more than twenty contemporaries wrote histories or other kinds of work on Alexander. Not one of those survives in the original. Of the many letters ascribed to Alexander, just one extract of one of them has a better than average claim to being genuine. The earliest surviving connected narrative account of Alexander's campaigns was composed in the first century BCE, some three hundred years after the events it relates; it is, besides, only incompletely preserved. Thus the sole connected narrative to have survived complete is a third-century CE epitome, or abridgement, of a first-century BCE work in Latin by a Romanized Gaul. Finally, what is generally today accounted the best of the more or less completely surviving histories of Alexander was written by a Greek philosopher–statesman in the second century CE, probably during the reign of the philhellenic emperor Hadrian. In short, 'it is as if the history of Tudor England could only be recovered from Macaulay's essays and the histories of Hume the philosopher' (Robin Lane Fox).

There are some brighter features in this generally gloomy landscape. Perhaps the greatest contribution made by the nineteenth-century philological approach to the field of ancient Greek and Roman history was its refinement of the concept and techniques of *Quellenforschung* (source investigation) and *Quellenkritik* (source criticism).

These had first been developed towards the end of the eighteenth century, especially at Göttingen in Germany. And perhaps the most important fruits of nineteenth-century source investigation and source criticism were borne, happily for us, by the enormous labour invested in the notorious problem of sorting out the written sources for Alexander. What has been described as the classic thesis of nineteenth-century German scholarship is the notion of classifying the majority of our main surviving narrative accounts of Alexander into one family known as 'the Vulgate'.

According to this classification, the histories of Diodorus, Trogus (the Romanized Gaul mentioned earlier, as summarized by Justin) and Curtius could all be traced back in their main lines ultimately to one source text: the contemporary but not eyewitness account written by Cleitarchus of Alexandria. The thesis has been challenged more recently, but not significantly shaken (see further below). Arrian, on the other hand, the Greek philosopher–statesman frequently mentioned in this work, is the principal extant representative of the alternative tradition on Alexander. He chose, rather, to base himself on the accounts of three privileged eyewitnesses: Ptolemy, Aristoboulus and Nearchus. Since all three were members of Alexander's entourage and remained loyal to the end, this tradition is called for convenience the 'Official' tradition.

Standing outside both the Vulgate and the Official traditions was Plutarch (c. CE 46–120), who in his *Life of Alexander* made eclectic use of both of those and of other sources besides. His artful biography also exemplifies another lesson that has been fully learned only in the late twentieth and early twenty-first centuries: that the facts never come to us 'straight', but are wrapped up or moulded in accordance with each individual writer's own preconceptions and aims. Plutarch himself, for instance, wrote moralizing biographies, and when we use what he says for purposes of historical reconstruction his overriding moralizing aims must never be overlooked. Finally, all accounts – eyewitness or not, contemporary or not, Vulgate or Official or neither

– somehow used the original narrative of Alexander's official historian, Callisthenes, at least for events down to 331 or perhaps 329.

Enormous problems still remain, and the picture is not of course as relatively neat and tidy as, for simplicity's sake, I have presented it. But the consensus of scholarly opinion that I shall now summarize is at any rate considerably more nuanced and sophisticated than that of the nineteenth century, above all thanks to its attention to and respect for ancient authors' literary mannerisms, narratological and other tropes, and rhetorical manoeuvres. At the end of this Appendix I discuss in possibly gut-wrenching detail two particularly indigestible source problems, chosen because they also have a crucial bearing on our main objective – namely, the better understanding of Alexander and his times.

Logically, and chronologically, any conspectus must begin with Callisthenes, a native of Greek Olynthus. Both the 'Greek' and the 'Olynthus' are crucial. In 348, as we have seen, Alexander's father Philip carried out its exemplary destruction, as the leading city of the Greek Chalcidian federation that was situated threateningly on his doorstep. The city was still in uninhabited ruins when Alexander hired Callisthenes as his official historian in the mid 330s. That he hired him and not someone else was due partly to Callisthenes's proven historiographical expertise. He had published a history of Greece from 387/6 to 357/6 and, in collaboration with his relative (great-uncle or uncle) Aristotle, had compiled a list of the victors at the quadrennial Pan-hellenic games held at Delphi in honour of Pythian Apollo. But his Greek nationality and not least his kinship with Aristotle were also vitally relevant factors. Aristotle's father had been court physician to Alexander's paternal grandfather Amyntas III. And as we know, Aristotle at Philip's invitation had taught Alexander when he was in his impressionable early teens.

By selecting Callisthenes Alexander was thus maintaining the family connection with Aristotle and perhaps repaying him a personal favour. At the same time he was also securing what must have seemed to be the services of a loyal Greek. This was a vital commodity as he was commencing a Panhellenic mission of revenge against the oriental 'barbarian'. Callisthenes may have had motives other than purely personal ones for accepting Alexander's invitation. Whatever we make of his alleged boast that Alexander would owe his remembrance solely to him, the story that he hoped to persuade his employer to rebuild his native city of Olynthus is quite possibly true. Yet it was all to end in tears, or worse, with the execution of Callisthenes for treason, ordered by Alexander in 327 (see pp. 73, 263–5). That execution had more effect on our tradition concerning the Macedonian conqueror than perhaps any other single episode. It meant that, in so far as the tradition was dependent on Greek rather than Macedonian sources, it was by and large a hostile one.

Callisthenes's *Exploits of Alexander* (*Praxeis Alexandrou*) was perhaps sent back to Greece in instalments. All that survives of it are a dozen or so 'fragments' (quotations by other, surviving writers, though there is never a guarantee that the quotations are word for word). These are not calculated to arouse the unqualified admiration of a modern critical historian. The Olynthian's main appointed task was almost certainly to sell an image of Alexander to the by and large sceptical if not downright hostile Greeks (see Chapter Five). It is not at all surprising, therefore, that his work should have been, to an extent at least, a rhetorical encomium. Clearly, Callisthenes aimed to present Alexander as a hero, though we cannot of course say how far it was his or Alexander's idea to cast him in the role of a Homeric hero, a new Agamemnon or, still better, an Achilles.

The ancient label of 'the flatterer' that was applied to Callisthenes (among others) no doubt hit the mark. The corollary of such a representation was a certain amount of divine apparatus and a certain amount of hagiography, as when he makes the sea off south-western Anatolia do formal obeisance to Alexander as if to a god (long before Alexander himself actually made any claim to divinity). Clearly, too, it was Callisthenes who after the Siwah oracle visit (see pp. 209–10) disseminated the story that Alexander was a son of Zeus. The extent to which he used documentary materials consigned to the official logbooks of the expedition cannot now be recovered, but this is not a burning issue. Far more inflammatory are the circumstances and manner of Callisthenes's premature death in 327. The latest events covered by him before the enforced termination of his labours belong, perhaps, to 329.

Callisthenes is by at least five years the earliest of the writers on Alexander of whose work 'fragments' have come down to us. The relative and absolute chronology of the other contemporary authors is now undeterminable with certainty. My own belief is that Cleitarchus (who lies behind the Vulgate tradition, as we saw) began to publish before the Official-tradition writers Ptolemy and Aristoboulus, who published in that order. For purposes of this exposition, however, I shall use another method of differentiation than the chronological. In the manner of Herodotus, I shall distinguish between eyewitness and non-eyewitness sources: that is, between those contemporary authors who went on the Asiatic expedition and those such as, most probably, Cleitarchus who did not.

The second of the eyewitness sources to consider is the Macedonian noble Ptolemaios son of Lagos, usually referred to in English simply as Ptolemy (see Figure 31). Apart from his stylus-pushing activities, he was also the founder (as Ptolemy I Soter, or 'Saviour') of a post-Alexander Macedono-Greek dynasty. This ruled Egypt from the late fourth century until the death by suicide in 30 BCE of its last and most famous representative, Cleopatra – officially Cleopatra VII. Having been one of Alexander's intimates from his teens, in 330, four years into the Persian expedition, Ptolemy was promoted to the general staff. He was therefore in an excellent position to know both Alexander and his expedition from the inside. The trouble was, such intimate knowledge could be an embarrassment, especially for the man who in 321, when it was en route home for the final obsequies in Macedon, would snatch Alexander's corpse at Damascus in Syria. Ptolemy had it reburied, with massive ceremonial, in what was to become his own royal capital of Alexandria (founded by Alexander in 332). He then tried to claim this peculiar link as a mark of his legitimacy as a – if not the – royal successor to Alexander.

Arrian chose Ptolemy as one of his three main sources on the grounds that 'it is more disgraceful for a king than for anyone else to tell lies'. This prima facie ridiculous statement has led some scholars to dismiss Arrian outright as congenitally naive, and so not worth bothering further with. But what he probably meant was that Ptolemy, being a king (self-proclaimed, to be sure), could least of anyone afford to be caught out blatantly lying. On the other hand, Arrian does seem to have overlooked the fact that a king might be more tempted than others, on occasion, to tell lies in which he could not be caught out.

It is only rarely possible to convict Ptolemy of outright lying; the two talking snakes which, he alleged, guided Alexander to the Siwah oasis are an obvious case in point (see below). But he was 'truly no detractor from his own glory' (the curt phrase of Curtius), and he can be convicted of both *suppressio veri* (suppression of the truth) and *suggestio falsi* (suggestion of what was untrue) – to use the technical language of the Roman rhetoricians, who were themselves pastmasters of those useful arts. On the whole, though, Ptolemy's bias can be allowed for, and the solid advantages of his militarily and terminologically competent narrative exploited, mainly through Arrian's extant account. But historians, alas, have to stop well short of using the fictional ploy of the novelist–academic Valerio Massimo Manfredi. His rather dull three-volume novel about Alexander (mentioned in Chapter Twelve) purports to be the very account of Ptolemy himself.

Our third eyewitness writer is Aristoboulus. Like Callisthenes but unlike Ptolemy, he was a Greek, though he became a citizen of the new, post-Alexander foundation of Cassandreia in the Chalcidice (not far from Olynthus). He suffers under the double disadvantage of having been eighty-four when he started writing ('Old men forget', to quote Shakespeare's Henry V) and of having earned the 'flatterer' label. Where

Ptolemy practised a selective and purposeful reserve, Aristoboulus tended to the opposite fault of sycophantic garrulity. Thus he stresses Alexander's chivalrous generosity towards the captured female members of the Persian royal family after the Battle of Issus in 333. He justifies various notoriously controversial murders and executions of leading Macedonians. He gives the more favourable version of Callisthenes's death (see below), and he maintains that Alexander subtly and purposefully loosened rather than crudely and in desperation slashed through the Gordian knot (see the Glossary). Perhaps the classic illustration of Aristoboulus's palliation of the unpalatable is his view that Alexander was not a regular toper – let alone a certifiable alcoholic, as he is considered by at least one modern historian (J. M. O'Brien) – but simply a social drinker.

The explanation of such palpably ludicrous euphemisms is that Aristoboulus was a pro-Macedonian Greek rather than a Macedonian, and more sensitive than Ptolemy to some Greeks' ferocious criticisms of his former employer. This did not deter Arrian from using him as his second main source, presumably because, as an engineer/architect with an interest in geography and natural history, Aristoboulus provided an additional and quite different perspective on the expedition. One of his more interesting commissions was to restore the tomb of Cyrus, founder of the Achaemenid Empire, at Pasargadae in 324 (see Figure 37). In my view, Aristoboulus wrote after 290 BCE, perhaps as many as twenty years after Ptolemy.

Our next two eyewitness sources, Onesicritus and Nearchus, are best taken together. They both served in the fleet that Alexander sent from modern Pakistan to Iran in the winter of 325/4, the former as chief helmsman, the latter as admiral, and Nearchus wrote his account at least in part to 'correct' that of Onesicritus. Both men, too, were Greek islanders, Onesicritus from tiny Astypalaea in the Aegean, Nearchus from Crete. But there the similarity ends.

Onesicritus was an adept of some version of the Cynic philosophy practised most notoriously in Alexander's day by Diogenes. (The meeting in Corinth between Alexander and Diogenes in the mid 330s became legendary. Alexander went over to try to engage Diogenes, who was living rough as usual, in earnest conversation. When Alexander asked the uncommunicative Diogenes what favour he could do him, Diogenes curtly asked him to stop blocking off his sunlight. Alexander's spin machine quickly got to work, claiming that Alexander had said that, if he had not been Alexander, the person he would most like to have been was Diogenes.) Onesicritus consciously imitated Xenophon's *Cyropaedia* (a fictional work ostensibly on the education of Cyrus the Great) and tried to turn his Alexander into a philosopher in arms. But he seems to have been remarkably mendacious, even for an Alexander-writer, and was another to earn, in the fullest sense, the dubious accolade of 'flatterer'.

Nearchus, like Ptolemy, had been an intimate of Alexander since their schooldays in Mieza. But unlike Ptolemy, he lost all his influence and status at Alexander's death and vented his frustrated ambition by composing self-interested memoirs. Nearchus's account of Alexander's venture into 'India' was, though, sufficiently intriguing and lively for Arrian to use it as the basis of the second half of his *Indian Affairs* (*Indica*), a separate work from his main Alexander history. Nearchus was taken even more seriously by most modern writers until Ernst Badian, the most severely critical and minimalist of modern historians of Alexander, felt the need to do a hatchet job. So he cut him down to a more appropriate size by stressing Nearchus's literary pretensions, his predilection for marvels and his distorted presentation of self: features that in combination made of his work a *Tendenzschrift* – a piece of writing with an ideological axe to grind – rather than an objective account of a crucial episode in Alexander's career.

My sixth and final eyewitness source is Chares, another Greek islander. He came from Mytilene on the island of Lesbos and rose in Alexander's personal service to become his chamberlain after his master had begun to adopt the ceremonial of the Persian court as part of his assumed role of King of Asia. Chares's racy *Stories of Alexander* was published in at least ten books and was read by Aristoboulus and cited by Plutarch, among others. But there is nothing known of it to suggest that it was other than a string of gossipy reminiscences and anecdotes of court life, the sort of thing that gets serialized in some of the Sunday papers today. Even as such, of course, it has its uses as a source of scandal-tainted episodes like the one leading to the death of Callisthenes.

Even if we did not have explicit references to documentary sources, it would have been possible to conjecture their existence from the numerous military and administrative details that Arrian took from Ptolemy and perhaps also from Aristoboulus, but that are not to be found in the Vulgate authors Diodorus, Curtius or Plutarch. The first of these is the *Ephemerides*, a title that may be translated as (Royal) Diaries, Journals or (as I prefer) Logbooks. Athenaeus, a Greek compiler working in Alexandria around CE 200, tells us these were kept by two Greeks, Eumenes from Cardia in the Hellespont and Diodotus from Erythrae in Ionia (the western coast of Asia Minor). Eumenes was Alexander's personal secretary and later became such a major player in the wars of Alexander's succession as to qualify as the subject of an extant *Life* by Plutarch. Scholars used to place great faith in the references to this source, and some even argued that it contained a day-by-day record of all important decisions made by Alexander and of all notable events reported to him. Such confidence is entirely misplaced. If not actually forged, or at least doctored, for propaganda purposes by Eumenes or another, at most and best they were a chronicle kept by the Babylonian priests that dealt only with occasions when the king was in or near Babylon – most conspicuously at his death in June 323.

Then there are the *Hypomnemata*, or personal Notebooks, allegedly kept by Alexander himself. At the least, their alleged contents – the so-called 'last plans', a list of Alexander's immediate and future projects at the time of his untimely death as read out to the assembled troops by Perdiccas soon after the event (see Chapter Ten) – had to seem plausible to those troops. Whether the Notebooks were authentic or not, we cannot say. We can be surer of the inauthenticity of the series of letters attributed directly and personally to Alexander, most of them preserved by Plutarch, who clearly had access to one or more collections of them. At the most generous reckoning a maximum usable total of fourteen, of which ten are to be found in Plutarch's *Life of Alexander*, have some claim to credence. Their authenticity matters when, for example, Alexander is alleged to have written directly to Darius after the Granicus battle of 334 claiming that he, not Darius, was the legitimate King of Persia, and Darius a mere usurper. Such *chutzpah* might well be thought characteristic of the young Alexander, but it would be nice to be able to document it with certainty.

NON-EYEWITNESS sources begin with Cleitarchus the son of Dinon, himself a respected historian of Persia. Cleitarchus was too young to accompany Alexander on his expedition, but this lack of first-hand experience was somewhat compensated for by his freedom from the pressures of writing more or less official history. Moreover, based as he was at Athens after 322, Cleitarchus was able to consult at leisure all those Greeks (politicians, ambassadors, artists, technicians, ordinary soldiers) connected either with Alexander or with the Persian side. He could therefore enrich his reading of Callisthenes and other eyewitness authors with an abundant oral tradition lacking in Arrian's sources. His sympathies at (occupied) Athens would have lain more with the pro-Macedonian tendency than with the circles favouring the diehard anti-Macedonian position of the late Demosthenes (died 322).

The hypothesis that he was the ultimate progenitor of the Vulgate literary tradition (as represented in the extant works of Diodorus, Curtius and Justin) has been impugned, chiefly by the late Nicholas Hammond. But it has been upheld convincingly by, for example, Paul Goukowsky. He has argued that Cleitarchus wrote his twelve or more books in the last decade of the fourth century – early enough, that is, for him to have been used at least by Aristoboulus and perhaps also by Ptolemy. It is an ingenious and attractive modern hypothesis that in 308 Cleitarchus accepted an invitation from Ptolemy, soon to be crowned king of Egypt, to come to Alexandria to create a picture of Alexander that would appeal to Greeks at a time when Ptolemy was attempting to resuscitate the long-defunct League of Corinth (see Chapter Five).

Cleitarchus was a far more exciting read for Hellenistic and Roman-period readers than the dry-as-dust Ptolemy, and so he became the most popular writer on Alexander in antiquity before the wide-spread dissemination of the *Alexander Romance* in the early Roman imperial period. He presented Alexander as a heroic king, predestined son of the Libyan god Amun, rival of his ancestor Heracles and of Dionysus, and conqueror of the most distant lands of the *oecumene* (the known inhabited world). The chief attraction of his history for posterity lay in its vivid descriptions and sensational incidents. For example, he portrayed Alexander's burning down of the palace complex at the former Persian ceremonial capital of Persepolis in 330 as more than just a symbolic act of policy that was later regretted (as it was depicted by Arrian, following Ptolemy). In Cleitarchus's account, it was ordered by Alexander when he was under the influence of drink, and at the suggestion of Thais, the upmarket Athenian prostitute who just happened to be the current partner of Ptolemy. Conceivably, Cleitarchus was in this instance historically accurate – Ptolemy's self-interested suppression of the alleged role of Thais would have been wholly understandable. But the general view of serious ancient writers was that Cleitarchus, though clever, was mendacious, and this view has found a strong echo in modern times.

Cleitarchus's work is itself lost. In so far as it survives at all, it is through the works of Diodorus, Curtius and Justin. Diodorus, a Greek of the first century BCE originally from Agyrrhium in Sicily, compiled at Rome a multi-book work rather oddly entitled *Library of History*. This was presumably so called because it contained all the history of the world that Diodorus thought any educated reader of the time could possibly wish to read. Alexander featured in the *Library*'s seventeenth book, which has not survived complete. Curtius – Quintus Curtius Rufus – wrote his *History of Alexander the Great* in ten books (the last eight survive) in highly rhetorical Latin. Justin (Marcus Junius Justinus) was a third-century CE epitomator of a lost first-century BCE Latin work by Trogus; the career of Alexander is treated in the eleventh and twelfth books of his extant epitome.

The precise chronology of the three surviving Vulgate sources is disputed. Possibly Diodorus published a little before Trogus at the end of the first century BCE, while Curtius probably wrote during the reign of either Claudius (the preferred view of his latest commentator) or Vespasian. Yet, to repeat, only Justin's epitome of Trogus has survived complete – for what that is worth. A sobering thought.

This is not to say that all three depended exclusively on Cleitarchus, or that they did so equally and in the same ways. Far from it. In accordance with his usual economical practice, Diodorus by and large did follow Cleitarchus as his main source for the Alexander years. Curtius was more independent both in choice and use of sources (as we shall see, he also used Ptolemy, among others) and in interpretation. For example, he abhorred the ruler cult promoted by Alexander's Hellenistic-period Successors and adopted, in their imitation, by Julius Caesar and the Roman emperors. Diodorus, by contrast, entirely swallowed the Hellenistic legitimating myth of the good king and applied it hagiographically to Alexander. Alongside the frequent agreements between Diodorus and Trogus/Justin, there are also serious disagreements. Trogus, for example, disliked aggressive imperialism as such and presented Alexander as a bloodstained tyrant perverted by his conquests, whereas Diodorus admired above all Alexander's moderation in success and his resistance to the manifold temptations towards luxury and despotism.

Our last two literary sources are both Greek, and both in their different ways ornaments of the age of Greek learning that is associated pre-eminently with the reign of the pro-Greek emperor Hadrian. This is an age – or a movement – conventionally known as the Second Sophistic because it harked back consciously to the age of the first Sophists, teachers of skills, especially rhetoric, in the fifth and fourth centuries BCE. Plutarch (c. CE 46–120) originated from the small town of Chaeronea in Boeotia (famed for Philip's victory of 338). He received an excellent rhetorical and literary education, and among the earliest works in his voluminous *oeuvre* are two short treatises on Alexander's 'fortune'. In these, he sought to rebut the charge that he owed his successes merely to good luck rather than to innate or acquired virtue.

Plutarch is much more famous, and much more useful to us, as the composer of fifty parallel *Lives* of famous Greeks and Romans of the more or less distant past. Alexander was an inevitable candidate for a Plutarchan biography, and Julius Caesar, who consciously sought to emulate him, his almost equally obvious 'pair'. Plutarch, as he himself emphasizes in his introduction to the *Alexander*, was writing 'lives, not histories'. More specifically, he was writing moralizing and edifying biographies, in which the prime focus of the author was on character and ethos, and the ideal reader was invited to contemplate moral examples either to follow or to avoid. The historical value of the *Alexander* depends, therefore, on the sources Plutarch used and on the use he made of them. He was at all events liberal both in their use and in their citation here, naming twenty-four previous authors in all.

The following passage (*Alexander*, Chapter 46) puts his reading on display. Admittedly, this concerns a matter of fact (or rather, blatant fiction) that many of us today might not think it worth giving a second thought to, but it was integral to Alexander's own myth and self-presentation:

> Here the queen of the Amazons paid him a visit, as most writers record, including Cleitarchus, Polycleitus, Onesicritus, Antigenes, and Istrus; but Aristoboulus and Chares the chamberlain,

Ptolemy, Anticleides, Philon of Thebes and Philippus of
Theangela, besides Hecataeus of Eretria, Philippus of Chalcis
and Duris of Samos, claim that this is a fiction. And it looks as
though Alexander's own testimony supports the latter group, as
in a very precise and detailed letter to Antipater he does say that
the Scythian king offered him his daughter in marriage but he
makes no mention of the Amazon.

Plutarch's pretensions to source-critical acumen are notable. But, given his moralizing aim, he was naturally not bound to give a comprehensive account of Alexander's career, even in summary form. Those episodes that he did choose to single out for mention are presented anachronistically, by being judged according to Plutarch's own moral criteria rather than by the standards of Alexander's time and place. Plutarch can be critical (in the other sense – of making negative criticisms) of Alexander, and there is dark as well as light in his account of his personality. But in general the *Life* is apologetic in tone. Its chief value for the modern historian lies in its unique record of Alexander's early life, especially the years from 338 to 336. The first half-dozen or so chapters covering these early years are pretty much the sole basis for what I take to be the finest modern historical novel about Alexander, *Fire From Heaven*, the first volume of Mary Renault's trilogy (see Chapter Twelve).

Arrian (as we know him for short) was (for long) Lucius (or Aulus) Flavius Arrianus Xenophon. He was born at Greek Nicomedeia in Bithynia on the southern shore of the Black Sea in the late 80s CE. As a callow twenty-year-old, Arrian took advantage of his family wealth in the then familiar upper-class way to complete his formal education by studying under a Greek philosopher. But his choice of philosopher was far from merely conventional. He became an avid student and follower of the ex-slave Stoic Epictetus in the wilds of north-west Greece; perhaps not coincidentally, this was not far from the home of Alexander's mother Olympias. It was clearly from his master Epictetus that Arrian derived the high moral standards by which he was to judge Alexander. But Epictetus was not Arrian's only model. The Athenian historian and pamphleteer Xenophon, himself a pupil of the philosopher Socrates, was no less influential, if in different ways. Xenophon's *Anabasis* ('March Up Country') was the literary model for his own account of Alexander's expedition, right down to the very title of his work and its division into just seven books. Like Xenophon, too, and not irrelevantly to this book's conception, he wrote among several other works a *Cynegeticus*, or treatise on hunting. Arrian even incorporated Xenophon's name as part of his own official formal name in eloquent homage to his virtual mentor.

Like Plutarch, Arrian operated between two worlds, but at a much higher political level: he held the chief magistracies at both Rome and Athens and exercised high military command in Asia Minor. We cannot say for certain when he composed his *Anabasis*. The old view was that it was a work of his retirement, as most of Xenophon's published writings probably were. But expert opinion has more recently swung round to the view that it was a work of his youth – a view that has the merit (as some see it) of explaining or excusing its defects as a work of explanation and analysis. The errors of fact or omission are harder to palliate or justify on either dating, of course; for example, the less morally admirable materialistic and acquisitive sides of the expedition are distinctly under-reported.

Whenever it was composed, it is today regarded almost universally as the best surviving ancient work on Alexander. What chiefly commends Arrian to the modern hunter of the historical Alexander is his painstaking attention to detail. This is revealed above all in his generally accurate use of technical vocabulary and in his relatively full treatment of administrative matters, such as the appointment of satraps (see the Glossary). It was probably this innate or acquired taste for factual detail that influenced Arrian's choice of first Ptolemy and secondarily Aristoboulus as his main sources.

The modern historian is also likely to be favourably impressed by

Arrian's freedom from hero worship of Alexander (see Chapter Eleven). Not that he was unprejudiced and impartial: the overall purpose of his work was to contribute to the greater glory and fame of Alexander, and he tends to try to explain away some of his less obviously admirable actions or traits on grounds of overriding expediency. But he does not allow this honorific purpose to obliterate criticism of what he sees as Alexander's increasing orientalism, his heavy drinking and his inability to control his emotions, especially his anger, ambition and pride. Perhaps his single most perceptive observation is that to Alexander 'the sheer pleasure of battle, as other pleasures are to other men, was irresistible' (6.13.4).

One final literary curiosity: a pamphlet on Alexander ascribed to a female writer. Known women writers in ancient Greece are almost as rare as hens' teeth, and those few who are known were almost without exception poets. One exception is the Hellenistic-period prose writer Nicoboule, who showed that she could give as good – or as bad – a scandalmongering account of Alexander as male authors like Chares the chamberlain.

QUITE different from these literary writers are the contemporary documentary sources, both Greek and non-Greek. Of course, official records can also lie in the sense that they can be economical with the truth. But so long as they are not forged – and even, in some circumstances, when they are – they have the merit of immediacy that literary narrative inevitably moderates. Unfortunately, the number of extant contemporary official documents that were produced either in Macedon or in Greek cities or by Greek-speaking communities during Alexander's reign is relatively small. But they have been well studied, and I have exploited them as appropriate in the text (Chapter Five, especially).

The number of extant official documents produced in non-Greek languages on the Persian Empire side of the equation is even smaller.

A flood of new light has been shed by the Treasury and Fortification Tablets from the bureaucratic archives at Persepolis, written on baked clay mainly in the local Elamite language; but that light chiefly illuminates the period from the late sixth to the mid fifth century, not the period of Alexander. Here, moreover, there is no compensation at all to be had from preserved historical narrations, since Greek-style historiography was not an oriental or Persian accomplishment. Two of the so-called historical Books of the Hebrew Bible, Ezra and Nehemiah, provide a Jewish angle on the Achaemenid Empire, though these too – like the heavily mythicized Esther – deal with earlier reigns than those of Alexander's opponent Darius III.

THE SPADE cannot lie, it has been said. But that is only because it cannot speak. It has to be given a voice, by the interpreter of the mute archaeological data. Some such data are more easily interpretable than others. No visitor to the extraordinary fourth-century BCE royal tombs at Vergina, or to the archaeological museums in Thessaloniki and Pella, can fail to register the stupendous concentration of gold amassed by the leading Macedonian nobles; or their willingness, and ability, to 'destroy' it by having it placed in their tombs in the form of goblets and other tableware used in the symposium, or personal jewellery. Likewise, the fate of Olynthus, destroyed in 348 by Philip and never resettled on the same site, speaks unambiguously. Paradoxically enough, dead Olynthus provides our best evidence on what everyday life was like in an above-averagely prosperous and powerful Greek city of the fourth century. At the other pole, geographically as well as historically, there is the abundant archaeological evidence excavated at Ai Khanum on the River Oxus in Afghanistan. This was a new, fourth-century foundation, a new Greek city, a new Alexandria almost certainly; it bears powerful witness to the extent of the cultural transformation of the Middle Eastern landscape that was effected by, and in the wake of, Alexander's conquests.

Between written and archaeological evidence comes the numismatic evidence – of coins which, apart from their intrinsic economic value, bore images and often superscriptions. These served to guarantee the coins' authenticity and to maintain their value as media of payment and exchange and means of storing wealth. Coins, therefore, are evidence not only for economic history, but also for art history, political history and cultural (especially ideological) history. Thanks to the ancient practice of hoarding, they survive in plentiful numbers on both the Persian and the Greek sides. Indeed Philip, once he had got hold of extraordinary amounts of the raw materials, went into overdrive in issuing silver and to a much smaller extent gold coinages. Alexander, besides vigorously following his father's lead in this, also 'liberated' the simply vast amounts of gold and silver bullion that had been thesaurized by the Persian Great Kings in their four major capitals – Susa, Persepolis, Ecbatana in Iran, and Babylon in Iraq. This had incalculable economic consequences both in his reign and after his death. But no less interesting and revealing in its way is the development of the repertoire of symbolic attributes with which Alexander chose to be represented in person on the obverse of his coinages. Indeed, the fact that, after favouring gods, he went over to having his own image stamped on coins leads us inevitably to ask whether he did so as himself another god (see Chapter Eleven).

There is no explicit evidence that Alexander employed an official die-cutter to manufacture 'authorized' images of himself on his coinages. There is evidence, though it is non-contemporary and suspect, that he did employ an official court gem-cutter, Pyrgoteles, an official court painter, Apelles, and an official sculptor, Lysippus – all Greeks – to produce images suitable for dissemination and reproduction throughout his ever-expanding realm (see Chapter Twelve). When that evidence speaks of an 'edict' by Alexander prescribing the use only of images produced by these three, it is clearly anachronistic, owing everything to Roman imperial rather than Macedonian royal practice. But a softer interpretation might equate Alexander's possible attempt to control the metaphorical language of the visual sphere with his certain employment of Callisthenes to control the written propaganda, and deliver the authorized version of his great and heroic deeds. At any rate, far, far more of Alexander's subjects could see than could read, and far more would catch sight of a sculpture or relief of him or hold a coin bearing his image than would hear, let alone read for themselves, the latest dispatch roll from the pen of Callisthenes. 'Propaganda' – or its contemporary derivative, 'spin' – is never a word to be used lightly, but it does seem the right word for this sort of control freakery.

To CONCLUDE, I explore two case studies in some detail in order to illustrate the evidentiary problems and hazards of a hunt for Alexander. The episodes chosen are both absolutely central to this book's aims and objectives. They involve matters at the very heart of Alexander's extraordinary enterprise, his conception and projection of it, and its reception both within and outside his innermost circle of adherents.

THE DEATH OF CALLISTHENES, 327

The extant sources record no fewer than five mutually inconsistent or incompatible methods and modes of Callisthenes's execution. As Robin Lane Fox once commented: 'There are few plainer insights into the hazards of a search for Alexander than that his own historian was said by informed contemporaries to have died in five different ways.' Indeed. Only seven years after Alexander landed in Asia, and rather less than four years after the final victory at Gaugamela, Callisthenes was put to death on grounds of high treason. Why he was put to death is therefore, obviously, a matter of the highest historical consequence, and one that has been fully explored in the text (especially Chapter

Five). The discussion here will be confined to the more technical question of *how* he was put to death – by what legal (or extra-legal) and physical means.

Arrian, to begin chronologically at the end (he is the latest source), makes this telling general remark (4.14.3):

> *Even the most trustworthy writers, men who were actually with Alexander at the time, have given conflicting accounts of notorious events with which they must have been perfectly familiar.*

The 'most trustworthy writers' Arrian had in mind were of course his two preferred authorities, Ptolemy and Aristoboulus. According to the latter, Callisthenes was bound in fetters and taken around with the army, later dying of disease. According to Ptolemy, he was tortured and hanged. Plutarch, after reporting these two variants, adds the testimony of a third eyewitness source, Chares the chamberlain. According to the latter, Callisthenes was not put to death immediately but kept in fetters for seven months until he died, lice-ridden, of disease about the time of Alexander's near-fatal wounding among the Mallian people in India (see Chapter Nine). Of the Vulgate accounts, that of Diodorus is lost in the manuscript lacuna, although we know from the surviving table of contents that he did describe the death. Curtius declares that Callisthenes was tortured and then put to death. Trogus/Justin, finally, paints an elaborate picture of Callisthenes being first mutilated according to Persian custom (nose and ears sliced off), then shut up in a cage with a dog and carried about with the army, until one of Alexander's seven personal bodyguards poisoned him to put him out of his misery.

Which of the five versions are we to believe? As between Aristoboulus and Ptolemy, we must prefer Ptolemy, since in the former we have a clear example of 'the flatterer' in action. By many Greeks the execution of Callisthenes on mere suspicion of guilt and without trial would have been considered a politically motivated breach of natural justice. So too, and in the same sense, we must reject Chares, since he is merely elaborating on the Aristobulus line. Trogus/Justin is out on its own in retailing a story of oriental-style mutilation, but this detail is also the clue to its fictitiousness. Such a mutilation had particular point as applied by Alexander to the Persian royal pretender Bessus in 329 (see Chapter Eight). It has no point as applied to the Greek Callisthenes and must therefore be rejected as an easily detectable example of the gratuitous blackening of Alexander's character to which Trogus was prone. The remaining Vulgate source, Curtius, though brief and unadorned, is actually far more interesting. He simply accepts and repeats the version of Ptolemy – an excellent illustration of both Curtius's relative independence within the Vulgate tradition and his occasional use of the Official Ptolemy.

But should we believe Ptolemy, as Curtius did, and accept that Callisthenes was tortured and hanged forthwith? We should, and for a reason given long ago by George Grote, one of the best nineteenth-century historians of ancient Greece: 'His partiality might permit [Ptolemy] to omit or soften what was discreditable to Alexander, but he may be fully trusted when he records an act of cruelty.' And, moreover, gratuitous and illegal cruelty, at that. For Alexander did not opt to have Callisthenes tried, as he certainly could and probably should have done, before either the assembled Macedonian army or (what would have admittedly been far more difficult to arrange and manage) the Council of the allies who were members of the League of Corinth.

WHAT DID REALLY HAPPEN AT SIWAH IN 332/1?

In the case we have just looked at it was relatively easy to decide between the five different versions of the episode, by applying straight-forward legalistic criteria of reliability. Moreover, the manner of Callisthenes's death, important though that was, was relatively less important than the reasons why he was executed. My second case study concerns Alexander's extraordinary detour through the western desert of Egypt to the oracular shrine of Ammon in the Siwah oasis, a journey of three hundred miles (four hundred and eighty kilometres) inland to the remote western border of Egypt and Libya in spring 331. This is at once far more complex historiographically, and historically even more crucial. It has direct implications for at least two of the chapters of this book, those on the divinity of Alexander (Chapter Eleven) and on Alexander the man (Chapter Ten), and is variously relevant to almost all the others as well.

The contemporary narrative sources, as ever, do not survive as such, but there are fairly reliable reports available of at least the main ones. However, they all tell different stories, and this really does matter: not just because all historians always want to know what actually happened in any particular case, but also because in this instance Alexander himself made a very big deal of what he – or his spokesmen – claimed had transpired between him and the god's mouthpiece, the priest of Ammon, in private. Thereafter he represented himself to the world in a significantly new guise, and he seems too to have perceived and related to the world differently. Most obviously, he added Ammon to the pantheon of divinities whose special guidance he regularly invoked on major occasions, and with whom he claimed to enjoy a special relationship.

I shall focus here on two of the main facets of the episode: first, what were Alexander's intentions in making this visit in person to the oracle through hazardous desert country at a time when the Persian Great King was launching a counter-offensive in his rear? and, second, what actually happened at the oracle? The third main facet, Alexander's subsequent and consequent behaviour, has been treated in Chapter Eleven.

Our preserved accounts are ultimately derived from three main fountainheads: Callisthenes as summarized in Strabo (a Greek geographer writing in the late first century BCE and early first century CE, so a contemporary of Trogus); Ptolemy/Aristoboulus, as preserved in Arrian; and Cleitarchus as reproduced in Diodorus, Trogus/Justin and Curtius. Plutarch, as usual, has drawn something from all three. The whole truth of the visit was, clearly, lost from the very start. Strabo prefaces his summary of Callisthenes with the comment that the Alexander historians were guilty of many flatteries. And the normally sober and rational Ptolemy has the gall to claim that, after getting lost in the desert, Alexander was guided to his destination by two talking snakes. By and large, though, the story of the march through the desert is an agreed one. Disagreement begins in earnest over the question of Alexander's motives for making the trip in the first place.

According to our fullest source, Arrian, Alexander went for three reasons. First, in order to ask the oracle something, because it was reputed to be infallible. Second, in order to rival Perseus and Heracles, from both of whom he was descended. And third, because he traced – or was seeking to trace (the Greek is ambiguous) – a part of either his descent or his manner of conception (again, the Greek is ambiguous) to Ammon, just as the legends traced that of Heracles and Perseus to Zeus. Arrian, on principle, followed Ptolemy and Aristoboulus where they agreed, so they presumably were agreed here, since he mentions no disagreement between them. From where, then, did they derive their agreed account of Alexander's motives? It is only logical to think at once of the earliest, and most official, account of all, namely that of Callisthenes.

Thus, it may be significant that the only point of agreement between Arrian (that is, Ptolemy/Aristoboulus) and Callisthenes (as reported in Strabo) is on the second of the three motives – Alexander's desire to rival Heracles and Perseus. As the rest of Strabo's summary shows, the Siwah trip was written up by Callisthenes only after Alexander had become King of the Persians in 330 (on top of being King of Macedon and general plenipotentiary of the League of Corinth). This is probably what explains the appearance, only here, of Perseus, who the Greeks thought was the ultimate ancestor of the

Persians. Callisthenes, in other words, either off his own bat or at Alexander's direction, used the Siwah visit anachronistically as part of the legitimating myth of Alexander's rule, and Ptolemy/Aristoboulus followed him. The mention of Heracles is less of a problem, since the Macedonian royal house of the Argeads traced its descent from him already, and he turns up in other Alexander-related contexts.

What, then, are we to make of Callisthenes's apparent silences about the other two motives mentioned by Arrian? His silence about the first – Alexander's wanting to ask the oracle some (unspecified) thing – is unimportant, since neither Arrian nor Callisthenes reveals either what it was in fact that Alexander asked or what response(s) he received. The third motive, however, that of tracing part of either his descent or the manner of his conception to Ammon, is important: it turns up not just in Arrian but indirectly in Curtius too, that is, in a Vulgate source. The question remains, therefore, of why the motive of desiring to learn more about his (putatively divine) paternity is absent from Callisthenes.

Leaving that on one side for the moment, we must turn to the divergent accounts of what went on once Alexander had arrived at the oracle. At this point Arrian suddenly and suspiciously – religious reserve? sceptical detachment? – dries up. After all the (relatively) full detail he has given on the motives underlying Alexander's *pothos*, violent desire, to consult the oracle of Ammon, we get just this: 'He put his question to the oracle and received (or so he said) the answer that his soul desired.' We move on – to the Vulgate sources, which at this point, no less suspiciously, wax positively garrulous.

According to Trogus/Justin, but only to him, Alexander had suborned Ammon's priest in advance to give the responses he required. All three agree in stating that the priest addressed Alexander as the son of a god (either Ammon, or Zeus identified syncretistically with Ammon), and that Alexander asked two questions, to both of which he received affirmative answers: namely, yes, Philip's murder had been avenged; and, yes, he, Alexander, would rule the whole world. Curtius and Trogus/Justin add that Alexander's friends then received the further oracular response that their king was to be worshipped as a god. How are we to choose between the Vulgate sources, going back ultimately to Cleitarchus, and Arrian, reproducing in whole or in part the Official version of Ptolemy and Aristoboulus?

If we look back to Callisthenes and compare what we know of his account with what we know of the Official and Vulgate versions, both similarities and differences emerge. The first and most important point is that Callisthenes states, as we might have inferred from Arrian, that Alexander did not divulge the content of his question, or questions, at the time. Openly – in the hearing of Alexander's entourage and perhaps within earshot of Callisthenes himself – the chief priest told Alexander he was the son of Zeus. This can be reconciled, if need be, with the various ways in which the Vulgate sources say that Alexander was addressed by the priest of Ammon as a son of Ammon. For the Greeks did sometimes identify Libyan Ammon/Amun with Greek Zeus (though on other occasions they were able to see them as separate deities too).

On the other hand, there is not in Callisthenes (as preserved) a whisper of Alexander's two questions as reported by the Vulgate sources. These should probably be rejected as inauthentic, on grounds either of inappropriateness or of anachronism, and their invention attributed probably to the ever fertile imagination of Cleitarchus. What, then, of the silence of Ptolemy/Aristoboulus on the (alleged) matter of the chief priest's addressing Alexander as son of Zeus? Might this be a case of censorship, since both found distasteful Alexander's undeniable later use of this divine filiation for purposes of which they, for different reasons, disapproved? At any rate, their silence should not be taken as by itself sufficient to disprove the Vulgate's allegation of the priest's mode of addressing Alexander.

Plutarch, as might have been expected, preferred the garrulity of the Vulgate tradition to the reserve, self-imposed or otherwise, of the Official tradition. But then, in Chapter 27, section 5, of the *Alexander*, he adds two pieces of 'evidence'. The first is an alleged letter to his mother Olympias, in which Alexander says that he has received from Ammon certain secret responses that he will divulge to her alone on his return to Macedonia. The second is a story found in a minority of the extant writers, to the effect that Ammon's priest did not really mean to address Alexander as 'son of Zeus' but tripped over the unfamiliar Greek words meaning 'My child/son', which came out sounding to Greek ears like 'O son of Zeus'. Of these items of evidence, the letter can safely be discounted as a forgery, even if it is a forgery based ultimately on Callisthenes's report of Alexander's studied silence about the secret responses. The story of the priest's verbal slip is harder to evaluate. If, on the one hand, it was genuine, then it might have been construed by any Greek or Macedonian listeners as itself an inspired omen of Alexander's future status. Alternatively, it might be rejected critically as an ingenious fiction designed to refute the pro-Alexander claim that his divine filiation had been given the seal of official approval by Ammon's priest.

More, much more, could be – and has been elsewhere – said. But I hope I have sufficiently achieved my fairly modest aim of illustrating the sorts of source problems the hunter after the 'real' Alexander can encounter. These are deep and murky waters. They have to be trawled, however, and have been, for the most part silently, throughout the main text of this book.

Table of Achaemenid Kings*

Reign dates before Cyrus II are approximate

650–620 BCE	Teispes
620–590	Cyrus I
590–559	Cambyses I
559–530	Cyrus II the Great
530–522	Cambyses II (son)
522	Bardiya (brother)
522–486	Darius I (distant relative of Cambyses)
486–465	Xerxes I (son)
465–424	Artaxerxes I (son)
424 (45 days only)	Xerxes II (son)
424–404	Darius II Ochus (bastard brother)
404–359	Artaxerxes II Arsaces (son)
359–338	Artaxerxes III Ochus (son)
338–336	Artaxerxes IV Arses (son)
336–330	Darius III Artashata (relative)

* After M. Brosius, *The Persian Empire from Cyrus to Artaxerxes I*, modified.

Dramatis Personae

Names cross-referenced within this list are in italic type; words cross-referring to the Glossary are in small capitals.

Alex. = Alexander III the Great

Abdalonymus – Prince from Sidon in Phoenicia (roughly modern Lebanon), appointed ruler of Sidon for Alex. in 332 BCE, allegedly on recommendation of *Hephaestion*. Traditionally believed to be the occupant of so-called Alexander Sarcophagus. *See* Figures 2 and 8.

Achaemenids – Persian royal house, supposedly originating with eponymous Achaemenes (Greek transcription of Persian name), from area of PASARGADAE. Actually documented first 'Achaemenid' monarch was Teispes (650–620). *See* Table of Achaemenid Kings.

Ada – Daughter of Hecatomnos, first native Carian under-SATRAP of mixed Greek–Carian HALICARNASSUS (birthplace of Herodotus) within the SATRAPY of LYDIA. Sister–wife of Idrieus, younger sister of Mausolus (of 'Mausoleum' fame) and Artemisia (who also married each other). Despite, or because of, his extreme difficulty in capturing Halicarnassus in 334, Alex. retained Ada in her satrapal role with honorific title of 'queen'. She in return quasi-formally adopted him as her 'son'.

Agis III – Spartan king of the Eurypontid house, r. 338–?331. Attempted inconclusively to liaise with Persian naval commanders in Crete and Aegean (333) and succeeded in raising revolt by some Peloponnesian states against MACEDON in 331, only to be comprehensively defeated and killed in battle – referred to unkindly by Alex. as a 'battle of mice' – by *Antipater* at Megalopolis in Arcadia (331 or 330).

Ahura Mazda – Name means 'Wise Lord' or 'Lord Wisdom' in Persian language; Hellenized as 'Oromasdes' or 'Oromazes' and equated by Greeks with Zeus. His cult was promoted especially by *Zoroaster*. Supreme Iranian deity of light, he was featured prominently in Old Persian inscriptions and represented in cartouche as a winged figure, e.g. in Darius I's monument at BISITUN. *See* Figure 12.

Alexander IV – Posthumous son of Alex. and *Roxane*. Made joint ruler of Empire with *Philip III Arrhidaeus* in 322 by *Perdiccas*, but never more than a tool of his grandmother *Olympias*, with whom he was taken prisoner in 316 by *Cassander*. Murdered in 311, aged only 11 or 12, after internment at AMPHIPOLIS. Tomb III at AEGAE has been implausibly assigned to him.

Alexander of Molossia – Brother of *Olympias* and king/general of Molossian federation of southern Epirus *c.*342–330/29; Molossian royal house claimed descent from Neoptolemus, son of Achilles. Client of *Philip II*, at whose court he was groomed to marry Philip and Olympias's daughter, *Cleopatra*. Died fighting in south Italy in 330.

Ammon – Hellenized form of Libyan–Egyptian sky god, Amun, sometimes equated by Greeks with Zeus. Alex.'s consultation of his oracular shrine at SIWAH, after life-threatening and strategically questionable march in winter 332/1, was pivotal episode in his personal life and political career. Alex. is depicted on immediately posthumous coinage (see COINS) wearing the ram's horns of Ammon. *See* Figure 24.

Anaxarchus of Abdera – Major philosopher from Abdera in northern Greece, adherent of empiricist–materialist school of Democritus (also of Abdera; ?470–385), and teacher of Pyrrhon, founder of Scepticism. Accompanied Alex. to Asia and remained with him to the end in Babylon. Wrote (lost) treatise on kingship, and actively sought to influence Alex.'s ideological self-projection (e.g., by suggesting that superhuman achievements conferred godhead).

Antigonus Monophthalmus – Macedonian noble, born *c.*382, a near-coeval of Philip II, under whom he prospered. Appointed SATRAP of Greater Phrygia by Alex., he saved his king's bacon in three desperate post-ISSUS encounters in 332. Fell out with the post-Alex. regent *Perdiccas* and remained major player in the Wars of the Alexandrine Succession until his death at Battle of Ipsus in central Phrygia in 301. Father of Demetrius Poliorcetes ('the Besieger'), whom he married off aged only 15 to a daughter of *Antipater*.

Antipater – Macedonian noble (in Greek, Antipatros), born ? early 390s; served Philip II in important capacities (e.g., in diplomacy with Athens, 346 and 338). Appointed Macedonian regent by Alex. in 335; from 334 de facto viceroy of Alex. in Europe. Quashed revolt of *Agis III*, but his relations with Alex. deteriorated later, and perhaps *Craterus* had been sent back from Asia in 324 to replace him. After Alex.'s death, was instrumental in winning LAMIAN WAR (323/2) and sided with Craterus against *Perdiccas*; died 319.

Apelles – Greek from Ionia (Colophon, later Ephesus). Painter of extreme verismo, he was commissioned by Philip II and became Alex.'s exclusive court portraitist, most famously – or controversially – depicting him mounted and wielding thunderbolt (attribute of Zeus). Also portrayed Alex. holding personified god of war as bound captive, and in company of the Dioscuri (Castor and Pollux, divine twin brothers of Helen of Troy) and the goddess Victory (Nike) personified.

Aristander – Greek *mantis* (seer) from Telmissus (modern Fethiye) in Lycia (southwest Anatolia), whose interpretations of supposed signs and omens acquired extraordinary authority with Alex. One reason for his success was skill at hedging his bets.

Aristoboulus – Served Alex. on Persian expedition as architect (e.g., restoring desecrated tomb of *Cyrus II* at PASARGADAE and in other capacities), settling after 316 as citizen of new foundation of Cassandreia (*Cassander*). Wrote up apologetic account of Alex. in extreme old age (84-plus) after Battle of Ipsus (301) in reaction against hostile anti-Alex. accounts. *Arrian* took him, together with *Ptolemy*, as one of his two main sources. *See the* Appendix.

Aristotle – Major Greek intellectual of his day (384–322), born at Stageira in Chalcidice but spent most of adult life at Athens, where he founded Lyceum institute for advanced study in the 330s. Son of personal physician to Amyntas III (father of Philip II), Aristotle (Aristoteles, in Greek) was appointed by Philip II to tutor Alex. at *Mieza* in 343 and remained in touch with his former pupil until latter's death. Credited with extant exchange of (invented) correspondence, he certainly did request and receive botanical and other natural-historical specimens from Alex. in Asia. His views on ideal kingship were at least influenced by firsthand experience of Alex., though he did not share latter's more enlarged views of the nature of barbarians (non-Greeks) and how to rule them. *See* Figures 7, 16, 37.

Arrhidaeus – *see* **Philip III Arrhidaeus**

Arrian – Lucius (or Aulus) Flavius Arrianus Xenophon (to give his full Roman name), Greek politician and intellectual from Nicomedeia in Asia Minor. Studied as young man with ex-slave Greek Stoic philosopher Epictetus, and as adult flourished under philhellenic emperor Hadrian (CE 117–138). His *Anabasis* ('March Up Country') and *Indica* ('Indian Affairs') are two of our major extant narrative sources for Alex. *See the* Appendix.

Arsites – Persian noble, SATRAP for Darius III of Hellespontine Phrygia (capital, Dascyleum); apparently overall commander, as *primus inter pares*, of Persian forces at RIVER GRANICUS battle in 334. Fled after defeat to Greater Phrygia where he committed suicide. Alex. replaced him as satrap with *Calas*.

Artabazus – Persian noble (*c.* mid 380s to *c.*325), son of Pharnabazus I (prominent in Thucydides and Xenophon), member of satrapal dynasty that ruled Hellespontine Phrygia from late 5th century to mid 4th. Grandson via mother Apame of Great King Artaxerxes II (r. 404–359), against whom he revolted in late 350s, fleeing to court of Philip II of Macedon. Returned to Persia in 343 and remained loyal to *Darius III* until latter's murder in 330; thereafter went over to Alex., who appointed him SATRAP of BACTRIA. Resigned as satrap in 327 and died soon after.

Artaxerxes III – Given name was Ochus, acquired throne name 'Artaxerxes' (Old Persian, Artakhshayathra) on succession to father Artaxerxes II in 359, reigned until 338. Put down SATRAPS' revolt in Asia Minor (see *Artabazus*) and, after crushing Phoenician revolt in 345, reconquered Egypt (in revolt since 404) in 343. Assassinated in 338 through machinations of Grand Vizier Bagoas (a eunuch, but not to be confused with Alex.'s *Bagoas*). In 324 at mass weddings in Susa, Alex. married a daughter of his.

Artaxerxes IV – Youngest son of *Artaxerxes III*, his given name was Arses; came to throne in 338 with regnal name 'Artaxerxes' thanks to multiple murders orchestrated by anorchic Grand Vizier Bagoas. Murdered on Bagoas's orders in 336.

Attalus – Macedonian noble, son-in-law of *Parmenion*, guardian of the Cleopatra to whom Philip II was married in 337. Antagonized Alex. by praying for offspring of the marriage to be 'legitimate' successor to Macedonian throne. Alex. had him murdered as soon as he indecently could after becoming king, in 336.

Bagoas – Younger of the two prominent Persian eunuchs of this name, introduced in 330 when still a teenager to Alex. at Zadracarta by Nabarzanes, *Darius III*'s Grand Vizier. An outstanding beauty, and possibly also an accomplished singer and dancer, he became almost certainly Alex.'s lover, as he had been Darius's. A figure of ambiguous acceptability to both leading Macedonians and leading Persians, but of unquestionably great influence with Alex. Eponymous subject of Mary Renault's historical novel, *The Persian Boy*.

Barsine – Noble Persian, daughter of *Artabazus*, wife of *Memnon*. Rumoured to have had an affair, after Memnon's death in 333, with Alex. that produced a son named Heracles: remarkable if true.

Batis – Eunuch, Arab, governor of Gaza in the Persian interest. His fierce resistance to Alex.'s siege in 332 was rewarded with excruciating death by being tied at the ankles and dragged behind chariot round and round Gaza's walls.

Bel-Marduk – 'Lord Marduk': name may mean 'bull-calf of the sun'; an agricultural god, chief deity of the Babylonians, worshipped in the Esagila temple. Alex. was careful to reverence him ostentatiously, especially during his final re-entry to, and stay at, Babylon in 324/3.

Bessus – SATRAP of BACTRIA and relative of *Darius III*, after murdering whom he briefly assumed the Achaemenid title as Artaxerxes (V) before being himself captured (by *Ptolemy*), then mutilated and executed by Alex. in 329.

Bucephalas – Massively expensive Thessalian stallion, with distinctive white marking (either a natural blaze on his muzzle or a brand-mark resembling ox-head shape after which he was named), whom Philip was persuaded to buy for his son against his better judgement. Served his master faithfully and successfully until his death in Pakistan in 326 in his late twenties or early thirties. Alexander rewarded him with lavish funeral and by naming after him new settlement on RIVER HYDASPES, called Bucephala. *See* Figure 6.

Calanus – Alex. included in his entourage barbarian as well as Greek sages (see *Anaxarchus of Abdera*) and most famous of the former was Indian Brahman ascetic Calanus of Taxila in the Punjab. Nothing became Calanus in life so much as his manner of leaving it: judging the time had come, at Persepolis in 324, he committed suicide by fire – a spectacular pyrification ceremony accompanied by gymnastic and musical competitions and by prodigious, sometimes fatal, potations.

Calas – Leading Macedonian, a commander of expeditionary force of 336 in succession to murdered *Attalus*; appointed SATRAP of Hellespontine Phrygia in 334 in succession to *Arsites*. Campaigned successfully against Paphlagonians.

Callisthenes – Native of OLYNTHUS; junior relative (nephew or great-nephew) of *Aristotle*, with whom he compiled a list of victors at Panhellenic Pythian Games (held at Delphi every four years since 582). Appointed Alex.'s official historian, perhaps on Aristotle's recommendation, but, despite lavish flattery, fell out in 327 with his master over the issue of PROSKYNESIS and was executed for alleged treason. *See the* Appendix.

Cassander – Son of *Antipater*, who sent him as his representative to Alex. at BABYLON in 323, but Alex. treated him with undisguised contempt. Major player in Wars of the Alexandrine Succession, having himself hailed 'king' of Macedon in 305; eponymous founder of Cassandreia (316). Died 297.

Chares – Greek courtier from Mytilene on Lesbos, who rose to be Alex.'s chamberlain. Wrote highly romanticized *Histories of Alexander* (lost, but used by *Plutarch* and by Athenaeus, Egyptian Greek compiler of dinner-table anecdotes). *See the* Appendix.

Cleitarchus – Son of Greek historian of Persia, Dinon, and himself author of an at least 12-book *History* of Alex., much plundered by authors within the VULGATE tradition of Alex. historiography, which sometimes corrects and can be used to supplement the OFFICIAL tradition represented by *Arrian. See the* Appendix.

Cleitus the Black – Leading Macedonian noble (so nicknamed to avoid confusion with Cleitus 'the White'), brother of Alex.'s wet nurse. Saved Alex.'s life at GRANICUS, but disapproved violently enough of trend of Alex.'s behaviour and policy after defeating Darius to oppose him openly at drinking bout in MARACANDA in 328. Alex. personally murdered him in his cups.

Cleomenes – Greek from Naucratis in Nile delta, placed in charge of eastern sector of Egypt by Alex. in 332/1. Allegedly profiteered from his position of supposed fiscal responsibility and became de facto SATRAP of Egypt based at the new foundation of ALEXANDRIA. *Ptolemy* in 323, after Alex.'s death, found Alexandria not big enough for both of them and had Cleomenes executed on grounds of suspected sympathy with *Perdiccas*.

Cleopatra – Daughter of Philip II and Olympias and full sister of Alex., she was married dynastically to *Alexander of Molossia*, her mother's brother. Ruled as regent in her husband's absence in Italy.

Cleopatra – Also known as Eurydice; seventh and last wife of Philip II, and niece and ward of *Attalus*, who negotiated her marriage to Philip at highly sensitive time of 337. She duly produced son, who was given the redolent name Caranus (after mythical founder of the Argead royal line), but by then Philip had been assassinated, Alex. had succeeded, and Alex.'s mother saw to both her death by suicide and the murder of Caranus.

Coenus – High-ranking Macedonian, son-in-law of *Parmenion*, sent back to raise reinforcements from Greece in 334. Sided with Alex. against his brother-in-law *Philotas* in 330, played important command role in guerrilla campaign in central Asia (see *Spitamenes*) and at the RIVER HYDASPES battle in 326. Made mistake of speaking up for mutinous Macedonians at the HYPHASIS and died soon afterwards.

Cossaeans – Mountain tribespeople of Iran south-west of ECBATANA, to whom the Achaemenid kings had traditionally paid annual sum for right of passage through their territory; Alex. repudiated this traditional agreement and violently targeted them in winter 324/3, his last campaign as it turned out.

Craterus – Son-in-law of *Antipater*, appointed to a command by Alex. in 334 and eventually rose to be a marshal of his Empire. Instrumental in removing *Philotas* and *Parmenion* in 330, he took leading commands in Sogdiana and India. Tasked to escort 10,000 demobbed Macedonians back to MACEDONIA after OPIS affair in 324, he may also have been appointed by Alex. to replace Antipater. His forces were key to victory in LAMIAN WAR. Died fighting *Eumenes* in Asia Minor in 321. *See* Figure 3.

Curtius Rufus, Quintus – Roman author (1st century CE) of a *History* of Alex. in ten books, of which the last eight survive. *See the* Appendix.

Cyrus II – Cyrus the Great, founder of the Achaemenid Empire (*c*.559–530). Achieved remarkable feat of earning a good press even from his or his successors' subjects (Jewish, Greek). Son of Median mother and Persian father, he reversed the relationship between Persians and their Median kinsmen, then expanded the Empire rapidly by conquest east, west and north, dying fighting Massagetae of east Caspian region. *See* Figure 37.

Darius III – Artashata (not Codomannus as previously believed) became Darius III in 336 following asassination of *Artaxerxes IV*. Derogated and derided according to usual principle that history is written by the winners, but it is not clear that Darius was unusually incompetent or ill-prepared to meet and beat off Alex. Having fled from GAUGAMELA in 331, as he had fled from defeat at ISSUS in 333, he was deposed in a coup by *Bessus*/Artaxerxes V, who left him for dead shortly before Alex. could catch up with him in 330.

Demosthenes – Demosthenes (384–322) became foremost democratic politician of Athens on a ticket of unrelenting patriotic opposition to first Philip of Macedon and then his son. Policy bore little positive fruit in military terms, but Athens, unlike Thebes, remained democracy and free of Macedonian garrison despite rebellions in 336 and 335; and Demosthenes retained popularity at home until he became embroiled in *Harpalus* affair of 324. Committed suicide as fugitive on island of Calaureia (Poros).

Diodorus of Sicily – Flourished in latter part of 1st century BCE; author of monumental *Library of History* dealing with Greek history from return of descendants of Heracles (notionally, 12th century in our terms) onwards. *See the* Appendix.

Dionysus – Member of Olympian pantheon, god of wine, disguise and metamorphosis with strong northern Greek associations. Alex., influenced initially by his mother, was always a devoted follower of Dionysus, in both spiritual and physical sense – and paid him sincerest compliment of trying not just to imitate but to outdo him, especially in India.

Eumenes – Greek from Cardia in the Hellespont (Dardanelles), sufficiently important to merit extant *Life* by *Plutarch*. Bureaucrat par excellence, who served as chief secretary both to Philip II and to Alex., but also appointed senior cavalry commander by Alex. in his last year. Went on to play leading role in Wars of Alexandrine Succession until his death in 316.

Harpalus – Upper Macedonian noble from ELIMIOTIS, friend of Alex. from boyhood, educated with him at MIEZA, exiled with him in 337/6. Deserted Alex. shortly before ISSUS battle, but reinstated as Grand Imperial Treasurer of Empire in 331 and controller of central treasuries at BABYLON. Committed second and final defection in 324, before Alex. could catch up with him in Babylon; fled to Cilicia and then Athens, bringing with him 5,000 talents. Mutual recriminations about disbursement – or peculation – of 700 talents brought down *Demosthenes*. Harpalus again fled, with mercenary army, to Crete, where he was murdered by a lieutenant.

Hephaestion – Boyhood friend of Alex., like *Harpalus*, but his developing relationship was of unusual, and probably sexual, intimacy. Emerged to prominence as cavalry commander in 330 after death of *Philotas*; entrusted with bridging the Indus in 327, appointed bodyguard of Alex. and then Grand Vizier. Married, like Alex., a daughter of *Darius III* in mass Susa weddings of 324. Died suddenly at Ecbatana in autumn 324 and accorded by Alex. magnificent funeral and (with *Ammon*'s sanction) posthumous heroic honours. *See* Figure 29.

Heracles – Universal Greek hero–god, ancestor of Macedonian royal house (Argeads), object of special devotion and emulation by Alex.

Hermolaus – One of Alex.'s ROYAL PAGES, ringleader of alleged conspiracy against Alex.'s life in 327 that also brought down *Callisthenes* by alleged association.

Homer – Fount of all Greek literature and much Panhellenic folk memory; attributed with many works, above all the two major epics, the *Iliad* and the *Odyssey*. Aristotle annotated special copy of the *Iliad* for Alex., who in many ways modelled himself on the unique Achilles and his overall commander at Troy, Agamemnon. Alex. kept this copy in golden chest captured from *Darius III* after ISSUS battle. One of Alex.'s boyhood tutors (*Lysimachus*) likened himself to Homer's Phoenix and Alex. to Achilles.

Isocrates – Long-lived (436–338) Athenian rhetorician, who in open letter urged Philip of Macedon to conquer at least the western chunk of Persian Empire in the name of all Greeks and Greek culture (see PANHELLENISM).

Justin – Marcus Iunianus Iustinus, to give his full Latin name, wrote in the high Roman Empire (?3rd century CE) extant epitome of the now lost *Philippic Histories* by Pompeius Trogus, an educated Gaul who acquired Roman citizenship soon after Julius Caesar's conquest and annexation in 1st century BCE. Trogus/ Justin belongs, with *Curtius* and *Diodorus*, to the VULGATE tradition of Alex. historiography. *See the* Appendix.

Leonidas – Relative of Alex.'s mother and, with *Lysimachus*, one of Alex.'s two principal boyhood tutors. Appropriately for namesake of famed Spartan king, he was a stickler for severe physical regimen and self-controlled abstinence. At animal sacrifice once rebuked his pupil for being too heavy-handed with expensive Arabian incense – a rebuke that the ever-mindful Alex. repaid by sending him 18 tons of frankincense and myrrh after capture of Gaza (see *Batis*).

Leonnatus – Related to Macedonian royal family through Philip II's mother, served as bodyguard successively to Philip and Alex. Helped kill *Pausanias* in 336, and participated at highest military and diplomatic levels throughout Alex.'s campaigns, earning SATRAPY of Hellespontine Phrygia in 323. Killed during LAMIAN WAR attempting to relieve the besieged *Antipater*.

Leosthenes – Athenian general, both mercenary commander and regular elected Athenian officer. Played key role in mobilizing Alex.'s demobbed mercenaries gathered at Taenarum (within Sparta's territory) for revolt against Macedon in 323 (see LAMIAN WAR), using to pay them money filched by *Harpalus*. He was killed and his cause defeated, but he was honoured with heroic state funeral.

Lycurgus – Principal Athenian statesman during the post-CHAERONEA battle (338) period. Oversaw revitalization of Athens's economy and culture and maintained strong anti-Macedonian stance.

Lysimachus – Greek from Acarnania; one of Alex.'s two principal boyhood tutors (with *Leonidas*), who played the *Homer* card for all it was worth. Insisted on visiting his old pupil during siege of TYRE (332) and had to be rescued by Alex. from death by exposure.

Lysippus – Sculptor from Sicyon working exclusively in bronze between c.370 and 315. Like *Apelles*, only less so, he was one of Alex.'s official court artists, responsible for a number of Alexander types, including original of the Azara herm. *See* Figures 7, 30.

Mazaeus – Persian noble (c.385–328), SATRAP of Cilicia and Syria under *Artaxerxes III* and *Darius III*. Entrusted with command of Darius's right wing at GAUGAMELA, he achieved transition to Alex.'s service so smoothly as to arouse suspicion that his surrender of Babylon was due to collusion. Rewarded with the key satrapy of Babylonia, the first Iranian to be appointed to satrapal post by Alex.; his wife was Babylonian and he appears to have been devoted to worship of *Bel-Marduk*.

Memnon – Greek military commander from Rhodes, in the service of *Artabazus*, whose daughter *Barsine* he married. Despite revolting with Artabazus against *Artaxerxes III*, he was restored to favour and then served *Darius III* effectively both by land and especially by sea, where he was placed in overall command of Persian fleet. Successfully defended besieged HALICARNASSUS in 334, but died at Mytilene on Lesbos in 333.

Nearchus – Cretan, another boyhood friend of Alex. Shared Alex.'s tribulations under Philip II and was rewarded for his loyalty with first the SATRAPY of Lycia/Pamphylia (334–329), then command of Alex.'s fleets first on the RIVER HYDASPES, and then from India to the Tigris and on to Iran in 325/4. Played leading role at BABYLON in 323, and after Alex.'s death served *Antigonus Monophthalmus*. His (lost) apologetic memoirs were used by Greek geographer Strabo (1st century BCE to 1st century CE) and especially *Arrian. See the* Appendix.

Nicanor – Native of Stageira, like *Aristotle*, who named him as future husband of his daughter in his will. Commissioned by Alex. to promulgate the EXILES' DECREE at Olympic Games of 324 and undertook other diplomatic missions.

Olympias – Sister of *Alexander of Molossia*, wife of Philip II (allegedly a love match) and mother of Alex., who, when king, complained that she charged him a high rent for the nine months he spent in her womb. Of immense energy and resource, with bitterly cruel and vindictive streak, she survived her repudiation by Philip by trying to ensure that Alex. remained devoted to her. Suspected of being somehow behind Philip's assassination in 336, she made sure that Alex. would not be troubled by any survivors of Philip's last (seventh) marriage (to *Cleopatra*). Relations with *Antipater* were also bad, and she remained in her native Epirus from 331 to 317. Embroiled in the Succession Wars, she was killed by relatives of her Macedonian victims in 316. Has given her name to the reconstructed Greek trireme (man-of-war) officially commissioned into the Greek navy and kept mainly in dry dock. *See* Figure 5.

Onesicritus – Greek from tiny Aegean island of Astypalaea; served Alex. as helmsman in India, then *Nearchus*, with whom he acrimoniously fell out. From mentor Diogenes he imbibed elements of Cynic philosophy that he tried to invest Alex. with in his (lost) memoirs. *See the* Appendix.

Parmenion – Upper Macedonian noble, premier general of Philip II, inherited and retained by Alex. as his deputy until 330, when he was murdered following execution of his oldest son *Philotas*. Parmenion was three times older and more than three times more cautious than Alex., giving rise to anecdotal evidence of regular disagreements between them on strategy and tactics. His loyalty was nevertheless unswerving.

Pausanias – Who, if anyone, was Pausanias's Svengali, will never be known for sure, nor will his motives; history records only that he, a member of the inner royal bodyguard, assassinated Philip at AEGAE in 336 and was in turn promptly killed (see *Leonnatus*).

Perdiccas – Upper Macedonian noble from Orestis; rose to be member of Alex.'s bodyguard by 330, and a marshal of the Empire. Succeeded *Hephaestion* in 324 as cavalry commander and Grand Vizier. Guardian of *Philip III* and of Alex.'s unborn child with *Roxane*, he became at Alex.'s death de facto regent. Killed in Egypt in 321 in the Succession Wars.

Perseus – Through a familiar etymological confusion, this mythological hero (son of Danae and Zeus, who succeeded in decapitating the Gorgon Medusa) became considered the eponym of the Persian people; as such, he found a place in the panoply of gods and heroes to whom Alex. was careful to pay his respects publicly.

Peucestas – Macedonian; saved Alex.'s life among the MALLI of the southern Punjab in 326, promoted to join elite bodyguard, and granted plum SATRAPY of Persis (325/4). Only leading Macedonian to adopt thoroughly Alex.'s orientalizing programme to extent of learning to speak Persian and wearing Persian dress. Survived long after Alex.'s death, but not as premier-division player.

Philippus of Acarnania – Physician; with *Aristandrus* the seer, one of the two key members of Alex.'s technical support staff. Like *Lysimachus*, he was a Greek from Acarnania. Performed his role most critically in late 333 before Battle of ISSUS, by purging Alex. when he was suffering from bronchial fever after taking unwise dip in ice-cold River Cydnus, which flowed through city of Tarsus.

Philip II – Son of Amyntas III (r. 393–369), succeeded technically as regent for nephew in 359 but in practice as King. Responsible for transforming Macedon into premier power of Aegean Greek world by 338 (Battle of CHAERONEA) and founding LEAGUE OF CORINTH. As HÊGEMÔN of League appointed to Persian command but assassinated at AEGAE in 336.

Philip III Arrhidaeus – Born in *c.*357, son of Philip II and one of his seven wives, Philinna of Thessalian Larissa. Did not trouble the record during reigns of either his father or Alex., but somehow found his way to BABYLON in 323 and, despite mental impairment, was formally declared king jointly with infant Alexander IV (son of Alex. and *Roxane*). A pawn in the great Succession game, he became another victim of *Olympias* in 317.

Philotas – Upper Macedonian noble, oldest son of *Parmenion*, sole commander of Companion Cavalry until death in 330. His condemnation for treason was trumped up mainly to get Parmenion out of the way.

Plutarch – Greek biographer and philosopher, *c.* CE 46–120, from CHAERONEA in Boeotia. Wrote many parallel *Lives*, most of which survive, including the pair of

Alexander and *Julius Caesar*. *Alexander* begins with programmatic declaration that Plutarch is writing 'lives, not histories', but his sort of moral biography was also very historical, and he is almost the sole surviving source for first 20 years of Alexander's life. *See the* Appendix.

Polyperchon – Upper Macedonian from Tymphaea, raised to command of his native battalion within the Companion infantry phalanx after ISSUS. Returned to Macedonia after OPIS demobilization (324), and, at first as deputy to *Craterus*, became major player in Succession Wars before dying in retirement in Peloponnese after 309.

Porus – Hellenized form of name of great Rajah of the Pauravas living between Rivers Hydaspes and Acesines (Chenab) in the Punjab. Enormously tall and fearless, he and his elephant-stiffened force gave Alexander a tough time at the HYDASPES battle in 326 before being utterly trounced. Alex. rewarded his courage by retaining him as Rajah and granting him an expanded realm over territories east of the Hydaspes, including perhaps Sind. In 318, assassinated by Macedonian commander of Taxila (former base of Indian ruler Taxiles, who actively cooperated with Alex.). *See* Figure 21.

Ptolemy – Macedonian noble, best known under throne name Ptolemy I Soter ('Saviour'), after he became founding king of Ptolemaic Egypt (305); another boyhood friend and schoolmate of Alex. (see *Harpalus, Hephaestion, Nearchus*). Accompanied Alex. to SIWAH in winter 332/1. One version of burning of the palace at PERSEPOLIS in 330 attributed it to the suggestion of Athenian courtesan Thais, then Ptolemy's partner. Captured pretender *Bessus* in 329. Rose to be a marshal of the Empire. At Susa weddings (324), was married to a daughter of *Artabazus*, but mother of his Egyptian dynastic line was the Macedonian Berenice (in standard Greek, Pherenice means 'Victory-bringer'). After Alex.'s death he cleverly hijacked his corpse (en route from Babylon to Macedonia) and had it buried first at Memphis (the old native capital), then at Alexandria (Alex.'s new capital). From Alexandria he ruled Egypt, first as SATRAP (replacing *Cleomenes*), finally as king (305–285). His lost and very retrospective memoirs of Alex. (responding to *Cleitarchus*) formed one of two main sources of the 'Official' tradition represented by *Arrian*. *See the* Appendix. It is the conceit of the trilogy of historical novels about Alex. by Valerio Massimo Manfredi that they are the (recovered!) journals of Ptolemy. *See* Figures 31, 36.

Roxane – Daughter of Sogdian baron Oxyartes whose seat lay athwart Alex.'s route eastwards in 327; married to Alex. as part of political settlement of the region (like his father, Alex. fought his wars by marriages). Romance had it that she was stunningly beautiful and that the marriage was a love match; alas, for the truth. She did her duty by producing a son and heir for Alex., but by then he was dead, and she and her son (*Alexander IV*) were victims of the Succession Wars and murdered on orders of *Cassander* in 311.

Seleucus I Nicator – Son of Antiochus, one of Philip's generals, and near-contemporary of Alex. Fought as commander with Alex., married Bactrian princess Apame in mass Susa weddings (324) and, uniquely, did not thereafter repudiate her. Gained SATRAPY of Babylonia in 321 and later (305) made himself king of an empire that embraced most of Alex.'s Asiatic domains.

Sisygambis – Mother of *Darius III*, taken prisoner by Alex. after ISSUS. Famous anecdote has her mistaking the taller *Hephaestion* for Alex., who replied that 'he too is another Alexander'. Alex. reportedly treated her and her daughter-in-law *Stateira* with studied courtesy, partly at least for political–dynastic reasons of his own. *See* Figure 27.

Spitamenes – Like *Roxane*'s father, a Sogdian baron, who after *Bessus*'s death (329) was most painful thorn in Alex.'s flesh as he conducted three-year mountain guerrilla campaign against local nationalist resistance from Afghanistan to Bokhara, from Lake Seistan to the HINDU KUSH. Executed and decapitated by Massagetae in 327 after *Coenus* had inflicted major defeat, though *Curtius* offers fancy tale that it was his own wife who executed him.

Stateira – Wife of *Darius III*, captured with mother-in-law (*Sisygambis*) and children after ISSUS (333), she died in captivity (331). Alexander married one of her daughters at Susa mass wedding ceremony (324). *See* Figure 27.

Triballi – The Triballian kingdom was centred in the Danube valley near its confluence with the Oescus. Byword for barbarous brutishness in sophisticated Athens, the Triballi under their king Syrmus were defeated in 335 as part of Alex.'s miraculous inaugural campaign as king in non-Greek north. False rumour that Alex. had been killed prompted second Greek rebellion against him in the south. Triballi contributed contingent to expeditionary force of 334.

Trogus – *see* Justin

Zoroaster – Born Zarathustra (in Iranian) at Zariaspa, capital of BACTRIA, between 1000 and 550 BCE. As prophet who 'possesses the sacred formulas', he was instrumental in spreading worship of *Ahura Mazda*, supreme deity of light and truth whose cult was promoted as political tool, especially by Darius I (see BISITUN).

Glossary

Words cross-referenced within this list are in italic type; names cross-referring to the Dramatis Personae are in small capitals.

Aegae – Site of original capital of Macedonian kingdom, before transfer to *Pella*; in northern Pieria, at modern Vergina, well placed to exploit western end of coastal lowland plain. Distinguished by remarkable royal tombs. *See* Figures 9, 18, 19. Site of theatre where Alex.'s father Philip was assassinated has been located.

Ai Khanum – Of the fabled 'thousand cities' of *Bactria* only Ai Khanum ('Lady Moon', in Uzbek) has come to light, excavated by French team under P. Bernard (1965–78). Well situated on left bank of *River Oxus* to control eastern marches of Bactria, it developed genuine urban centre with gymnasium and hero shrine to the city's founder Cineas, the latter inscribed with Apolline maxims brought out from Delphi in Greece by Clearchus of Soli in Cyprus, a pupil of ARISTOTLE'S. Has been identified plausibly as genuine foundation of Alex.'s, possibly Alexandria Oxiana.

Alexander Romance – Alternatively known as 'Pseudo-Callisthenes', since falsely ascribed to original official historian (*see* CALLISTHENES), this is generic title for a work of historically based fiction originating in Hellenistic Alexandria and spreading from there in Roman period. Known in numerous variants in Greek, Syriac, Armenian, Latin and other vernacular recensions, it contains some surprising factoids such as the seduction of OLYMPIAS by last Pharaoh of Egypt, Nectanebis II, which would make Alex. half-Egyptian by birth.

Alexandria Arachosia – Alexandria of the Arachosians, founded by Alex. in 329 on site of Old Kandahar (Afghanistan), former capital of Achaemenid *satrapy* of Arachosia. Famed later as findspot of Graeco-Aramaic edict of Mauryan Buddhist ruler Ashoka (*c.*268–232 BCE).

Alexandria Areia – Alexandria of the Areians, founded by Alex. near Herat (ancient Artacoana) on important staging-point on route to Kandahar (see *Alexandria Arachosia*).

Alexandria (Egypt) – Or rather 'Alexandria by Egypt', since it was never integrated fully into the old Egyptian order. Founded in Nile delta at Canopic mouth in 331 (official date 7 April), by Alex. in person, to be his new capital of Egypt. Grew to be one of three largest cities of ancient world, with population of over half a million. PTOLEMY I Soter developed it as both his practical power base and international cultural showcase. Famous for its Pharos (lighthouse), Serapeum (shrine of Serapis, amalgam of cults of Osiris and of sacred Apis bull), gymnasium, museum and library. The Tomb of Alexander, constructed here by Ptolemy to house the corpse of his late master, has been lost to science since 3rd century CE.

Alexandria Eschate – Founded close to modern Khodjend (formerly Leninabad) in ex-Soviet Central Asia on ancient *Jaxartes* river. Garrison town, largest of seven seized and fortified on Alex.'s orders.

Amphipolis – Surrounded on three sides by River Strymon, hence its name ('Surround-city'). Its importance due partly to strategic location on main north Aegean coastal route, partly to its close access to gold and silver mines of Mt Pangaeum, partly to port facilities at Eion three miles (five km) away, through which shipbuilding timber was readily exported. Originally Thracian, then taken over by Athenians in 437, but liberated by Spartans in 424. Independence surrendered to Philip II in 357. Alex. used it as his principal Greek mint.

Aornus, Rock of – Mighty rock – Bar-sar ib Pir-Sar today – beside a bend of upper River Indus on Swat border. Going one better than Heracles, allegedly, Alex. took it by assault in spring 326, ending its role as refuge and quelling resistance of local towns.

Arabia, Arabs – Tributary to Achaemenid Persia under name 'Arabaya', the northern Arabian peninsula was opened up to Greek conquest and settlement by Alex., but he died before he could carry out his plans. Preliminary exploratory missions penetrated both Persian Gulf and Red Sea. From the interior came valuable incense and spices. BATIS, Persian governor of Gaza, was an Arab.

Babylon – Its heyday as capital of Neo-Babylonian Empire (605–539 BCE) had long passed before Alex. made it capital of his new kingdom of Asia. Area enclosed within double-enceinte city walls with their eight gates amounted to almost 1,000 acres (400 hectares). Alex. entered in 330 and again in 324, through brilliantly decorated Ishtar Gate (adorned with brightly coloured glazed-brick reliefs) next to old palace of Nebuchadnezzar. Ishtar Gate was linked directly by processional route to the Esagila (temple of BEL-MARDUK). Alex died in Babylon on 10 June 323.

Bactra – Modern Balkh, and scene of Alex.'s abortive attempt in 327 to institute *proskynesis*.

Bactria – Vast region of what is today northern Afghanistan, lying between *Hindu*

Kush mountains to the south and *River Oxus* on the north. Adjacent on the north is ancient Sogdiana, home of ROXANE. Alex. fought fierce guerrilla battles here, and control of the region was tough; under Seleucid Successors breakaway Graeco-Bactrian kingdom was formed, which produced wonderfully veristic dynastic coinage.

Bisitun – In ancient Media at modern Behistun *c*.19 miles (30 km) east of Kermanshah. On cliff overlooking a main route is long trilingual (Elamite, Babylonian and Old Persian) inscription of Darius I, surmounted by relief depicting him under the protection of AHURA MAZDA. *See* Figure 12.

bodyguards – Both at home in Macedonia and on campaign in Asia, Alex. was protected by bodyguards of varying degrees of intimacy and privilege. Appointment to inner bodyguard with title *Somatophylax* (*see* LEONNATUS, PERDICCAS, PTOLEMY) was tantamount to admission to inner circle of the king's most intimate *Companions*.

Brahmans – Ascetics and sages of the Indus valley whom Alex. encountered at Taxila and elsewhere. Most famed was CALANUS.

Bucephala – Town founded on the *Hydaspes* at or near spot where Alex.'s favourite charger, BUCEPHALAS, died in 326. No trace of town, perhaps just a temporary fort, has been found.

Chaeronea – Site of famous lion memorial commemorating spot where Theban Sacred Band (150 pairs of lovers) were killed to a man in a losing battle against Philip II in 338. *See* Figure 17.

coins – Major source and resource for study of Alex., who issued them for both practical economic and symbolic–propagandist purposes. He adopted the Athenian weight standard for both gold and silver coinages, striking coins with same designs at more than one mint, of which most important were *Amphipolis* in Greece and *Babylon* in Asia. *See* Figures 21, 24, 31, 36.

Companions – There were various grades and conditions of Companions; the originals were the Macedonian king's intimate friends. Title extended by Philip II to Companion Cavalry and Foot Companions.

conspiracies – It is possible to write a history of Alex.'s relations with his leading Macedonian and non-Macedonian courtiers, officers and other functionaries almost entirely in terms of conspiracies, alleged or genuine. Alex. acceded in 336 amid a welter of such suspicions; he had PHILOTAS and PARMENION executed in 330, and CALLISTHENES in 327, on grounds of treasonous conspiracy, and carried out something of a purge of *satraps* in 325/4. But allowance must be made for source bias and for uniqueness of Alex.'s developing positions of power.

Corinth, League of – Modern title for the organization – part pragmatic military alliance, part symbolic forum for Panhellenic peace and unity – established at Corinth in 338/7 by Philip II. Formally, it was delegates of Greek allies seconded to the Council of the League who voted to appoint Philip commander of a Panhellenic (see *Panhellenism*) expedition of revenge, reparation and conquest against Persian Empire. They too who condemned Thebes to annihilation in 335. *Exiles' Decree* exposed League for the sham it was.

Dascyleum – *c.*20 miles (32 km) south of Greek Cyzicus, *satrapal* capital of Hellespontine Phrygia. Famed for its hunting park.

Ecbatana – Modern Hamadan in Media, which overlies the ancient city and prevents its excavation. Developed extensively as royal residence by Great King Artaxerxes II (404–359), the site commands the route between western Iran and central Asia via Khorasan.

Elimiotis – One of the four 'cantons' of Upper (western) *Macedonia*; the others are *Lyncestis*, Orestis and Tymphaea. Absorbed and integrated by Philip II, the region produced such leading figures among Alex.'s entourage as COENUS and HARPALUS.

Ephemerides – Literally 'Journals' (same word as for 'newspapers' in modern Greek); but better 'Logbooks'. Ostensibly official royal diaries compiled or supervised by EUMENES. Cited by four of our extant sources, and possibly used by PTOLEMY in his lost history, they are of relatively restricted interest since they focus only on Alex.'s last days in *Babylon* and are apparently concerned above all to refute accusation that he was poisoned.

Exiles' Decree – In 324, to coincide with Olympic Games, Alex. sent back to Greece NICANOR bearing an order to Greek subjects grouped within *League of Corinth* to readmit their exiles. Decree was blatant infringement of supposed guarantee of autonomy that Alex. had given the cities, and, as surviving contemporary official documents show, its practical administration was a nightmare involving court cases and other, less legal altercations.

Gaugamela – In northern Iraq, not far from today's Mosul, this was the scene of Alex.'s decisive set-piece victory on 1 October 331.

Gedrosia – Short title for the region of modern Makran (southern Iran and Afghanistan, including Baluchistan) through which Alex. oddly chose to march en route back from the Punjab to central Iran in autumn 325. At that season it is almost entirely arid, and many of Alex.'s troops and other camp followers perished amid extreme discomfort.

Gordian knot – Gordium, capital of Phrygia, prospered extremely under King

Midas (8th century BCE) but was destroyed early in 7th century and attained only modest importance under ACHAEMENIDS. Yoke of funeral wagon of Gordius, mythical founder of Phrygian dynasty, was fastened to its pole by exceptionally intricate knot – which in 333 Alex. either unloosed or slashed through, according to differing versions of the legend.

Granicus, River – Relatively minor river in north-west Anatolia, in 334 scene of first of Alex.'s major pitched battles, in which he defeated a Persian force under ARSITES.

Halicarnassus – Mixed Carian–Greek settlement, birthplace of Herodotus, seat of Hecatomnid dynasty that included Queen ADA, and site of famous Mausoleum. Alex. encountered fierce resistance here from MEMNON in 334.

hêgemôn – Greek for 'leader', as in general of the *League of Corinth*, or leading state of an alliance.

Hindu Kush – Mountain range marking eastern limit of Achaemenid Empire before Alex.'s conquest. Greeks thought of it somehow as extension of Caucasus Mountains, hence their name for the range, 'Indian Caucasus'.

Hydaspes, River – River of the Punjab (modern Jhelum), where Alex. defeated PORUS in 326.

Hypaspists – 'Shield Bearers' (*Hypaspistai*), elite infantrymen of the Macedonian army, stationed in line of battle between Foot Companions and Companion Cavalry on right wing. Also used by Alex. for special operations requiring speed and surprise.

Hyphasis, River – River of the Punjab (modern Beas), where demoralized and foot-sore Macedonians in 325 issued their ultimatum to Alex., refusing to trek any further east.

Hypomnemata – These 'Notebooks' surfaced dramatically immediately after Alex.'s death at *Babylon*, in the hands of de facto regent PERDICCAS. They contained allegedly Alex.'s 'last plans', i.e. those he had drafted at the time of his early death. Perdiccas intended them to be rejected, as unattainable, and they were. *See the* Appendix.

Illyria – Territory of the Indo-European-speaking Illyrians on western side of Balkan range running south from the head of the Adriatic to Epirus. Their elderly king Bardylis, whose capital lay north of Lake Lychnitis and who controlled many Illyrian tribes as well as his own Dardanians, was soundly trounced by PARMENION in 358. Alex. reasserted Macedonian control in person over Bardylis's son Cleitus in 336/5.

India – Rather grandiose term for what was mainly the Punjab, so far as Alex.'s invasion and conquest of 'India' in 326/5 were concerned. Persian Empire had once extended to the Indus, but Alex. was entering territory controlled by powerful independent native rajahs such as PORUS.

Issus – Town in Cilicia near site of major battle between Alex. and Darius III in 333, from which Darius fled leaving wife and other members of immediate family as hostages in Alex.'s hands. *See* Figures 8, 20, 27, 35.

Jaxartes, River – Alex. and his forces were probably the first Greeks to discover this river (modern Syr-Darya) that played role of boundary for upper *satrapies* of Persian Empire. Alex. planted *Alexandria Eschate* on its banks.

Lamian War – Known after town in Thessaly where ANTIPATER was temporarily besieged during widely supported Greek revolt from Macedon led by Athens (*see* LEOSTHENES) following Alex.'s death (323/2). Macedon won decisively both by land and by sea.

Lydia – Once a kingdom, then Achaemenid *satrapy* (like Phrygia – see *Gordian knot*), it remained a satrapy within Alex.'s Empire, based on old capital Sardis that had long (since the reign of King Croesus in 6th century) been strongly Hellenized. Sardis was western terminus of *Royal Road*.

Lyncestis – Upper Macedonian canton (see *Elimiotis*), named for the native lynx. The sons of Aeropus from its princely house were put in the frame, or framed, by Alex. in the murky circumstances of his accession in 336.

Macedon, Macedonia – Macedon here means the Macedonian state; Macedonia, the territory forming the link between Balkans and southern peninsula of mainland Greece. Controversy continued to rage in Alex.'s day as to whether or not the Macedonians were – entirely – Greeks. Only the king, at any rate, was permitted to compete at the all-Greek and only-Greek Olympic Games. Macedonian language was certainly Indo-European and possibly dialect form related to north-west Greek, but in idiomatic usage could be unintelligible to most standard Greek-speakers. Names were entirely Greek, though sometimes pronounced idio-syncratically: PHILIP, for example, was pronounced Bilip.

Magi – An originally Median priesthood, which served the Persian Empire as its official priests alongside acolytes of AHURA MAZDA.

Malli – Alex.'s major target in 325 after mutiny at the HYPHASIS, the Malli (Malavas) were an Indian people living on either side of River Hydraotes (Ravi) in the Punjab. Alex. was almost killed in assaulting and entering their main town.

Maracanda – Chief town of ancient Sogdiana (modern Samarkand on old Silk

Route in Uzbekistan) and used as Alex.'s main base for guerrilla campaigns of 329/7. Also site of lethal flare-up in 328 between Alex. and CLEITUS THE BLACK.

Mieza – Site (probably modern Lefkadia, west of Pella) where Alex. was tutored with select band of friends by ARISTOTLE between c.343 and 340.

mutinies – Alex. suffered two serious mutinies, first in 326 at the *Hyphasis*, second in 324 at *Opis*. Their rarity speaks for the general support from his ordinary Macedonians that Alex. was normally able to count on through thick and – more often – thin. See *conspiracies*.

Ocean – Greeks believed the earth was surrounded by vast encircling sea, fed by all known rivers, that they called 'Ocean'. Alex. could plausibly be thought to have been yearning (see *pothos*) to press on eastwards until he reached Ocean – that thought may well have contributed to *Hyphasis* mutiny.

Official sources – Comprise CALLISTHENES, PTOLEMY, ARISTOBOULUS and NEARCHUS: all members of Alex.'s immediate entourage on campaign. Contrast *Vulgate sources*.

Olynthus – Chief city of Chalcidian federation before its total destruction by Philip in 348. Home city of CALLISTHENES.

Opis – Where the second of Alex.'s two most serious mass *mutinies* took place, in 324; roughly on site of modern Baghdad.

Oxus, River – In central Asia (modern Amu Darya), forming northern boundary of *Bactria* and flowing north-west into (what is left of) Aral Sea. Not to be confused, as it apparently was by Herodotus, with Armenian Araxes (Aras) river. On or near the Oxus in 1877 was discovered huge hoard of gold and silver objects of 5th–4th-century Achaemenid origin, now in British Museum.

Paeonia – Roughly equivalent to modern Serbia, its conquest and containment were crucial to Macedon's maintenance of power in the north Balkans. Paeonian troops were given important role by Alex., e.g. as cavalrymen at *Gaugamela*.

Pages, Royal – Institution (of Persian inspiration) devised by Philip and energetically maintained by Alex., whereby sons of Macedonian nobles did service at court as junior bodyguards and ceremonial attendants. Teenage Pages both were groomed for future high office in royal service and served as hostages for good behaviour of their potentially rebellious fathers. Occasionally things went very wrong, as in alleged conspiracy of Pages led by HERMOLAUS in 327, in which CALLISTHENES became fatally embroiled.

Pangaeum – Generic name for mountainous region (peak, 6,400 feet, 1,956 m) of Thrace, about 15 miles (25 km) long, that contained rich seams of both gold and silver. Philip was the first Macedonian king to benefit from their proximity and used the proceeds to hire mercenaries and bribe foreign politicians. Major source of silver for minting Alex.'s Greek coinage (see *coins*) at *Amphipolis*.

Panhellenism – Developed as political ideal especially after Persian invasions of early 5th century, it advocated Hellenic solidarity against 'barbarians', as in declaration of war on the Persian Empire by Philip which Alex. carried through to its total conquest. Could also be a double-edged sword for Alex., whose governing ideology for ruling his new Empire was not narrowly or exclusively Hellenic.

Pasargadae – North-east of *Persepolis*. Original capital of Achaemenid Persian Empire, founded by CYRUS II the Great *c*.550. *See* Figure 37.

Pella – New capital of the Macedonian kingdom, founded in late 5th century by King Archelaus (413–399). Philip greatly developed it as imperial capital, in tandem with old capital at *Aegae* that continued to function as ceremonial capital.

Persepolis – Ceremonial capital of the Achaemenid Persian Empire (Parsa, in Persian), founded by Darius I. Palace built by Darius and added to by his son Xerxes and other successors bears reliefs depicting representatives of subject peoples bringing tribute (Figure 13). Alex. torched it in 330, controversially, as he was by then king of Persians as well as of the Macedonians and Greeks.

pothos – Meaning strong desire or yearning, this term is attached in some sources to some of Alex.'s more grandiose or out-of-the-way projects, such as his visit to *Siwah*.

proskynesis – Greek term for obeisance, or bowing down, a gesture of respect and devotion which Greeks believed was appropriately made only to gods, but which Persians performed routinely to the Great King, who was not – despite Greek and Macedonian misconstrual to the contrary – worshipped as living god. Misunderstanding, wilful or otherwise, of Alex.'s attempt at *Bactra* in 328 to get his Macedonian and Greek courtiers to perform this gesture to him led to execution of CALLISTHENES, and the attempt's failure.

Royal Road – Ran west from Persian Susa to Lydian Sardis, over some 2,000 miles (over 3,000 kilometres). Herodotus says there were 111 relay stations at which a messenger might change horses, and that he might hope to cover the whole distance in ten days whereas an army on foot took nearer three months.

sarissa – Wooden pike with long iron point, made in two sections joined together by metal dowel, and over 16 feet (5m) long; characteristic weapon of Macedonian Foot Companions, who wielded it with both hands (unlike much shorter Greek hoplite spear). *See* Figure 23.

satrap – Originally, Median term taken over by Persians and then by Alex. for viceroy or ruler of tributary region known as a satrapy (there were over 20 in all). Under Achaemenids satraps tended to be members of ruling Persian dynasty, but Alex. promoted some relatively humble Macedonians as well as re-employing noble Persians such as MAZAEUS.

sexuality – Alex.'s sexual orientation and behaviour are still today extremely sensitive subjects. Given his position of unique power, he was rather moderate in his indulgence of sexual appetites with partners of both sexes. Sources single out his relationships with HEPHAESTION, BAGOAS the eunuch and ROXANE.

Siwah – Large oasis in western desert of Egypt, within cultural area of Libya. Its oracle of the Libyan–Egyptian god AMMON (Amun) was famed already in the time of Herodotus and consulted by Lysander of Sparta (d. 395), among other powerful figures, before Alex. made historic visit in 332/1. Whatever exactly the priest divulged to him, Alex. behaved thereafter as if he had a special relationship with Ammon, even possibly of filiation (at the expense of his natural father Philip).

Sparta – Formerly one of the two great powers of old Greece, it was reduced to impotence by Philip and Alex. (see AGIS III), who exploited also hostility of other Greeks towards it.

Successors – Title of Kings who succeeded to Alex.'s carved-up empire (ANTIGONUS MONOPHTHALMUS, PTOLEMY I, SELEUCUS I NICATOR)

Susa – In so far as Persian Empire had single permanent administrative capital (kings moved around on regular seasonal cycle from capital to capital within Iran), the 'city of lilies' was it. Located in the region called Elam, its language was one of three used for the *Bisitun* inscription (*see* Figure 12), and the main one used for bureaucratic administrative records incised in cuneiform lettering on sun-dried clay kept at Persepolis (known as the Fortification and Treasury Tablets). Scene of Alex.'s stage managed mass weddings in 324.

Tyre – Major Phoenician city for many centuries; Alex., having captured Old Tyre on the mainland, took New Tyre (on an offshore island) after a prodigiously long and difficult seven-month siege in 332.

Vulgate sources – As opposed to the 'Official' tradition of sources on Alex. stemming ultimately from CALLISTHENES and passing by way of PTOLEMY and ARISTOBOULUS to ARRIAN, the Vulgate tradition stemmed ultimately from CLEITARCHUS and descended to DIODORUS, CURTIUS and JUSTIN. *See* the Appendix.

Bibliography

Abbreviations

Badian (ed.) 1976 – E. Badian (ed.) *Alexandre le Grand: image et réalité* (*Entretiens Hardt* 1976)

Bosworth and Baynham (eds) 2000 – A. B. Bosworth and E. Baynham (eds) *Alexander the Great in Fact and Fiction* (2000)

Griffith (ed.) 1966 – G. T. Griffith (ed.) *Alexander the Great: The Main Problems* (1966)

Muir and Sewter (eds) 1965 – J. V. Muir and E. R. A. Sewter (eds) *Alexander the Great* (special issue of *Greece and Rome* n.s. 12.2 (1965))

Roisman (ed.) 2003 – J. Roisman (ed.) *Brill's Companion to Alexander the Great* (2003)

Worthington (ed.) 2003 – I. Worthington (ed.) *Alexander the Great. A Reader* (2003)

GENERAL READING

(Works relevant to all or most chapters)

1. Monographs

A. B. Bosworth *Conquest and Empire: The Reign of Alexander the Great* (1988, and repr.)

P. Briant *Alexander the Great: The Heroic Ideal* (1996, French original 1987)

P. Green *Alexander of Macedon, 356–323 BC. A Historical Biography* (1974, rev. edn 1991)

J. R. Hamilton *Alexander the Great* (1973)

N. G. L. Hammond *Alexander the Great. King, Commander and Statesman* (2nd edn 1989)

———— *The Genius of Alexander the Great* (1997)

R. Lane Fox *Alexander the Great* (1973)

———— *The Search for Alexander* (1980)

R. D. Milns *Alexander the Great* (1968)

Cl. Mossé *Alexander: The Destiny of a Myth* (2004, French original 2001)

J. M. O'Brien *Alexander the Great: The Invisible Enemy. A Biography* (1992)

E. Rice *Alexander the Great* (1997)

F. Schachermeyr *Alexander der Grosse. Das Problem seines Persönlichkeit und seines Wirkens* (1973); with A. B. Bosworth, 'Ingenium und Macht: Fritz Schachermeyr and Alexander the Great' *American Journal of Ancient History* 13 (1988 (publ. 1996)) 56–78

R. Stoneman *Alexander the Great* (1997)

W. W. Tarn *Alexander the Great*, 2 vols: I. *Narrative*; II. *Sources and Studies* (1948; vol. I repr. in pb. 1979)

U. Wilcken *Alexander the Great*, ed. E. N. Borza (Eng. trans. 1932, repr. 1967) (includes Borza 'An introduction to Alexander studies' ix–xxviii)

I. Worthington *Alexander the Great. Man and God* (2003)

Bosworth is generally rated the most authoritative scholar currently working on matters Alexandrine, not least because he is producing a definitive historical commentary on the best of the surviving ancient narrative sources, Arrian (see the Appendix). His notes give full citations to the ancient sources but his main text is sufficiently readable for the book to have been reprinted in the Cambridge University Press's cheap Canto paperback imprint. Bosworth is a prime exponent of the 'realist' – almost brutalist – school of Alexander historiography. See Chapter Ten. After Bosworth, Green is the fullest and most lively work of scholarship, with plenty of comparative reference. Tarn once dominated the field, and his appendices are still useful, but his view of a reasonable and gentlemanly Alexander has been exploded in a series of articles by Badian (1958, 1964, 1971 et al., below). Hammond too errs on the side of hagiography. Schachermeyr grapples with the problem of the modern Germanic exaltation of Alexander as a man of destiny and of power. Briant's little book is in two parts, first a very brief narrative, then a section of documents; it is brilliantly illustrated throughout and wonderful value for money. Milns, Rice and Stoneman are also very succinct indeed. Lane Fox's 1973 presentation of Alexander as the New Achilles won literary prizes, but in style of presentation it veers uncomfortably towards the genre of the historical novel. Lane Fox 1980 was written to accompany an official Greek-organized travelling exhibition of Alexander artefacts prompted by the discoveries of Manolis Andronikos at Vergina (ancient Aegae) and is therefore very well illustrated. The ever source-critically alert Mossé concentrates on images of all sorts and all periods, especially medieval and modern French, as well as the possible contemporary realities. O'Brien presents Alexander rather lopsidedly as an alcoholic, excessively devoted to the wine god Dionysus ('Dionysus chose wine as the vehicle through which he would unveil and magnify the defects of a brilliant man who was spiritually blind'). The two most soberly reliable introductions, if a little dated, are Wilcken and Hamilton (the latter being my own recommendable favourite). Most recent is Worthington, who emphasizes throughout Alexander's debt to and rivalry with his father.

2. Articles and chapters

E. Badian 'Alexander the Great and the creation of an empire' *History Today* 1958: 369–76, 494–502

A. B. Bosworth 'Alexander the Great' *Cambridge Ancient History* vol. VI. *The Fourth Century* BC (2nd edn 1994) chs 16–17 (ch. 17 repr. in Roisman (ed.) 2003)

S. Hornblower *The Greek World 479–323 BC* (3rd edn 2002) ch. 19

C. B. Welles 'Alexander's historical achievement' in Muir and Sewter (eds) 1965: 216–28

Bosworth and Hornblower are written for scholars and university students. Badian, published in a leading general history magazine, and Welles in Muir and Sewter (eds) are more widely accessible.

3. Collections of articles

W. L. Adams and E. N. Borza (eds) *Philip II, Alexander the Great and the Macedonian Heritage* (1982)

E. Badian *Studies in Greek and Roman History* (1964)
———— (ed.) 1976

E. N. Borza (ed.) *The Impact of Alexander the Great. Civilizer or Destroyer?* (1974)

Bosworth and Baynham (eds) 2000

J. Carlsen et al. (eds) *Alexander the Great: Reality and Myth* (1993, repr. 1997)

Griffith (ed.) 1966

K. B. Leyton-Brown and R. I. Cleveland (eds) *Alexander the Great: An Exercise in the Study of History* (1992)

Muir and Sewter (eds) 1965

T. Quirico (ed.) *Alessandro Magno. Storia e Mito* (1995–6)

J. Roisman (ed.) *Alexander the Great: Ancient and Modern Perspectives* (1995)
———— (ed.) 2003

M. Sordi (ed.) *Alessandro Magno tra storia e mito* (1984)

Worthington (ed.) 2003

All are written or edited chiefly for scholars and university students, but Muir and Sewter (eds) is perhaps the most accessible. Worthington (ed.) contains useful editorial matter as well as reprints both of modern works and of ancient sources. It and Roisman (ed.) are cited again and again below.

4. Surveys of modern work

E. Badian *Classical World* 65 (October–November 1971) 37–56, 77–83
———— in Badian (ed.) 1976 ch. 7
P. Goukowsky *Revue des Etudes Grecques* 96 (1983) 225–41
J. Seibert *Alexander der Grosse* (1972)

Purely for scholars and advanced university students.

5. Websites

wso.williams.edu:8000/~junterek/
www.isidore-of-seville.com/ImagesofAlexander/
www.pothos.org

For sources, see the Appendix

SPECIFIC READING

Preface

1. Hunting and Alexander the huntsman

J. K. Anderson *Hunting in the Ancient World* (1985)
P. Briant 'Chasses royales macédoniennes et chasses royales perses: le thème de la
    chasse au lion sur la chasse de Vergine' *Dialogues d'Histoire Ancienne* 17
    (1991) 211–55
———— 'Les Chasses d'Alexandre' *Ancient Macedonia* 5 (1993) 267–77
M. B. Hatzopoulos *Cultes et rites de passage en Macédoine* (1994) 92–111
O. Palagia 'Hephaestion's pyre and the royal hunt of Alexander' in Bosworth and
    Baynham (eds) 2000: 167–206

2. Alexander as alcoholic

J. M. O'Brien *Alexander the Great: The Invisible Enemy. A Biography* (1992)

One: The Fame of Alexander

E. Badian 'Alexander the Great and the creation of an empire' *History Today* 1958: 369–76, 494–502

Partha Bose *Alexander the Great's Art of Strategy. Lessons from the Great Empire Builder* (2002)

G. Cary *The Medieval Alexander* (1956)

P. Green 'Caesar and Alexander: Aemulatio, Imitatio, Comparatio' *American Journal of Ancient History* 3 (1978) 1–26

F. L. Holt *Alexander the Great and the Mystery of the Elephant Medallions* (2003) ch. 1 ('Man of Mystery')

M. A. Jackson *Life Lessons from History's Heroes* (2003)

D. Spencer *The Roman Alexander. Readings in a Cultural Myth* (2002)

R. Stoneman (ed.) *Legends of Alexander the Great* (1994)

——— 'The legacy of Alexander in ancient philosophy' in Roisman (ed.) 2003: 325–46

C. B. Welles 'Alexander's historical achievement' in Muir and Sewter (eds) 1965: 216–28

Badian and Welles are included here for those who want a reliable and critical orientation. Holt opens with an excellent selection of aspects of Alexander's posthumous fame, though not even he picks up on his exploitation by Bose and Jackson as a model master-planner of modern business strategy. Ancient Rome (Green and Spencer) and medieval Europe (Cary) pay homage to Alexander in a host of often startlingly inconsistent ways. Stoneman in Roisman (ed.) is a rare philosophical treatment. Several of the leads given in this chapter are picked up again in Chapter Twelve, on Alexander's many legacies.

Two: Alexander's World

J. K. Anderson *Military Theory and Practice in the Age of Xenophon* (1970)

J. Buckler *The Theban Hegemony, 371–362 BC* (1980)

——— *Aegean Greece in the Fourth Century BC* (2003)

P. Cartledge *Agesilaus and the Crisis of Sparta* (1987)

J. M. Cook *The Persian Empire* (1983)

J. Dillery *Xenophon and the History of His Times* (1995)

N. Hammond and G. T. Griffith *A History of Macedonia* vol. II. 550–336 BC (1979)

L. Tritle (ed.) *The Greek World in the Fourth Century: From the Fall of the Athenian Empire to the Successors of Alexander* (1997)

Tritle (ed.) is a very useful collection, restoring the maligned fourth century to its rightful position of importance often usurped by the fifth. Buckler 2003 covers much of the same ground, beginning with the end of the Atheno-Peloponnesian War and ending with the death of Philip II. Buckler 1980 is still indispensable for Thebes's contribution. On military matters, Anderson is basic. Cartledge traces Spartan history over a century or so down to 360, focusing on the career and reign of King Agesilaus II, one of the two most powerful Greek individuals of his day. Dillery deals handsomely with our major literary source for Aegean Greek history in the period 411 to 362, who among much else was a client of Agesilaus and wrote a posthumous encomium of him. Griffith in Hammond and Griffith 1979 is a simply wonderful account of Philip II. Cook remains a useful survey (for much more on the Persian Empire, see Chapter Eight).

Three: Young Alexander (356–334 BCE)

A. R. Anderson 'Bucephalas and his legend' *American Journal of Philology* 51 (1930) 1–21
E. Badian 'Harpalus' *Journal of Hellenic Studies* 81 (1961) 16–43
———— 'The death of Philip II' *Phoenix* 17 (1963) 244–50
E. D. Carney 'Olympias' *Ancient Society* 18 (1987) 35–62
J. R. Hamilton 'Alexander's early life' in Muir and Sewter (eds) 1965: 117–24
I. Worthington 'Alexander, Philip, and the Macedonian background' in Roisman (ed.) 2003: 69–98

Hamilton and Worthington set the scene of Alexander's background, upbringing and youth. The articles by Badian 1963, Carney and Anderson deal with three of the most important persons in Alexander's life, his father, mother and favourite (four-footed) mount. Badian 1961 discusses a key boyhood friend, who was later to play Alexander false, not once but twice. Much of the suggested reading for the next chapter is also relevant for this.

See also above, General Reading 1 Monographs.

Four: Alexander and the Macedonians

Some of the reading suggested for Chapter Twelve is also relevant to this one.

M. Andronikos *Vergina: The Royal Tombs* (1984)
E. Badian 'The death of Parmenio' *Transactions and Proceedings of the American Philological Association* 91 (1960) 324–38
———— 'Conspiracies' in Bosworth and Baynham (eds) 2000: 50–95 (partially repr. in Roisman (ed.) 2003: 277–95)

E. Borza *In the Shadow of Olympus: the Emergence of Macedon* (1990)
——— *Before Alexander: Constructing Early Macedonia* (1999)
E. Carney 'Macedonians and mutiny: discipline and indiscipline in the army of
  Philip and Alexander' *Classical Philology* 91 (1996) 19–44
——— *Women and Monarchy in Macedonia* (2000)
J. R. Ellis *Philip II and Macedonian Imperialism* (1976)
——— 'Macedon and north-west Greece' and 'Macedonian hegemony created'
  Cambridge Ancient History vol. VI (2nd edn 1994) 791–875
R. M. Errington *A History of Macedonia* (1990)
R. Ginouvès and M. Hatzopoulos (eds) *Macedonia from Philip II to the Roman
  Conquest* (1994)
G. T. Griffith 'The Macedonian background' in Muir and Sewter (eds) 1965:
  125–39
N. G. L. Hammond *The Macedonian State: Origins, Institutions, and History*
  (1989)
——— and G. T. Griffith *A History of Macedonia* vol. II. *550–336 BC* (1979)
  esp. chs XI (G.) and XX (H.)
M. B. Hatzopoulos *Cultes et rites de passage en Macédoine* (1994)
——— *Macedonian Institutions under the Kings*, 2 vols (1996)
——— and L. Loukopoulos (eds) *Philip of Macedon* (1980)
W. Heckel 'The conspiracy against Philotas' *Phoenix* 31 (1977) 9–21

The excavations of Manolis Andronikos at Vergina transformed our understanding of the Macedonian monarchy. The greatest living Greek expert on Macedonian institutions is Hatzopoulos. He is closely followed by the Englishman Hammond and the Australian Ellis. For general histories of Macedonia see Borza 1990 and 1999, Errington, and Ginouvès and Hatzopoulos (eds). Griffith 1965 is an excellent brief survey of the Macedonian background. Griffith in Hammond and Griffith 1979 is terrific on Philip II, Hatzopoulos and Loukopoulos (eds) a splendidly illustrated collection devoted to the same key figure. Hamilton 1965 looks at Alexander's early life. Badian 2000 investigates the general problems of conspiracies against Alexander, real and alleged, while Carney 1996 examines Macedonian soldierly (in)discipline; Worthington (ed.) 2003 devotes a whole chapter to 'Alexander and conspiracies'. Badian 1960 seeks to unravel the murder mystery of Parmenion's death, Heckel that of Philotas. Cherchez les femmes? see Carney 2000.

Five: Alexander and the Greeks

E. Badian 'Alexander the Great and the Greeks of Asia' in Badian (ed.) *Ancient
  Society and Institutions. Fest. V. Ehrenberg* (1966) 37–62

──────── 'Agis III' *Hermes* 95 (1967) 170–92

──────── 'Greeks and Macedonians' in B. Barr-Sharrar and E. N. Borza (eds) *Macedonia and Greece in Late Classical and Early Hellenistic Times* (Studies in the History of Art, no. 10) (1982) 33–51

──────── 'Agis III: revisions and reflections' in I. Worthington (ed.) *Ventures into Greek History. Fest. N. G. L. Hammond* (1994) 258–92

V. Ehrenberg *Alexander and the Greeks* (1938) esp. ch. 1

M. Faraguna 'Alexander and the Greeks' in Roisman (ed.) 2003: 99–130

M. A. Flower 'Alexander the Great and Panhellenism' in Bosworth and Baynham (eds) 2000: 96–135

P. M. Fraser *Cities of Alexander the Great* (1996)

J. M. Hall *Hellenicity* (2002)

F. Hartog *Memories of Odysseus: Frontier Tales from Ancient Greece* (2001)

A. J. Heisserer *Alexander the Great and the Greeks. The Epigraphic Evidence* (1980)

P. Vasunia *The Gift of the Nile: Hellenizing Egypt from Aeschylus to Alexander* (2001)

F. Walbank 'The problem of Greek nationality' *Phoenix* 5 (1951) 41–60, repr. in his *Selected Papers* (1985) 1–19

I. Worthington 'The Harpalus affair and the Greek response to the Macedonian hegemony' in Worthington (ed.) *Ventures into Greek History. Fest. N. G. L. Hammond* (1994) 307–30

Flower, Hall, Hartog, Vasunia and Walbank tackle in different ways the issue of Greek identity, and how far it was developed, or compromised, by Alexander. Badian 1966, Ehrenberg, Faraguna and Worthington examine the more practical problems of the Greeks' relations with Alexander as his subjects; Heisserer is a useful collection of the relevant documentary evidence. Fraser takes a minimalist position on the number of cities actually founded in person by Alexander, and therefore on their immediate cultural as opposed to strategic significance. Opinions vary widely on the degree of threat posed by Spartan king Agis III's revolt: Badian 1967 and 1994 hold firmly to the view that it did represent a major threat.

Six: Alexander: Conqueror of Persia (334–327 BCE)

See above, General Reading 1 Monographs; and Chapters Seven and Eight in this bibliography.

Seven: The Generalship of Alexander

M. Austin 'Hellenistic kings, war, and the economy' *Classical Quarterly* n.s. 36 (1986) 450–66

—— 'Alexander and the Macedonian invasion of Asia: aspects of the historiography of war and empire in antiquity' in J. Rich and G. Shipley (eds) *War and Society in the Greek World* (1993) 197–223, repr. in Worthington (ed.) 2003: 118–35

E. F. Bloedow 'The siege of Tyre in 332 BC: Alexander at the crossroads in his career' *La Parola del Passato* 301 (1998) 255–93

A. B. Bosworth 'The Indian campaigns, 327–325 BC' in Roisman (ed.) 2003: 159–68

P. Briant 'The Achaemenid empire' in K. Raaflaub and N. Rosenstein (eds) *War and Society in the Ancient and Medieval Worlds. Asia, the Mediterranean, Europe and Mesoamerica* (1999) 105–28

P. A. Brunt *Loeb Arrian* I (1976): lxix–lxxxii; App. II (the naval war)

—— *Loeb Arrian* I (1976): App. XIII (cavalry reforms)

A. R. Burn 'Notes on Alexander's campaigns 332–330' *Journal of Hellenic Studies* 72 (1952) 81–91

—— 'The generalship of Alexander' in Muir and Sewter (eds) 1965: 140–52

A. M. Devine 'Grand tactics at the Battle of Issus' *Ancient World* 12 (1985) 39–59

—— 'The Battle of Gaugamela: A tactical and source-critical study' *Ancient World* 13 (1986) 87–116

—— 'The Battle of the Hydaspes: A tactical and source-critical study' *Ancient World* 16 (1987) 91–113

—— 'Alexander the Great' in J. Hackett (ed.) *Warfare in the Ancient World* (1989) 104–29

D. W. Engels *Alexander the Great and the Logistics of the Macedonian Army* (1978)

J. F. C. Fuller *The Generalship of Alexander the Great* (1958)

P. Grabsky *The Great Commanders* (1994)

G. T. Griffith 'Alexander's generalship at Gaugamela' *Journal of Hellenic Studies* 67 (1947) 77–89

N. Hammond *Alexander the Great: King, Commander, Statesman* (1996)

W. Heckel *The Marshals of Alexander's Empire* (1993)

—— *The Wars of Alexander the Great* (2002)

J. Keegan *The Mask of Command* (1987)

J. Lucas (ed.) *Command. From Alexander the Great to Zhukov: The Greatest Commanders of World History* (1988)

A. Mayor *Greek Fire, Poison Arrows and Scorpion Bombs. Biological and Chemical Warfare in the Ancient World* (2003)

R. D. Milns 'The army of Alexander the Great' in E. Badian (ed.) *Entretiens Hardt* 1976: 87–130 (discussion 131–6)

N. Sekunda and J. Warry *Alexander the Great. His Armies and Campaigns 334–323 BC* (1998)

B. Strauss 'Alexander: the military campaign' in Roisman (ed.) 2003: 133–58

Alexander's generalship as a whole is variously evaluated by Burn 1965, Devine 1989, Fuller (a modern commander rather than academic scholar), Grabsky (a popular account), Hammond, Heckel 2002, Keegan (an expert in military history of the modern period), Lucas, Sekunda and Warry, and Strauss. Briant examines the Achaemenid opposition. Bloedow, Bosworth, Brunt, Burn 1952, Devine 1985–7, and Griffith examine particular campaigns. Heckel 1993 studies the high command, Milns the army as a whole and its changes over time, and Brunt the cavalry in particular. Engels was the first to quantify the value of doing away with baggage trains. Austin emphasizes the material basis and aims of warfare in Alexander's day. Besides the excellent discussion of the siege of Tyre (quoted in Chapter Seven), Mayor has a chapter entitled 'Alexander the Great and the arrows of doom', which treats the use of poisoned arrows against Alexander by Scythians and Indians.

Eight: Alexander and the Persians

E. Badian 'Harpalus' *Journal of Hellenic Studies* 81 (1961) 16–43

—— 'The administration of the Empire' in Muir and Sewter (eds) 1965: 166–82

—— 'Darius III' *Harvard Studies in Classical Philology* 102 (2000) 241–68

H. Bengtson et al. *The Greeks and the Persians* (1969) chs 16–20

H. Berve *Das Alexanderreich auf prosopographische Grundlage*, 2 vols (1926)

A. B. Bosworth 'Alexander and the Iranians' *Journal of Hellenic Studies* 100 (1980) 1–21

—— *Alexander and the East: The Tragedy of Triumph* (1996)

P. Briant *Histoire de l'empire perse de Cyrus à Alexandre* (1996)

—— 'The Achaemenid Empire' in K. Raaflaub and N. Rosenstein (eds) *War and Society in the Ancient and Medieval Worlds. Asia, the Mediterranean, Europe and Mesoamerica* (1999) 105–128

M. Brosius *Women in Ancient Persia (559–331 BC)* (1996)

—— (ed.) *The Persian Empire from Cyrus to Artaxerxes I* LACTOR (London Association of Classical Teachers. Original Records) 16 (2000)

—— 'Alexander and the Persians' in Roisman (ed.) 2003: 169–93

P. Brunt *Loeb Arrian* vol. I (1976) lxiii–lxix

J. M. Cook *The Persian Empire* (1983)

J.-Y. Empereur *Alexandria. Past, Present and Future* (2002, French original 2001)

P. M. Fraser *Cities of Alexander the Great* (1996)

E. A. Fredricksmeyer 'Alexander the Great and the Kingship of Asia' in Bosworth and Baynham (eds) 2000: 136–66

R. N. Frye *The Heritage of Persia* (1966, repr. 1976) chs 3–4

————— *A History of Ancient Iran* vol. 1 (1984)

R. Ghirshman, V. Minorsky and R. Sanghvi *Persia: The Immortal Kingdom* (1971)

P. Green 'Alexander's Alexandria' in *Alexandria and Alexandrianism* (Getty Museum/Center Symposium 1993, publ. 1996) 3–25

W. Heckel *The Marshals of Alexander's Empire* (1993)

F. L. Holt *Alexander the Great and Bactria: The Formation of a Greek Frontier in Central Asia* (1988)

S. Hornblower *Mausolus* (1982)

————— 'Persia' *Cambridge Ancient History* VI (2nd edn 1994) 45–96

A. Kuhrt *The Ancient Near East, c.3000–330 BC*, 2 vols (1997), esp. 647–701 ('The Achaemenid Empire')

R. Lane Fox *The Search for Alexander* (1980) ch. 27 (Ai Khanum)

D. M. Lewis *Sparta and Persia* (1977) ch. 1

A. K. Narain 'Alexander and India' in Muir and Sewter (eds) 1965: 155–65 (partially repr. in Worthington (ed.) 2003: 161–9)

H. Sancisi-Weerdeburg and A. Kuhrt (eds) *Achaemenid History*, several vols, ongoing (1987–)

Shapur Shabaz 'Iranian interpretations of Alexander' *American Journal of Ancient History* n.s. 2 (1977) 5–38

W. Vogelsang *The Rise and Organisation of the Achaemenid Empire: The Eastern Iranian Evidence* (1992)

J. Wiesehöfer *Ancient Persia from 550 BC to 650 AD* (1996)

Narain and Shabaz are very rare cases of non-western scholarly views of Alexander's role in their countries' early history. For general accounts of the Achaemenid Persian Empire see Bengtson et al., Briant 1996 and 1999, Brunt, Cook, Frye 1966 and 1984, Hornblower 1994, Vogelsang, and Wiesehöfer. For Alexander's opponent Darius III, see Badian 2000. The role of women is the focus of Brosius. Kuhrt expertly places this Empire within a vast chronological and geographical context of Middle Eastern history. Ghirshman et al. is not merely a celebratory puff for the then Shah's regime (though it is that too); the photography (by William MacQuitty) is magnificent. Hornblower 1982 provides an illuminating micro-study of one corner of the Empire, Caria, towards its end. Brosius (ed.), Lewis, and Sancisi-Weerdenburg and Kuhrt (eds) pay special attention to the primary Persian documentation that has been emerging to scholarly view over the past half-century. Fredricksmeyer puts forward a persuasive view of Alexander as King of Asia. Badian dissects the administration – and maladministration – of Alexander's new empire. Berve remains indispensable for research on all known significant individuals; Heckel focuses on the military top brass. Fraser, Holt and Lane Fox are helpful on Alexander's eponymous city foundations, and on the cultural dimension of his conquests more generally. For Alexandria in Egypt see Empereur (himself responsible for recovering many artefacts through underwater archaeology in the old harbour) and Green.

Nine: The Final Years (327–323 BCE)

A. B. Bosworth 'The death of Alexander the Great: rumour and propaganda' *Classical Quarterly* n.s. 21 (1971) 112–36

A. W. Erskine 'Life after death: Alexandria and the body of Alexander' *Greece and Rome* 49 (2002) 163–79

F. L. Holt *Alexander the Great and the Mystery of the Elephant Medallions* (2003)

J. Reames-Zimmermann 'The mourning of Alexander the Great' *Syllecta Classica* 12 (2001) 98–145

Holt is among the most original recent contributions to Alexander scholarship. Bosworth, Erskine and Reames-Zimmermann look variously at the circumstances, process and aftermath of Alexander's death.

See also above, General Reading 1 Monographs.

Ten: Alexander the Man

A. R. Anderson 'Bucephalas and his legend' *American Journal of Philology* 51 (1930) 1–21

E. Badian 'Alexander the Great and the unity of mankind' *Historia* 7 (1958a) 425–44 (= Griffith (ed.) 1966: 287–306)

———— 'The eunuch Bagoas' *Classical Quarterly* n.s. 8 (1958b) 144–57

———— 'Alexander the Great and the loneliness of power' *Studies in Greek and Roman History* (1964) 192–205

E. J. Baynham 'Why didn't Alexander marry a nice Macedonian girl before leaving home? Observations on factional politics at Alexander's court in 336–334 BC' in T. W. Hillard et al. (eds) *Ancient History in a Modern University (Macquarie University, NSW, Australia)* vol I. *The Ancient Near East, Greece, and Rome* (1998) 148–55

P. A. Brunt 'The aims of Alexander' in Muir and Sewter (eds) 1965: 205–15
(partial repr. in Worthington (ed.) 2003: 45–53)

E. D. Carney *Women and Monarchy in Macedonia* (2000)
—— 'Women in Alexander's court' in Roisman (ed.) 2003: 227–52

L. Edmunds 'The religiosity of Alexander' *Greek, Roman, and Byzantine Studies*
12 (1971) 363–91

E. A. Fredricksmeyer 'Alexander and Philip: emulation and resentment' *Classical
Journal* 85 (1990) 300–15
—— 'Alexander's Religion and Divinity' in Roisman (ed.) 2003: 253–78

W. Heckel *The Last Days and Testament of Alexander the Great. A
prosopographic study* (1988)

F. L. Holt 'Alexander the Great Today: in the interests of historical accuracy?'
Ancient History Bulletin 13.3 (1999) 111–17

L. Llewellyn-Jones in S. Tougher (ed.) *Eunuchs in Antiquity and Beyond* (2002)

O. Palagia 'Hephaestion's pyre and the royal hunt of Alexander' in Bosworth and
Baynham (eds) 2000: 167–206

C. A. Robinson 'The extraordinary ideas of Alexander the Great' *American
Historical Review* 1957: 326–44

J. Roisman 'Honor in Alexander's campaign' in Roisman (ed.) 2003: 279–321

W. W. Tarn 'Alexander the Great and the unity of mankind' *Proceedings of the
British Academy* 19 (1933) 123–66 (= Griffith (ed.) 1966: 243–86)

I. Worthington 'How "great" was Alexander?' *Ancient History Bulletin* 13.2
(1999) 39–55

Badian 1958a pours buckets of cynical scorn on Tarn for his starry-eyed view of Alexander the dreamy believer in the unity of mankind, but it remains very striking all the same that Alexander, like only a very few of his followers, was willing to extend Greek–oriental collaboration, on a permanent and relatively egalitarian basis, to the home and even the bedroom. This was just one of his 'extraordinary ideas' (Robinson). For the so-called 'last plans' see Heckel. Alexander's sexuality, that is his sexual orientation and behaviour, seems to have been pretty normal for a Greek/Macedonian of his times. He probably enjoyed a homosexual relationship with the older Hephaestion in his teens and perhaps later; he had good political reasons for not marrying a nice Macedonian girl before he left for Asia in 334 (aged only twenty-two, when the usual marrying age for a man was late twenties); and he bedded the Iranian wife (Barsine) of one of his major enemies (Memnon), before marrying an oriental woman in his mid twenties, for political–strategic reasons (Carney). Where he was indeed odd was in uniting maritally several times over with Iranian women; in forming a very intimate relationship with a member of a species – eunuchs – that Greeks despised (Badian 1958b, Llewellyn-Jones); in extravagantly mourning a former lover (Palagia); and in naming a city after a horse (Anderson). Religion was a constant driving force for Alexander, though his religiosity often tipped over into superstition (Edmunds, Fredricksmeyer 2003). Alexander's aims remain ultimately unfathomable (Brunt). Holt and Worthington argue the toss – Holt pro, Worthington, con – over his true 'greatness'. Roisman rightly injects a note of sanity by establishing the moral code of honour according to which Alexander would have acted.

Eleven: The Divinity of Alexander

E. Badian 'The deification of Alexander the Great' *Ancient Macedonian Studies in Honor of Charles F. Edson* (1981) 27–71

J. P. V. D. Balsdon 'The "divinity" of Alexander' *Historia* 1 (1950) 363–88 (= Griffith (ed.) 1966: 179–204

L. Bruit Zaidman and P. Schmitt Pantel *Religion in the Ancient Greek City*, ed. and trans. P. Cartledge (1992 and repr.)

P. A. Brunt *Loeb Arrian* I (1976), App. XI (*proskynesis*)

P. A. Cartledge, *Agesilaos and the Crisis of Sparta* (1987) ch. 16

G. L. Cawkwell 'The deification of Alexander the Great: a note' in I. Worthington (ed.) *Ventures into Greek History. Fest. N. G. L. Hammond* (1994) 293–306

A. Chaniotis 'The divinity of Hellenistic rulers' in A. W. Erskine (ed.) *A Companion to the Hellenistic World* (2003) 431–45

L. Edmunds 'The religiosity of Alexander' *Greek, Roman, and Byzantine Studies* 12 (1971) 363–91

E. A. Fredricksmeyer 'Alexander's religion and divinity' in Roisman (ed.) 2003: 253–78

P. Goukowsky *Essai sur les origines du mythe d'Alexandre* II. *Alexandre et Dionysos* (1981)

C. Habicht *Gottmenschentum und griechische Städte* (2nd edn 1970)

J. R. Hamilton 'Alexander and his "so-called" father' *Classical Review* n.s. 3 (1953) 151–7 (= Griffith (ed.) 1966: 235–41)

S. Price *The Religions of the Ancient Greeks* (1999)

G. de Ste Croix *The Class Struggle in the Ancient Greek World* (1981, 1983)

Bruit and Schmitt, and Price, both of which translate ancient texts and documents *in extenso*, provide excellent introductions to ancient Greek pre-Christian (or pagan) religion. Habicht is an indispensable study of the official divinization/ deification of mortal men. Badian's view that Alexander was the first Greek to be deified in his lifetime has been superseded; Cawkwell's equally firm view that Alexander did not order his deification is, surprisingly, simply denied by Chaniotis. Balsdon remains a balanced overview more than fifty years on. On *proskynesis* see Brunt, on Alexander's rivalrous relationship with Dionysus, see Goukowsky. Ste Croix explains the background of *stasis* (civil strife or war, class struggle on the political plane) that helped to generate Lysander's deification on Samos; Cartledge situates it in relation to Spartan attitudes to the divine, and especially their heroization of dead kings (such as Agesilaus). Hamilton gives a typically sound account of Alexander's treatment of Philip (the 'so-called father' of his title). Edmunds's and Fredricksmeyer's accounts of Alexander's religiosity apply also to Chapter Ten above.

Twelve: The Legends and Legacies of Alexander

1. The ancient myth of Alexander

Badian (ed.) 1976

Bosworth and Baynham (eds) 2000

J. Carlsen et al. (eds) *Alexander the Great. Reality and Myth* (1993, repr. 1997)

P. Goukowsky *Essai sur les origines du mythe d'Alexandre* I. *Les origines*; II. *Alexandre et Dionysos* (1978–81)

D. Spencer *The Roman Alexander: Reading Cultural Myth* (2002)

Many of the essays in the collections by Badian, Bosworth and Baynham, and Carlsen et al. have been individually cited elsewhere. Goukowsky focuses on the ancient beginnings of the Alexander myth (or rather myths), Spencer on its Roman-period versions (see also Chapter One above).

2. The Hellenistic world

A. B. Bosworth 'Ptolemy and the will of Alexander' in Bosworth and Baynham (eds) 2000: 207–41

————— *The Legacy of Alexander. Politics, Warfare, and Propaganda under the Successors* (2002)

B. Brown *Royal Portraits in Sculpture and Coins: Pyrrhos and the Successors of Alexander the Great* (1995)

P. Cartledge, P. Garnsey and E. Gruen (eds) *Hellenistic Constructs* (1997)

A. Cohen *The Alexander Mosaic. Stories of Victory and Defeat* (1997)

A. Erskine (ed.) *A Companion to the Hellenistic World* (2003)

P. Green *Alexander to Actium* (1990, corrected edn 1993)

C. Habicht *Athens from Alexander to Antony* (1997)

D. Ogden *Polygamy, Prostitutes and Death. The Hellenistic Dynasties* (1999)

N. Powers 'Onesicritus, naked wise men, and the Cynics' Alexander' *Syllecta Classica* 9 (1998) 70–85

M. I. Rostovtzeff *Social and Economic History of the Hellenistic World* 3 vols
(corrected edn 1953)

G. Shipley *The Greek World after Alexander* (2000)

A. F. Stewart *Faces of Power. Alexander's Image and Hellenistic Politics*
(1993)

——— 'Alexander in Greek and Roman Art' in Roisman (ed.) 2003: 31–66

M. True and K. Hamma (eds) *Alexandria and Alexandrianism* (1996)

C. B. Welles *Alexander and the Hellenistic World* (1970)

M. Wheeler *Flames Over Persepolis* (1968)

Erskine (ed.) is an up-to-date survey; older but still valuable is Cartledge et al.
(eds). Green and Shipley are the best single-authored accounts in English of the
period as a whole, but Welles is still useful, and Habicht is an excellent account
of Hellenistic Athens in particular. Rostovtzeff remains invaluable as a formidably
learned marriage of the then known written and archaeological evidence. Hellenistic royal imagery is treated by Brown and Stewart. Bosworth 2002 looks at the
Successors generally, Bosworth 2000 at one Successor in particular (also a major
source on Alexander – see the Appendix). Powers examines a distinctive post-
Alexander philosophical tradition (its originator, Onesicritus, is also a source on
Alexander). Ogden is a fascinating account of marital politics. Cohen examines in
detail one very famous visual representation of Alexander – excavated in a private
villa at Pompeii but based on a lost original that could have been a public history
painting. True and Hamma (eds) looks at one of Alexander's major material as
well as spiritual legacies. Wheeler is lively on such post-Alexander cultural
phenomena as the fusion art of Gandhara.

3. The Alexander Romance

E. J. Baynham 'Who put the Romance in the Alexander Romance? The
Alexander Romance within Alexander historiography' *Ancient History
Bulletin* 9 (1995) 1–13

R. Stoneman (ed. and trans.) *The Greek Alexander Romance* (1991)

No further comment required here.

4. Post-Antiquity

Partha Bose *Alexander the Great's Art of Strategy* (2003)

G. Cary *The Medieval Alexander* (1956)

L. M. Danforth *The Macedonian Conflict: Ethnic Nationalism in a
Transnational World* (1995)

——— 'Alexander the Great and the Macedonian conflict' in Roisman (ed.)
2003: 347–64

E. M. Goodwin *Encyclopedia of Mosaic* (2003)

C. Grell and C. Michel *L'École des princes ou Alexandre disgracié*, with foreword 'Les Alexandres' by P. Vidal-Naquet (1988), repr. in his *Les grecs, les historiens, les démocraties* (2000) 111–34

L. Gunderson *Alexander's Letter to Aristotle about India* (1980)

M. A. Jackson *Life Lessons from History's Heroes* (2003)

I. J. Kazis *The Gests of Alexander of Macedon* (1962)

M. Lascelles 'Alexander and the Earthly Paradise in medieval English writings' *Medium Aevum* 5 (1936) 31–47, 79–104, 173–88

S. McKendrick (ed.) *The History of Alexander the Great: An illuminated ms of Vasco da Lucena's trans. of the ancient text of Quintus Curtius Rufus* (1996)

F. de Polignac 'Alexandre dans la littérature arabe. L'Orient face à l'hellénisme' *Arabica* 229.3 (1982) 296–306

———— 'L'homme aux deux cornes. Une image d'Alexandre du symbolisme grec à l'apocalypse musulmane' *Mélanges de l'École française de Rome* 96 (1984) 29–51

C. Reynaud *Alexandre le Grand dans les littératures occidentales et proche-orientales* (1999)

D. J. A. Ross *Alexander Historiatus. A Guide to Medieval Illustrated Alexander Literature* (2nd edn 1988)

R. Stoneman (ed.) *Legends of Alexander the Great* (1994)

———— 'The legacy of Alexander in ancient philosophy' in Roisman (ed.) 2003: 325–46

M. Wood *In the Footsteps of Alexander the Great* (1997)

Gunderson examines in detail an ancient pseudepigraphic Alexander, supposedly writing from India to his old teacher back home (well, in Athens). Reynaud's general survey of Alexander in European and Near Eastern literature can be usefully followed up in more specialized detail by consulting Cary (medieval Europe), Lascelles (medieval England), Kazis (gest literature), Grell and Michel (eighteenth-century France), and Stoneman (philosophy ancient and medieval). Particularly interesting is de Polignac on the Arabic and Muslim literary and visual receptions. Illustrated literature is discussed in Ross and McKendrick (ed.); the Otranto mosaic is illustrated (a detail) in Goodwin. Very different modern approaches are represented by Danforth (contemporary exploitation of Alexander for purposes of ethnic politics), Bose and Jackson (supposed lessons for contemporary businesspeople), and Wood (supposedly treading in Alexander's footsteps – with the aid of modern technology, naturally).

5. Historical novels

Mary Butts *The Macedonian* (1931, repr. USA 1994)

Tom Holt *Alexander at the World's End* (1999)

V. M. Manfredi *Alexander* 1. *Child of a Dream*; 2. *The Sands of Ammon*; 3. *The Ends of the Earth* (2001, Italian originals, 1998)

Klaus Mann *Alexander. Roman der Utopie* (1929)

Mary Renault *Fire From Heaven* (1970), *The Persian Boy* (1972), *Funeral Games* (1981)

Holt's novel is both the funniest/wittiest and the most deflating, even trivializing. He invents a fictional grandson of the real Athenian comic poet Eupolis (who flourished in competition with Aristophanes at the end of the fifth century BCE). This Euxenus tutors Alexander, inspires him with the idea of world conquest as a new Achilles – and ends up at the eastern end of the world created by Alexander, at Alexandria the Furthest (Eschate, the modern Khodjend on the Syr-Darya in central Asia – see picture in Heckel 1988, Chapter 10). Manfredi's trilogy has as its rabbit-out-of-a-hat conceit the notion that it is the lost history of Ptolemy. This perhaps explains, though it does not excuse, its dullness and sexual censorship. Mary Renault, herself lesbian, had no problems with Alexander's bisexuality: the eponymous 'Persian Boy' is Bagoas the eunuch, whom Alexander took over from Darius III and with whom he was very much taken (see Badian 1958b in Chapter Ten). Klaus Mann, son of Thomas, went even further: his Alexander was what would be called today a gay. Butts has been described as 'a Bohemian British expatriate' (she wrote in Paris), and her hope, in which she confesses she failed, was to 'give some hint of the final nature of the man'.

6. What if?

J. Ober 'Conquest denied. The premature death of Alexander the Great' in R. Cowley (ed.) *What If? The World's Foremost Historians Imagine What Might Have Been* (2001) 37–56

Arnold Toynbee 'If Alexander had lived on' in Toynbee, *The Greeks and Their Heritages* (1981)

Fascinating to compare and contrast these diametrically opposed counterfactual scenarios. Toynbee, sharing W. W. Tarn's quasi-romantic vision of Alexander, imagined that he might have gone on to conquer China and send ships to circumnavigate Africa (as the Phoenicians already had under Persian King Darius I). He would then have been in a position actually to fulfil his one-world dream, as 'a kind of benevolent advance man for a United Nations, ancient style' (Robert Cowley). The soberly realistic Ober, in the sharpest possible contrast, has Alexander killed at the Granicus aged twenty-two, so that 'the brilliant Hellenistic period, that cultural seedbed of the West, would have been stillborn' (Cowley again).

Appendix: Sources of Paradox

1. General

W. Heckel and J. C. Yardley (eds) *Alexander the Great. Historical Sources in Translation* (2003)

C. A. Robinson *Historians of Alexander the Great* I (1953)

I. Worthington *Alexander the Great. A Reader* (2002)

2. The eyewitnesses (fragmentary/non-extant)

Aristoboulus 139J(acoby) (*Die Fragmente der Griechischen Historiker*, ed. F. Jacoby, serial nos 117–53; Jacoby vol. IIBi (text), vol. IID (with German commentary))

Callisthenes: 124 J

Chares 125J

Nearchus 133J

Onesicritus 134J

Ptolemy 138J

Most major fragments (many originally in Strabo *Geography* bks XI, XV) are translated in C. A. Robinson *Historians of Alexander the Great* I (1953)

> See also:

L. Pearson *The Lost Histories of Alexander the Great* (1960); rev. E. Badian, *Studies in Greek and Roman History* (1964) 250–61

P. Pédech *Historiens Compagnons d'Alexandre. Callisthène–Onésicrite–Néarque–Ptolémée–Aristobule* (Paris 1984)

3. Non-eyewitness:

Cleitarchus, 137 Jacoby (progenitor of the extant 'Vulgate' tradition: Diodorus, Trogus/Justin and Curtius)

4. Contemporary documents (real or supposed)

The letters, etc. of Alexander: J. R. Hamilton *Commentary on Plutarch's Life of Alexander* (1969, repr. 1998) lix–lxx

Ephemerides (Jacoby 117): A. B. Bosworth *Classical Quarterly* n.s. 21 (1971) 112–36 ('The death of Alexander the Great: rumour and propaganda'); A. B. Bosworth, in Badian (ed.) 1976: 1–34

Hypomnemata (Diodorus 18.4): E. Badian *Harvard Studies in Classical Philology* 72 (1968) 183–204 ('A king's notebooks')

'Mercenaries source': P. A. Brunt 'Persian accounts of Alexander's campaigns' *Classical Quarterly* n.s. 12 (1962) 141–55

5. Epigraphic, numismatic, archaeological sources

A. R. Bellinger *Essays on the Coinage of Alexander the Great* (1963)

P. Briant *Alexander the Great* (1996, French original 1987)

M. Brosius (ed.) *The Persian Empire from Cyrus to Artaxerxes I* LACTOR (London Association of Classical Teachers. Original Records) 16 (2000)

J. M. Camp *The Archaeology of Athens* (2001) 142–60

A. J. Heisserer *Alexander the Great and the Greeks. The Epigraphic Evidence* (1980)

R. Lane Fox *The Search for Alexander* (1980)
────── 'Text and image: Alexander the Great, coins and elephants' *Bulletin of the Institute of Classical Studies* 41 (1996) 87–108

K. Liambi 'The numismatic politics of Alexander the Great' *Istorika* (20 March 2003) 26–37 (in Greek)

Al. N. Oikonomides *The Coins of Alexander the Great* (1981)

M. J. Price *The Coinage in the Name of Alexander the Great and Philip Arrhidaeus*, 2 vols (1991)

M. Stamatopoulou and M. Yeroulanou (eds) *Excavating Classical Culture. Recent Archaeological Discoveries in Greece* (2002) (This includes A. Kottaridi 'Discovering Aegae', A. Lilimpaki-Akamati 'Recent discoveries in Pella', M. Tsibidou-Avloniti 'Excavating a painted Macedonian tomb near Thessaloniki' and D. Pandermalis 'New discoveries at Dion'.)

A. F. Stewart *Faces of Power. Alexander's Image and Hellenistic Politics* (1993)
────── 'Alexander in Greek and Roman Art' in Roisman (ed.) 2003: 31–66

E. von Schwarzenberg 'The portraiture of Alexander' in Badian (ed.) 1976: 223–78

6. Major extant literary sources (all non-contemporary, in chronological order)

(a) Texts/translations

Diodorus *Library of History* Book XVII: (ed.) C. Th. Fischer, Teubner; (ed.) C. Bradford Welles, Loeb Classical Library; (ed.) P. Goukowski, Budé

Q. Curtius Rufus *History of Alexander*: (ed.) Th. Vogel, Teubner; ed. J. C. Rolfe, Loeb Classical Library; trans. W. Heckel and J. Yardley, Penguin; E. Baynham, *Alexander the Great. The Unique History of Quintus Curtius Rufus* (1998)

Plutarch *Life of Alexander*: (ed.) K. Ziegler, Teubner; (ed.) B. Perrin, Loeb Classical Library (Plutarch vol. VII); trans. I. Scott-Kilvert, Penguin Classics; R. Waterfield, *The Age of Alexander*, Oxford World Classics

Arrian *Anabasis*: ed. A. G. Roos, rev. G. Wirth, Teubner; (ed.) P. A. Brunt, Loeb
  Classical Library, 2 vols, 1976–83; trans. A. de Sélincourt, rev. J. R.
  Hamilton, Penguin Classics 1971 (based on 'Official' Ptolemy: A. B.
  Bosworth, *Alexander and the East: The Tragedy of Triumph* (1996) 31–65;
  and on Aristoboulus)
Trogus/Justin *Philippic Histories*: (ed.) O. Seel, Teubner; (ed.) M. Galdi, Corpus
  Paravicinum

(b) Commentaries
Diodorus: trans. P. Goukowsky Books XVII–XVIII (Belles Lettres, 1976–8)
Curtius: J. E. Atkinson *A Commentary on Q. Curtius Rufus Historiae Alexandri
  Magni*, Books 3 and 4 (1980), Books 5 to 7.2 (1994)
Plutarch: J. R. Hamilton (1969, 2nd edn 1999)
Arrian: A. B. Bosworth 2 vols (Books I–V) so far (1980–95); P. Brunt, 2 vols,
  Loeb Classical Library (1976, 1983)

7. The Alexander Romance

W. Kroll (ed.) (Pseudo-Callisthenes) *Historia Alexandri Magni* (1926)
R. Stoneman (trans.) *The Greek Alexander Romance* (Penguin Classics 1991)
A. B. Wolohijan (trans.) (1969, Armenian version)

8. Historiographical books and articles

J. E. Atkinson 'Q. Curtius Rufus' "Historia Alexandri Magni"' *Aufstieg und
  Niedergang der römischen Welt* II 34.4 (1998) 3447–83
E. Badian 'Nearchus the Cretan' *Yale Classical Studies* 24 (1975) 147–70
E. Baynham *Alexander the Great. The Unique History of Quintus Curtius Rufus*
  (1998)
———— 'The Ancient Evidence for Alexander the Great' in Roisman (ed.) 2003:
  3–29
A. B. Bosworth *From Arrian to Alexander. Studies in Historical Interpretation*
  (1988)
———— and Baynham (eds) 2000
T. S. Brown 'Clitarchus' *American Journal of Philology* 71 (1950) 134–55
P. A. Brunt (ed. and trans.) *Arrian. History of Alexander*, Loeb Classical
  Library, 2 vols (1976, 1983)
———— 'On historical fragments and epitomes' *Classical Quarterly* n.s. 30
  (1980) 477–94
J. Carlsen et al. *Alexander the Great. Reality and Myth* (Danish Institute, Rome;
  1993, repr. 1997)
T. Duff *Plutarch's Lives. Exploring Virtue and Vice* (1999)

N. Hammond *Three Historians of Alexander the Great: The So-called Vulgate Authors. Diodorus, Justin and Trogus* (1983)
—————— *Sources for Alexander the Great: An Analysis of Plutarch's Life and Arrian's Anabasis* (1993)
J. Mossman 'Tragedy and epic in Plutarch's Life of Alexander' *Journal of Hellenic Studies* 108 (1988) 83–93, repr. in B. Scardigli (ed.) *Essays on Plutarch's Lives* (1995)
P. Pédech *Historiens compagnons d'Alexandre* (1984)
K. S. Sacks *Diodorus Siculus and the First Century* (1990)
D. Spencer *The Roman Alexander* (2002)
P. Stadter *Arrian of Nicomedia* (1980)
P. Vidal-Naquet 'Flavius Arrien entre deux mondes', postface to Arrian, *Histoire d'Alexandre. L'Anabase d'Alexandre le Grand*, trans. P. Savinel (1984)

9. Particular problems

(a) Death of Callisthenes

D. Golan 'The fate of a court historian: Callisthenes' *Athenaeum* 66 (1988) 99–120

(b) Alexander's visit to Siwah

W. W. Tarn *Alexander the Great* (1948) vol. II, App. 22,1 'Alexander's deification': at 347–59 (= Griffith (ed.) 1966: 151–63); P. Langer *The Ancient World* vol. 4 (1981) 109–27

Index

Page numbers in *italics* denote glossary/dramatis personae entries

INDEX

PAUL CARTLEDGE

The Spartans

An Epic History

PAN BOOKS

While Athens promoted democracy, individualism and high culture, its great rival Sparta embodied militarism, segregation and brutal repression. In *The Spartans*, leading world specialist Professor Paul Cartledge offers an account of an extraordinary people which will appal, impress and fascinate in equal measure.

'Paul Cartledge brings his infectious interest and searing
scholarship to one of the most intriguing civilizations
in the ancient world'
Bettany Hughes

'Cartledge's crystalline prose, his vivacious storytelling and
his lucid historical insights combine here to provide a first-rate
history of the Spartans'
Publishers Weekly

OTHER PAN BOOKS
AVAILABLE FROM PAN MACMILLAN

PAUL CARTLEDGE
THE SPARTANS   0 330 41325 2   £7.99

VICTORIA CLARK
THE FAR-FARERS   0 330 48976 3   £8.99

ROBERT SERVICE
STALIN   0 330 41913 7   £9.99

All Pan Macmillan titles can be ordered from our website,
www.panmacmillan.com, or from your local bookshop
and are also available by post from:

Bookpost, PO Box 29, Douglas, Isle of Man IM99 1BQ
Credit cards accepted. For details:
Telephone: +44 (0)1624 677237
Fax: +44 (0)1624 670923
E-mail: bookshop@enterprise.net
www.bookpost.co.uk

Free postage and packing in the United Kingdom

Prices shown above were correct at the time of going to press.
Pan Macmillan reserve the right to show new retail prices on covers
which may differ from those previously advertised in the text
or elsewhere.